Miracles of the Virgin in Medieval England

Law and Jewishness in Marian Legends

Legendary accounts of the Virgin Mary's intercession were widely circulated throughout the Middle Ages and borrowed heavily, as hagiography generally, from folktale and other literary motifs. Mary is represented in these texts in a number of different ways, rarely as the meek and mild mother of Christ, but often as a bookish, fierce, and capricious advocate.

This is the first book-length study of the place of medieval Miracles of the Virgin in a specifically English literary and cultural history. While the English circulation of vernacular Marian legends was markedly different from continental examples, this book shows how difference and miscellaneity can reveal important developments within an unwieldy genre. Boyarin argues that English miracles in particular were influenced by medieval England's troubled history with its Jewish population and the rapid thirteenth-century codification of English law, so that Mary frequently becomes a figure with special dominion over Jews, text, and legal problems. The shifting codicological and historical contexts of these texts make clear that the paradoxical sign 'Mary' could signify in surprisingly different and surprisingly consistent ways, rendering Mary both *mediatrix* and *legislatrix*.

ADRIENNE WILLIAMS BOYARIN is Assistant Professor of English at the University of Victoria (British Columbia).

Miracles of the Virgin in Medieval England

Law and Jewishness in Marian Legends

ADRIENNE WILLIAMS BOYARIN

D. S. BREWER

First published 2010
D. S. Brewer, Cambridge

ISBN 978–1–84384–240–8

D. S. Brewer is an imprint of Boydell & Brewer Ltd
PO Box 9, Woodbridge, Suffolk IP12 3DF, UK
and of Boydell & Brewer Inc.
668 Mount Hope Ave, Rochester, NY 14604, USA
website: www.boydellandbrewer.com

The publisher has no responsibility for the continued existence or accuracy of
URLs for external or third-party internet websites referred to in this book,
and does not guarantee that any content on such websites is,
or will remain, accurate or appropriate.

A CIP catalogue record for this book is available
from the British Library

This publication is printed on acid-free paper

Printed in Great Britain by
CPI Antony Rowe, Chippenham and Eastbourne

For Gabriel and Ephraim, as is all.

Blessed sister, holy mother …
Suffer us not to mock ourselves with falsehood
Teach us to care and not to care
Teach us to sit still
Even among these rocks
                    T. S. Eliot, 'Ash Wednesday'

Right now I am painting the Virgin Mary. I paint her in blue, with
the usual white veil, but with the head of a lioness. Christ lies in her
lap in the form of a cub. If Christ is a lion, as he is in traditional
iconography, why wouldn't the Virgin Mary be a lioness? Anyway it
seems to me more accurate about motherhood than the old bloodless
milk-and-water Virgins of art history. My Virgin Mary is fierce, alert
to danger, wild. She stares levelly out at the viewer with her yellow
lion's eyes. A gnawed bone lies at her feet.
                    Margaret Atwood, *Cat's Eye*

Contents

Illustrations

Acknowledgements

I am grateful to the following libraries and their staffs: the Bancroft and Doe Libraries at the University of California, Berkeley; the Bodleian Library at the University of Oxford; the British Library; the Lambeth Palace Library; and the McPherson Library at the University of Victoria. The British Library granted permission to reproduce the images gathered here and, along with the Bodleian and Lambeth Palace Libraries, to print the texts edited in Appendices 1–3. I am grateful also for funding from: the Kenneth E. and Dorothy V. Hill Fellowship Fund; the Program in Medieval Studies at the University of California, Berkeley; the Regents of the University of California; internal research grants from the University of Victoria; and my mother and in-laws, who also made several research trips possible over the years.

This work began too long ago in a corner of the Bancroft Library in Berkeley, where I opened a small thirteenth-century book of Latin Miracles of the Virgin that had not then been identified and began to translate and catalogue its texts. Since then, I have read and catalogued and forgotten and recalled enough miracle stories to make me dizzy many times over (and yet there are so many more!). I have also accumulated many Marian knick-knacks and curios. Friends, family, students, and colleagues have given me coffee-table books, refrigerator magnets, small plastic statues, candles, icons, belt buckles, newspaper clippings, posters and photographs, modern novels and short stories, and tiny reproductions of medieval windows and illuminations. Most of these were gifted with humor, some with thoughtfulness, but nevertheless they have been welcome visions in the midst of days' work, and have often made me pause to consider the similar varieties of tone in the medieval experience of Mary. Thank you to everyone who contributed to my accidental collection.

I have accumulated, also, many friendships and debts of thanks. I remain grateful to my teachers Jennifer Miller, Anne Middleton, Niklaus Largier, and Robert Brentano, who, before his death late in 2002, introduced me to the 'old school' medieval historians and to a style of teaching and approaching history that will always be with me. My colleagues at the University of Victoria have been extraordinarily encouraging of all my endeavors and have taught me many lessons in collegiality and productivity. I thank those who have, in one way or another, helped me to finish this book, especially: Christopher Douglas, Iain Higgins, Gary Kuchar, Erik Kwakkel, Robert Miles, J. Allan Mitchell, Stephen Ross, and Lisa Surridge. To Kathryn Kerby-Fulton I owe many professional opportunities, and I hope that I can one day repay (or at least pay forward) the unexpected support that she has given me in the early stages of my career. Many others have graciously offered time and consideration, citations, comments, corrections, criticism, encouragement, or camara-derie, particularly: Sheila Adams, Arthur Bahr, Anne Clarke Bartlett, Roger Dahood, Julian Deahl, Kasey Evans, Matthew Fisher, Sharon Goetz, Monica Green, D. Rae Greiner, the late Nicholas Howe, Steven Justice, Ruth Mazo Karras, David Lawton, Rebecca Metzger, Miri Rubin, Jerry Singerman, Rosalynn Voaden, and the anonymous readers for Boydell & Brewer, whose suggestions and comments were motivating, doable, and have unquestionably made this a better book. Certainly not least in this list are those who helped the manuscript through production: my diligent and meticulous research assistants Katrina Shearer and Katrina Bens; the extraordinary office staff of the English Department at the University of Victoria, especially Katharine Waring; and the extremely kind Caroline Palmer, Rohais Haughton, and Vanda Andrews at Boydell & Brewer. My daycare provider Barbara Donahue also deserves special mention, as do many others who help working mothers with young children. This book would not have been possible without Barb's love for my boys, nor without the day-to-day peace of mind that that gave me.

I do not have sufficient words to acknowledge my greatest obligations. I am extremely lucky to count my family among my closest friends, and to have married into a family that could hardly be more understanding of academic work. My brothers and my sisters-in-law have buoyed me up in difficult times and have never for a moment made me doubt their interest or their love, and my mother has been unflinchingly supportive in every way and at every stage of my education and career, even as her own protracted (successful) medical battles should have kept her attention elsewhere. I am grateful to her in ways and with depth that I know only she understands. To my husband Shamma Boyarin I owe more personal and intellectual debts than I can say or remember. I am absolutely sure that he never thought he would spend so many nights of his life talking about the Virgin Mary, and he is due some intercession for his devotion. This book is dedicated to our sons, who have grown alongside it. May they be sensitive readers and complex thinkers, and may their questions never cease.

Abbreviations

BHL	*Bibliotheca hagiographica Latina antiquae et mediae aetatis*, Subsidia hagiographica 6 and 70, I–III (Brussels, 1898–1901)
BL	London, British Library
Bodl.	University of Oxford, Bodleian Library
CSMD	The Oxford *Cantigas de Santa Maria* Database [online] (Oxford, 2005). Available from: http://csm.mml.ox.ac.uk
CT	*Canterbury Tales*
EETS	Early English Text Society
	os Original Series
	es Extra Series
	ss Supplemental Series
Foxe, *A&M*	John Foxe, *Acts and Monuments [...]*, *The Variorum Edition* [online] (hriOnline, Sheffield, 2004). Available from: http://www.hrionline.shef.ac.uk/johnfoxe/
JMEMS	*Journal of Medieval and Early Modern Studies*
MÆ	*Medium Ævum*
MED	*Middle English Dictionary* [online] (Ann Arbor, MI, 2001). Available from: http://quod.lib.umich.edu/m/med/
MLN	*Modern Language Notes*
MWME XXIV	Thomas D. Cooke (with Peter Whiteford and Nancy Mohr McKinley), 'XXIV. Tales: 3. Pious Tales: I. Miracles of the Virgin', *A Manual of Writings in Middle English, 1050–1500*, IX, ed. Albert E. Hartung (New Haven, CT, 1993), pp. 3177–258, 3501–51.
N&Q	*Notes & Queries*
PL	*Patrologia cursus completus*, series *Latina*
PMLA	*Publications of the Modern Language Association*
SEL	*South English Legendary*

Biblical citations follow the Douay-Rheims. Translations are the author's unless otherwise noted.

Introduction

Eadem enim peccata mea, o domina,
cognosci a te cupiunt propter curationem,
parere tibi fugiunt propter execrationem.

Because of these sins of mine, Lady,
I desire to come to you and be cured,
but I flee from you for fear of being cursed.
St Anselm, Orationes sive meditationes[1]

When Anselm wrote his influential prayers to the Virgin Mary, he was not yet in England. Anselm of Bec could not have known, in the decades before William Rufus made him Archbishop of Canterbury, what importance he would have for England, for the growth of medieval private devotion, and for the development of Marian devotion in particular. Anselm's personal and conversational appeal to Mary, and especially his consciousness of Mary's doubleness – the simultaneity of her mercy and judgment, and the sinner's inability to know which he may provoke – anticipated what R. W. Southern called the 'caprice' of later medieval Marian literature, wherein Mary could intervene with cure or curse for 'the just and the unjust alike'.[2] When Southern commented that '[o]f all Anselm's prayers there can be no doubt that the most important and original are those to St Mary', he surely had in mind his earlier work on the English origins of the Miracles of the Virgin.[3]

St Anselm's indirect influence is everywhere evident in Southern's arguments concerning the earliest Latin collections of tales of Mary's miraculous intervention. It is St Anselm's nephew, the younger Anselm, who is responsible for the earliest gathering of such stories, and, according to Southern, the nephew's endeavor was in great part due to 'his long association with St. Anselm and his friends' and his resulting 'enthusiasm … [for] the propagation of the cult of the Blessed Virgin Mary in all its branches'.[4] The younger Anselm was a Norman, educated in Chiusa, and later Abbot of Bury St Edmunds, where he compiled his collection of Marian miracles. He had traveled frequently with his uncle in the early years of the twelfth century, and he, along with Eadmer of Canterbury, was among the earliest public proponents

---

[1] F. S. Schmitt, ed., *S. Anselmi Cantuariensis Archiepiscopi opera omnia*, III (Edinburgh, 1946), p. 14, lines 33–4. The translation is Benedicta Ward's, *The Prayers and Meditations of Saint Anselm* (London, 1973), p. 108, lines 56–8.

[2] *The Making of the Middle Ages* (New Haven, CT, 1953), p. 248.

[3] Foreword, *The Prayers and Meditations of Saint Anselm*, ed. and trans. Benedicta Ward (London, 1973), p. 12; and 'The English Origins of the Miracles of the Virgin', *Mediaeval and Renaissance Studies* 4 (1958), pp. 176–216.

[4] 'English Origins', p. 199.

of the celebration of the feast of the Conception of Mary in the West. These facts made him uniquely qualified to bring together a series of tales that in some parts seems 'entirely continental', in which 'no branch of th[e] cult [of the Virgin] is neglected', and which borrows two stories from the *Dicta Anselmi*.[5] Though the Provincial Council of Canterbury claimed in 1328 that St Anselm had instituted the feast of the Conception of Mary,[6] it seems more likely that it was his influence on his nephew that made both liturgical and literary innovations in Marian devotion the claim of England.

Such innovations were hardly unexpected. England had always been precocious in its Marian doctrine and devotion. Several studies have demonstrated England's connection, from a very early date, to both Eastern and Italian Marian thought and shown that England took up the idea of devotion to the Virgin Mary with an exceptional zeal.[7] By the time of the Norman Conquest, six feasts of the Virgin were known and celebrated in England. The feasts of the Purification, Assumption, Annunciation, and Nativity were observed by the end of the seventh century, soon after their establishment in Rome, and the feasts of the Presentation and the Conception were, in some centers of the country, celebrated by the early eleventh century (long before St Anselm arrived), even though they were not at that time recognized throughout the West.[8] The Anglo-Saxon church accepted and incorporated into its liturgy apocryphal accounts of Mary's life,[9] and the early observance of the feasts of the Presentation and the Conception suggests the influence of Eastern doctrine and makes it look as though England influenced continental devotional practice, rather than the other way around.[10]

---

5   Ibid., pp. 184, 199, 205–16.

6   Edmund Bishop, *Liturgica historia* (Oxford, 1918), p. 238.

7   See, for instance, Thomas Edward Bridgett, *Our Lady's Dowry, or, How England Won and Lost that Title* (London, 1890); Herbert Thurston, 'Our Popular Devotions – The Rosary', *The Month* 96 (1900), pp. 403–18, 513–27, 620–37; S. J. P. van Dijk, 'The Origin of the Latin Feast of the Conception of the Blessed Virgin Mary', *Dublin Review* 465 (1954), pp. 251–67, 428–42; Emile Mâle, *Religious Art from the Twelfth to Eighteenth Century* (New York, 1958); Hilda Graef, *Mary: A History of Doctrine and Devotion* (New York, 1963); Mary Clayton, *The Cult of the Virgin Mary in Anglo-Saxon England*, Cambridge Studies in Anglo-Saxon England 2 (Cambridge, 1990); and, most recently, Miri Rubin, *The Mother of God: A History of the Virgin Mary* (New Haven, CT, and London, 2009), especially pp. 103–12.

8   Information on the development of Marian feasts in England is conveniently gathered in Clayton, *Cult of the Virgin*, pp. 25–51. See also Clayton's 'Feasts of the Virgin in the Liturgy of the Anglo-Saxon Church', *Anglo-Saxon England* 13 (1984), pp. 209–33.

9   The celebrations of the Assumption, Nativity, Presentation, and Conception of Mary show that this is true, and there is ample evidence that apocryphal texts narrating Mary's parentage, birth and early life, death, and Assumption circulated widely in Anglo-Saxon England, most significantly in the *Protevangelium Iacobi*, in certain versions of the text known as the *Transitus*, and in the *Gospel of Pseudo-Matthew*. To give some idea of the chronology, it is clear that both Bede and the author of the *Old English Martyrology* knew well the apocryphal accounts of Mary's birth and death and possibly had these texts at hand. See Clayton, *Cult of the Virgin*, pp. 5–24, and Rubin, *Mother of God*, pp. 111–12.

10 This theory is held by Bishop, *Liturgica*, pp. 238–59 and van Dijk, 'Origin of the Latin Feast'. I describe one example of this pattern of transmission in Chapter 2, as part of my discussion of the 'Legend of Theophilus', pp. 42–5.

In legendary accounts of both the early and later Middle Ages, despite official claims of St Anselm's influence, English texts boast that the feast of the Conception was established first in England by divine decree. The story of the English founding of the feast is well attested in early Latin manuscripts of Marian miracles found in England and elsewhere, and it resurfaces in the vernacular in the late fourteenth century, most notably as an addition to the *South English Legendary*.[11] The evident propaganda of these accounts suggests that English churchmen found it important and necessary to defend their position on the validity of Marian apocrypha in their public and private devotions. Though the legend of the 'English' feast began to spread not long after the Conquest, the feast itself seems to have been abolished by incoming Norman ecclesiastics, along with the feast of the Presentation, as these were probably not considered doctrinally sound by those in close range of, but outside of, England.[12] In such situations, divinely inspired accounts of how and why a practice began could no doubt prove convincing and necessary, if not conducive to a sense of national identity.

Remarkable English Marian liturgies and private devotions survive from very early dates. Alcuin of York (*fl.* 790) composed and probably himself encouraged the first votive mass to the Virgin; and the *Regularis concordia* (*c.*970), the great document of Benedictine reform in England, introduced the Saturday mass for Mary, along with prescriptions for Marian antiphons following lauds and vespers.[13] There is evidence that the Office of the Virgin originated in England, and the earliest complete Hours of the Virgin is English, pre-Conquest.[14] Several unique antiphonal compositions come out of England as well, and the doctrine of the Immaculate Conception was first articulated there, by Eadmer of Canterbury (1060–1128). Several Marian iconographic traditions have their earliest survivals in England too, notably representations of Mary sorrowing at the cross, of her death, and of her perusing scripture at the moment of the Annunciation.[15] Even if the fact of such survival does not prove novelty or originality of practice, it does attest

---

[11] I treat this legend in more detail below, pp. 19–23, and the *SEL* version is printed in Appendix 1.

[12] There is no evidence of these feasts in *The Monastic Constitutions of Lanfranc*, ed. and trans. David Knowles (London, 1951), and post-Conquest calendars at Winchester and Exeter, where pre-Conquest evidence had suggested otherwise, do not record them. Mary Clayton, *Cult of the Virgin*, pp. 49–50, numbers these among 'the feasts peculiar to Anglo-Saxon England' that Lanfranc's reform at Canterbury erased.

[13] See Thomas Symons, ed. and trans., *Regularis concordia*, Medieval Classics (London and New York, 1953), p. 20.

[14] Fifteen eleventh- and twelfth-century Marian Offices have been published in E. S. Dewick, ed., *Facsimiles of Horae de Beata Maria Virgine from English Manuscripts of the Eleventh Century*, Henry Bradshaw Society 21 (London, 1902). The earliest full set of Hours, from MS BL Tiberius A. III, appears there in facsimile. For discussion of these, and arguments concerning their originality, see Clayton, *Cult of the Virgin*, pp. 54–68.

[15] Such images may in fact be Eastern in origin (with early examples not surviving the iconoclastic controversy). See Clayton, *Cult of the Virgin*, pp. 173–4, 154–5; and Michael Clanchy, *From Memory to Written Record* (Cambridge, 1993), p. 191 n. 26.

to a zealous and coherent insular Marian devotion, a tradition in which it is unsurprising that England might come to be called 'Our Lady's Dowry'.[16]

The topic of this book, however, is England's place in one particular Marian devotional innovation and peculiarly medieval literary phenomenon: collections of so-called Miracles of the Virgin, those short accounts of Mary's miraculous intercessory powers that the younger Anselm had a hand in propagating. These texts and stories were popular in the medieval world in every sense of the word. The first Latin collections of Miracles of the Virgin appeared in the first half of the twelfth century, and, from the decades of their origins through at least the fifteenth century, Marian miracle tales were compiled, throughout Christendom, into increasingly larger anthologies.[17] Vernacular collections are extant in English, Norse, German, Anglo-Norman and French, Provençal, Italian, Spanish, Arabic, and Ethiopic languages.[18] They were extraordinarily widely circulated. The lines of dissemination and translation both of collections and of the individual stories that they comprise are almost impossibly complex, presenting, as a whole, what Southern called a 'picture of such bewildering confusion'.[19] But it is not my intention to make sense of the whole.

---

[16] See Bridgett, *Our Lady's Dowry*, and Mark Turnham Elvins, *Catholic Trivia: Our Forgotten Heritage* (London, 1992), pp. 149–58.

[17] The earliest collections contained between fourteen and seventeen miracles, but, at the other extreme, a collection might have as many as 427 miracles, as is the case with the Galician-Portuguese *Cantigas de Santa Maria* of Alfonso X, for which see Walter Mettmann's edition (Coimbra, 1959–72); the English translation by Kathleen Kulp-Hill, *The Songs of Holy Mary of Alfonso X, The Wise*, Medieval and Renaissance Studies (Tempe, AZ, 2000); and the *CSMD*. For an eloquent explication of the cultural saturation of these tales, see R. W. Southern, *Making of the Middle Ages*, pp. 246–57. Benedicta Ward also gives a good overview of the genre and its distinctions in *Miracles and the Medieval Mind* (London, 1982), pp. 132–65. See also H. L. D. Ward, *Catalogue of Romances in the Department of Manuscripts in the British Museum*, II (London, 1883), pp. 586–94; Evelyn Faye Wilson, ed., *The Stella Maris of John of Garland* (Cambridge, MA, 1946), pp. 3–76; and Peter Whiteford, ed., *The Myracles of Oure Lady*, Middle English Texts 23 (Heidelberg, 1990), pp. 7–23.

[18] Some edited examples include, respectively: Ruth Wilson Tryon, 'Miracles of Our Lady in Middle English Verse', *PMLA* 28 (1923), pp. 308–88; Whiteford, *Myracles of Oure Lady*; E. A. W. Budge, ed., *Maríu Saga*, Norske Oldskriftselskabs Samlinger (Christiana, 1871); Franz Bär, *Die Marienlegenden der Strassburger Handschrift Germ. 863* (Strasbourg, 1913); H. Kjellman, ed., *La deuxième collection anglo-normande des Miracles de la Sainte Vièrge et son original latin*, Bibliotheca Ekmaniana Universitatis Upsaliensis (Paris and Uppsala, 1922); Jean Miélot, *Les Miracles de Nostre Dame* (Paris, 1928); Jacob Ulrich, 'Miracles de Nostre Dame en provençal', *Romania* 8 (1879), pp. 12–28; Ezio Levi, ed., *Il libro dei cinquanta Miracoli della Vergine*, Collezione di opere inedite o rare dei primi tre secoli della lingua (Bologna, 1917); Gonzalo de Berceo, *Milagros de Nuestra Señora* (Barcelona, 2002); L. Villecourt, 'Les collections arabes des miracles de la Sainte Vierge', *Analecta Bollandiana* 42 (1924), pp. 21–68, 266–87; and E. A. W. Budge, ed. and trans., *The Miracles of the Blessed Virgin Mary and the Life of Hannâ*, Lady Meux Manuscripts (London, 1900). See also the series of Icelandic miracles (*Maríuvísur* I–III) in Kellinde Wrightson, ed., *Fourteenth-Century Icelandic Verse on the Virgin Mary*, Viking Society for Northern Research Text 14 (London, 2001). For a fairly complete bibliography of Marian miracles in various languages, see Wilson, *Stella Maris*, pp. v–ix, and, more recently, José Canal, ed., *El libro de laudibus et miraculis Sanctae Mariae de Guillermo de Malmesbury, OSB*, 2nd edn (Rome, 1968), pp. 9–15.

[19] 'English Origins', p. 176.

I am interested in Southern's unassailable and now canonical argument, which he made in an attempt to 'state some facts about the early history of these collections with the least possible complication',[20] that the genre we call 'Miracles of the Virgin' is of English origin. Southern proved that the earliest common groupings of Marian miracles were brought together by three English monastics – the younger Anselm already mentioned (d.1148), Dominic of Evesham (*fl. c.*1125) and William of Malmesbury (d. *c.*1143) – and that a certain Master Alberic of London combined (or found combined) the three collections. The poet William Adgar then translated the combined work into Anglo-Norman verse and cited Alberic as his source.[21] Adgar's work, sometimes called *Le Gracial*, is the earliest known vernacular collection of Miracles of the Virgin. It was completed no earlier than the last decade of the twelfth century, and it was probably used, at least partially, by Gautier de Coinci (d.1236) in his *Miracles de sainte Vierge*.[22] But after this, the picture is less clear, most puzzlingly because, whereas continental evidence shows massive collections of such stories in many vernaculars throughout the Middle Ages, the Anglo-Norman examples are few and relatively early in the period of the genre's vernacular popularity,[23] and English-language examples do not show up in any significant way until the late fourteenth century.

This is especially surprising since what was consistently being produced in Middle English during the intervening centuries was exactly the kind of large religious and historical compilations that collections of Miracles of the Virgin would seem to complement. The earliest Middle English versions, however, are a single tale in Bodleian Library MS Digby 86 (*c.*1280), a group of seven tales in the *South English Legendary* (*c.*1280), seven tales scattered throughout the *Northern Homily Cycle* (compiled *c.*1315), and two tales in the Auchinleck manuscript (National Library of Scotland MS Advocates 19.2.1, *c.*1330–40). The next to appear are Chaucer's 'Prioress's Tale' (*c.*1390), a group in the Vernon manuscript (Bodleian Library MS Eng. poet. a. 1, *c.*1390), and some twenty-three tales attached to various homilies in

---

[20] Ibid.

[21] 'Selunc le liure mestre albri / Ke de saint pol oi del almarie.' Quoted in Ward, *Catalogue of Romances*, p. 710. The authoritative manuscript (MS BL Egerton 612) has been edited by Carl Ludwig Neuhaus, *Adgar's Marienlegenden nach der Londoner Handschrift Egerton 612* (Heilbronn, 1886), and more recently by Pierre Kunstmann, *Le Gracial*, Publications médiévales de l'Université d'Ottawa 8 (Ottawa, 1982). One other copy of the collection from the first half of the thirteenth century survives (MS BL Additional 38664), as does a fragmentary excerpt of Adgar's 'Theophilus' and prologue (London, MS Dulwich College 22).

[22] For a recent study of Adgar's collection that takes up some of the central questions of the present study, see Jennifer Shea, 'Adgar's *Gracial* and Christian Images of Jews in Twelfth-Century Vernacular Literature', *Journal of Medieval History* 33.2 (2007), pp. 181–96. For Gautier de Coinci's collection, see *Les miracles de Nostre Dame*, ed. V. F. Koenig, 2nd edn, Textes littéraires français (Geneva, 1966–70), in four volumes.

[23] There are three Anglo-Norman examples: the earliest manuscript of Adgar's collection dates *c.*1200 (see also n. 21); the anonymous collection in MS BL Royal 20 B. XIV, edited by Kjellman, was probably composed between 1300 and 1325; and the collection of Everard de Gately is certainly no later. For this last, see Paul Meyer, 'Notice du MS Rawlinson Poetry 241', *Romania* 29 (1900), pp. 27–47.

John Mirk's *Festial* (*c.*1385). It is not until well into the fifteenth century that the tales begin to show up in considerable numbers.[24] Even then, English-language Miracles of the Virgin are, in general, not to be found in the form of collections, creating a gap of nearly 250 years between the creation of an apparently English genre and its popularity in the English language, and a complementary diffusion of the genre – evidenced by its miscellaneity – that is found nowhere else.

Peter Whiteford has summarized the situation clearly: 'In Latin, and in most of the other European languages, the greatest stores of miracles are to be found in collections devoted to the cult of the Virgin, and these occupy single manuscripts in their own right, or form major items within *mariales*. It is otherwise with the English miracles.'[25] And it is not only the English-language miracles that show signs of this otherness, for even the Anglo-Latin collections were relatively static, copied and circulated to be sure but displaying few signs of growth or evolution.[26] Put simply, there is a large gap in chronology between the early Latin collections of Marian miracles compiled in England and later vernacular instances of individual miracles, which tend to occur in England *outside* of Marian collections, even as such collections gained widespread currency on the continent.

Though Southern, in his classic standard of medieval history *The Making of the Middle Ages*, confidently described the twelfth- and thirteenth-century development and popularity of Miracles of the Virgin as symbolic of profound cultural transformation, surprisingly little has been made of his implicitly related argument for their English origins. Southern explained medieval intellectual evolution by way of literary change – the stopping points being the *Chanson de Roland*, the romances of Chrétien de Troyes, and the Miracles of the Virgin – and he called Marian miracles '[o]ne of the most novel and influential forms ... of popular literature', a group of texts 'at the very centre of medieval personal devotion'.[27] But if, as he concluded in his later essay on the topic, the moment of William Adgar's Anglo-Norman translation of a collection of Miracles of the Virgin was the moment at which England had made one of its 'chief contributions to the popular literature of the Middle Ages',[28] why was England itself all but immune to the continental and vernacular trends it had apparently contributed? No large collections similar to those that grew on the continent ever gained popularity in England. There was simply no drive to produce them in the English vernacular in

---

24 This is dramatically illustrated in the 'Catalogue of Middle English Miracles' appended to White-ford, *Myracles of Oure Lady*, pp. 97–133.

25 Ibid., pp. 20–1.

26 See my discussion of the early Latin collections below, pp. 15, 62–74.

27 *Making of the Middle Ages*, pp. 246, 248.

28 'English Origins', p. 205. Shea, 'Adgar's *Gracial*', p. 181, uses Southern's framing of the 'popular' Miracles of the Virgin within 'the world of courtly romance literature' to introduce her argument for reading the Jewish and Christian characters of Adgar's Anglo-Norman verse collection as romance character types.

any generic way. Middle English accounts of Mary's legends exist mainly in the sermon, legend cycle, or miscellany, and they therefore seem to 'lack a discernible line of development'.[29] There is considerable disparity, historical and scholarly, between the supposed English origins of these texts and their English afterlives.

In what follows, I will explore some peculiarities in the character of the genre as it developed in England and suggest that these partially account for the paradoxes that previous scholarship has presented. I am interested less in the generic provenance of these texts than in what might distinguish English examples from the others that were so widely circulated, and especially in what can productively be made of Middle English examples that survive, as they survive. There are two lines of inquiry here. The first has to do with problems of transmission and evidence – the problems of any claim to origins – and the second has to do with the content and contexts of English Miracles of the Virgin, with their recurring concerns and stock characters, and with the culture that produced certain unique texts and thematic trends. There are also two threads of argument taken up in response. My basic claims, which will often intertwine but not always neatly, are: first, that the miscellaneity of English-language examples is not necessarily evidence of a lost or damaged corpus (as past scholars have implied) but more certainly of a genre that always functioned in English variably and as an exemplary mirror of English ideas about Marian intercession; and, second, that a conspicuous and influential subset of English Marian miracles consistently characterizes the Virgin Mary as an intercessor interested in, and supremely situated to take care of, matters legal, textual, and Jewish. The miracles that support this second claim will not only reveal one line of development for Middle English miracles but also make clear how these texts (and others like them) can penetrate deeply held religious ideologies of gender, authority, and difference.

In performing comparative analyses of individual legends in their codicological and historical contexts (which I will do very frequently), I will break most radically from the scholarly tradition surrounding Marian miracle narratives by beginning with the basic and enabling assumption that they need to be considered and interpreted *as texts*. Usually introduced as a literary phenomenon but dismissed from the realm of serious study as 'popular rather than learned', as 'the stuff of popular homiletics', or as a kind of 'vulgarization' of hagiographical literature only representative of the 'universal' medieval notion of Mary's power and mercy,[30] the texts I will examine have simply not been read and are not well known in their particu-

---

29 Whiteford, *Myracles of Oure Lady*, p. 23.
30 See respectively Beverly Boyd, ed., *The Middle English Miracles of the Virgin* (San Marino, 1964), p. 10; Miri Rubin, *Gentile Tales: The Narrative Assault on Late Medieval Jews* (New Haven, CT, 1999), p. 7; and Ward, *Miracles and the Medieval Mind*, p. 133.

lars. Recently, certain Miracles of the Virgin have been used in discussion of medieval anti-Semitic rhetoric (most notably in Miri Rubin's and Anthony Bale's work),[31] but the vast majority of scholarship on the subject has been concerned to edit, catalogue, and draw manuscript stemmata. The tendency has been to trace lines of dissemination and development and persistently to reintroduce the genre. I will offer, however, several readings of Anglo-Latin and Middle English examples and analyses of several texts not previously edited. These will produce an image of the genre and its interaction with its English contexts that is ultimately positioned on the historical backdrop of the rapid thirteenth-century codification of English law, the 1290 expulsion of the Jews from England, and the Protestant Reformation.

My first chapter outlines the problems created by the usual scholarly assumptions about the nature of the genre, introduces Miracles of the Virgin as they appeared in late medieval England, and juxtaposes the concerns of the early Latin collections with several readings of later Middle English miracles. It shows that the apparent lack of development in the Middle English corpus is the marker of a kind of exemplary literature that seeks to allude to its prior and authoritative corpus but not to imitate or reproduce it. In England, Miracles of the Virgin first functioned as clerical texts and had the status of pseudo-monastic literature, and this fact, in concert with England's troubled history with its Jewish population, created generic markers in many English versions that are not found in continental examples. In particular, I contend not only that Mary is in many English examples a figure with special dominion over text, legal problems, and Jews, but also that these domains are specially related in the English contexts. Often conceived of as a Jew herself, Mary maintains a relationship to text and law in the same way that the absent English Jew does, and she therefore becomes the exemplary Jewish convert who labors to teach, to convert, and to punish when necessary.

In Chapter 2, I argue that the Anglo-Saxon conception of Mary's ability to intercede on the sinner's behalf influenced the Latin compilations that developed in the twelfth century. Beginning with Mary Clayton's analyses of the Anglo-Saxon cult of Mary, I examine in detail Latin and Old English versions of the 'Legend of Theophilus' (in which a clerk contracts his soul to the devil through a Jewish intermediary and then repents through Mary), and I argue that the Latin version of this legend, as it existed in Anglo-Saxon *and* medieval England, established an important type of miracle – and an important type of Mary – for English authors. Ælfric, when he incorporated the 'Legend of Theophilus' into his first sermon on Mary's Assumption, demonstrated the collectability of this legend and also emphasized its characterization of Mary as a legal advocate with special connection to the documentary text and legal literalisms associated with her Jewish identity.

---

[31] See Rubin's *Gentile Tales*, pp. 7–39, and *Mother of God*, especially pp. 161–88 and 228–42; and Bale's *The Jew in the Medieval Book: English Antisemitisms, 1350–1500* (Cambridge, 2006).

The Latin legendary text on which Ælfric depended presented a complex and elaborate account of many of the Marian attributes that were and would remain appreciated in English Marian miracles.

Chapters 3 and 4 contend that, throughout the Middle Ages, both art-historical and literary-vernacular evidence reinforced Mary's connection to writing and to law. Beginning with the six Marian miracles of the *South English Legendary* (*c*.1280), all found under the rubric 'St Theophilus', I show that later groupings of Marian miracles maintain the thematic concerns of the Theophilus legend by using it to exaggerate Mary's legal/textual authority and symbolic connection to Jews, but especially to exploit Mary's sense of justice and legal advocacy. Late medieval iterations of Theophilus show that Mary was especially appreciated for the connection to contract law that the story established for her (because she could retrieve the soul-selling charter from the devil), and fifteenth-century homiletic literature and illustrative programs show how this could work with her other, more familiar intercessory modes. The legend could overlap imaginatively with Mary's motherhood and with her Jewish identity, most remarkably in portrayals of her as a legal 'corpus' (bearing a book at, or expelling text from, her breast), or as a type of Moses – not only a *mediatrix* but a *legislatrix*. Using in particular the mid-fifteenth-century religious miscellany British Library MS Additional 37049, I demonstrate how Miracles of the Virgin could work with illustrations to emphasize and instruct on Mary's position as legal advocate and bearer of text. Such use of Marian legends, I argue, created a valorization of the written word and the performative text that enacted Mary's intercessory powers.

The final chapter focuses on the evidentiary problem created by the miscellaneity of Miracles of the Virgin as they survive in England, and it suggests that scholarly assumptions about the shape of the Middle English corpus (as significantly affected by the sixteenth-century destruction of manuscripts and distaste for the cult of the Virgin Mary) may betray confusion about how the genre was understood. Development of Middle English Marian miracles should be conceptualized in light of certain late medieval and early modern ambivalences about the genre. These miracle stories had a literary appeal that could be separate from the belief- and truth-claims of devotional and liturgical texts. The resulting lack of stable contexts and patterns of transmission around Middle English examples – and those examples that are the focus of this study are a case in point – in fact reveals how dynamic they could be and how difficult it is, consequently, to imagine fixed (destructible) parameters of the genre. Using 'The Prioress's Tale' as an extremely influential model of an English Marian miracle, then, I show how Chaucer negotiated the movement of these texts from monastic-devotional to literary-secular realms, and how his experiment with the genre and its reception implicates usage that is characteristic (and not accidental) in the surviving corpus. Moreover, Chaucer's text embraced most brilliantly the Mary that had come down through the 'Legend of Theophilus', and fifteenth-century iterations of 'The Prioress's

Tale' show that its status as a Marian miracle was often privileged over its connection to Chaucer.

The last chapter concludes with discussion of the Shrine of Our Lady of Walsingham, England's most popular medieval Marian pilgrimage site, around which many miracles apparently happened. The shrine provides a social backdrop to the Marian narratives, and what evidence remains of its late medieval and reform-era history allows us to consider how English Marian devotion was perceived at the time. As Miracles of the Virgin often seemed to give Mary an inappropriate amount of power in the determination of Christian salvation, their circulation could certainly impact a community focused on her intercession, ultimately in disastrous ways. Walsingham, however, also allows us to see important distinctions between the transactions implicit in the public life of Marian veneration and pilgrimage and those associated with the circulation of texts that were exemplary and therefore not localizable. Miracles of the Virgin, because they were embedded in the corpus of English religious literature in such a way that they could only function in relation to other texts and contexts, fared better than Marian shrines.

There are far-reaching implications here. It will no doubt be noticed that, while this study can occupy only one small point on any general portrait of the medieval Virgin Mary, Mary's role in these accounts of her miracles often complicates standard readings of the high medieval Virgin Mary as a merciful and comforting mother. In the texts that are the subject of this study, Mary is cunning, bookish, sometimes violent and punishing, and above all powerful and capricious. Her role as one with power over text and law, and her resulting authority as an advocate at the Last Judgment, is most uniquely exploited in these examples. Mary emerges as the champion of the performative text that liberates, as against Jewish and also legal literalisms. At the same time, and even more critically, these texts suggest that her (English) identity in the Middle Ages was at least sometimes conceived of as inseparable from Jewish identity, and that these texts therefore represent one way of negotiating the relationships between real and (more often) imagined social communities.

These implications are not disconnected from the fact that exemplary literature and its functions, and limitations, are necessarily on display in an examination of Miracles of the Virgin. Subjecting individual miracles to the same rigorous readings to which we might subject a more stable text means that each reading can only reveal the traces of a moment in time. As one incisive press reader reminded me, I must be careful about the largeness of my conclusions when I am 'examining a subset of legends … out of a much bigger set of stories … out of a frighteningly large whole'. The caution matters to any scholar working on a similar corpus. Such work has its own methodological problems: it is study not only of texts but also of the process that I habitually call 'versioning' (an unsophisticated term for the mysterious means by which multiple versions of a story or group of stories proliferate through time). This will sound familiar to anyone who works on religious literature or folktales (for instance), for 'versioning' is widespread and char-acteristic of many genres and periods;[32] it is an inescapable fact of certain scholarly endeavors that one finds the same thing over and over, variously adapted to local contexts, regions, or ideological agendas; and, if we seek the worth and functions of both the texts and the process, in minute particulars and specific contexts, we must perhaps be satisfied with what we can make of moments in time, which, in any case, are not untrue.

As recent decades have witnessed medievalists working seriously and closely with this kind of literature – legends, *vitae*, sermons, sermon *exempla*, miscellaneous narrative pieces and poems, common devotional pieces – it becomes more and more evident that such literature has often been underes-timated or undervalued in literary and historical studies in large part because its content can only be generalized and flattened out in any discussion that seeks to describe or summarize it. As Tolkien asserted in his famous lecture on *Beowulf*, 'all stories, great and small' are rendered 'wild, or trivial, or typical' in summary treatment, and 'comparison of skeleton "plots" is simply not a critical literary process at all'.[33] We are certain to misconstrue the past if our modes of reading do not fit its circumstances, if we read in ways that contradict it, or only according to what C. S. Lewis in 1964 called the 'book–author unit, basic for modern criticism', a reading mode that copes only marginally well with uncertainty and instability and has a difficult time accommodating versioning and miscellaneity.[34] What matters most to my reading mode here is the knowledge that, even within a subset of a frighten-ingly large whole, exemplary literature is as various as it is repetitive. It is as sensitive and susceptible to its contexts as it is obstinately present and predictable. The status of Miracles of the Virgin as exemplary means not banality and repetition but rather mutability and flexibility that can absorb and expose shifting social and religious contexts. This is what I hope to show.

---

[32] It will also sound familiar to anyone acquainted with Paul Zumthor's *mouvance* concept, or with theories of medieval *translatio*, both of which engage problems of variation, transmission, and instability in medieval texts in historically sensitive ways. These are, however, still more concerned with textual genealogies and (broadly construed) authorship and/or composition than I will be here and are not easily relatable to the proliferation of 'popular' religious or devotional materials. See Zumthor's *Essai de poétique médiévale*, Collection poétique (Paris, 1972), Chapter 2; and, for an important example, Rita Copeland, *Rhetoric, Hermeneutics, and Translation in the Middle Ages: Academic Traditions and Vernacular Texts* (Cambridge, 1991), especially pp. 179ff.

[33] J. R. R. Tolkien, '*Beowulf*: The Monsters and the Critics', Sir Israel Gollancz Memorial Lectures, *Proceedings of the British Academy* 22 (1936), pp. 13–14.

[34] *The Discarded Image: An Introduction to Medieval and Renaissance Literature* (Cambridge, 1964), p. 210. My thanks to my colleagues Iain Higgins and J. Allan Mitchell for helping me think through these paragraphs.

1

The Idea of English Miracles of the Virgin

> Quid me tantopere miraris? Ego sum maxima feminarum.
> Vis scire quanta?
>
> Why are you gazing at me so intently? I am the greatest
> of women. Do you wish to know how great?
> > The Virgin Mary in *The Life of Christina of Markyate*[1]

The collective label 'Miracles of the Virgin' implies an easily gathered body of work, but it is unclear whether it was ever such a thing for readers of English. Paul Strohm has claimed that, by the late Middle Ages, the English term 'miracle' probably suggested not miracle stories generally but writings on the Virgin specifically: 'We learn to expect that a *miraculum* of the early Middle Ages will probably involve miraculous cures at the tomb of a saint and that a *miracle* of the fourteenth century will more likely involve the Virgin.'[2] But he readily admits that it is difficult to tell whether this had generic force, for it is rarely clear whether the term refers to the miraculous event or to the narrative.[3] There *was* an acknowledged category: Marian legends inserted into sermons or found among religious miscellanies often begin with phrases like 'i rede in þe myraculs of oure lady', and, in a series of tales, a phrase like 'also in þe same boke' might be repeated.[4] The authors who claimed this great source volume recognized some corpus of appropriate stories, and they expected their audiences to do so as well. These narratives do tend to fit a certain mold – a character performs some special devotion but later commits some horrendous sin, or falls in with horrendous

---

1. C. H. Talbot, ed. and trans., *The Life of Christina of Markyate: A Twelfth Century Recluse*, Medieval Academy Reprints for Teaching 39 (Toronto and Buffalo, 1998), pp. 78–9.
2. 'Passioun, Lyf, Miracle, Legende: Some Generic Terms in Middle English Hagiographical Narrative', *Chaucer Review* 10.1–2 (1976), p. 165. This is a two-part essay, each part with the same title, spread over two issues of the journal.
3. Ibid., pp. 67, 158–61.
4. See MS BL Harley 2250, fol. 87r, col. 2; MS BL Additional 37049, Charter Group (see Appendix 3). Other examples include the *SEL* 'Founding of the Feast of the Conception' ('as þe bok us tolde'); MS BL Additional 37049, fol. 27r ('it is red in þe myrakils of oure lady'); and MS Bodl. e Museo 180, fol. 62v ('we fynde among þe myrakils of oure lady'). Related texts are printed in Appendices 1, 2, and 3.

sinners, and Mary intercedes, often *in extremis*[5] – but a search for any book to which authors advert yields no sure results. While numerous Latin collections of Marian miracles and copious compendia of general Marian materials were circulating in England,[6] no surviving collection or grouping seems definitely linked to another, and attempts to trace the sources of Middle English versions of individual tales are often futile. Any story of Mary's intercession – heard or read, old or new – could fit into the notional book.

Middle English Miracles of the Virgin appear as scattered pieces. In general, they are *exempla* tagged onto sermons or items in miscellanies and loosely related compositions. At their most coherent, they come in legend cycles like those of the *South English Legendary* or the *Northern Homily Cycle*, but even these are few and crowded amidst non-Marian material.[7] No English Marian miracle plays survive, though dramatic performances of these narratives 'delighted audiences across the breadth of medieval Europe for well over three centuries'.[8] There are only three significant English-language collections that might be compared to the original Anglo-Latin and later continental vernacular models: the Vernon manuscript once contained a group of forty-one miracles, of which only nine survive; there is a group of eighteen very abbreviated verse tales in British Library MS Additional 39996; and the late medieval print collection of Wynkyn de Worde, first published in 1496, is the only extant self-contained collection in English.[9] But these are anomalies. Even the famous English poetic examples show that there was no drive to produce the genre as collected or collectible: Lydgate wrote *one*, Hoccleve wrote *one*, Chaucer wrote *one*. Though the *Manual of Writings in Middle English* catalogues 171 Miracles of the Virgin that survive in Middle English (and variant versions inflate the number threefold or more),[10] this is not a genre that looks like a genre. It takes wide reading and persistent searching to find its component parts. Many of the English examples remain unedited, and literary analysis of the texts within their English context is wanting.[11]

---

5   The genre is defined similarly in *MWME* XXIV, p. 3178, though the description is too restrictive.
6   For a list of such manuscripts, see Ward, *Catalogue of Romances*.
7   The *SEL* usually includes seven Marian tales, but these are appended to a 'Life of Theophilus', and, in a typical manuscript, appear amidst scores of other legends. The *Northern Homily Cycle*, similar in bulk to the *SEL*, usually includes six Marian tales, but these are not always consecutive and are incorporated into poetic homilies.
8   See Stephen K. Wright, 'The Durham Play of Mary and the Poor Knight: Sources and Analogues of a Lost English Miracle Play', *Comparative Drama* 17 (1983), pp. 254–65 (here p. 254).
9   See Whiteford, *Myracles of Oure Lady*.
10   See *MWME* XXIV.
11   Aside, that is, from copious work on 'The Prioress's Tale' (which I will address in Chapter 5). It should also be noted that Beverly Boyd has published two studies in addition to her work on 'The Prioress's Tale' and her collection of miscellaneous tales in *Middle English Miracles*: 'Hoccleve's Miracle of the Virgin', *Texas Studies in English* 35 (1956), pp. 116–22; and 'The Literary Background of Lydgate's "The Legend of Dan Joos"', *MLN* 72 (1957), pp. 81–7. O. S. Pickering's study of a mixed prose and verse Marian miracle in the religious miscellany MS Leeds University Library Brotherton 501 is also an important and overlooked case: 'A Middle English Prose Miracle of the Virgin, with Hidden Verses', *MÆ* 57.2 (1988), pp. 219–39. Pickering prints

This situation no doubt arises exactly because the Middle English miracles are so frequently found in sermon and miscellany contexts, and it is extremely difficult to make general claims about how any given genre functions in such contexts. While it could be that 'the extent to which the miscellany is responsible for preserving the Middle English miracles', as Peter Whiteford has put it, is 'partially to be attributed to the destruction of [Marian] manuscripts in the sixteenth century', one cannot ignore the fact that the tales were immensely popular as miscellaneous items and *exempla*, and that this is, as Whiteford understates, 'an interesting circumstance'.[12] There is little evidence to indicate that large vernacular collections akin to those that survive on the continent ever existed in England. Indeed, while collections 'in Middle English or in Latin ... would have been ripe for destruction',[13] there are many extant Anglo-Latin collections.[14] What has been identified as the 'lack of an observable line of development' in the Middle English miracles is not necessarily due to the loss of those intermediate manuscripts that might have held the answers, or to the curious idea that the notional books of sources might have existed.[15] The lack itself may signal a different kind of development, and one of the first questions to pose should be what kinds of developments *are* discernible.

That the early Latin collections of Miracles of the Virgin remained available throughout the Middle Ages, and that there was in England simply 'no effort to replace those monastic compilations', suggests that the genre maintained strong connections to its monastic origins and in some senses remained a type of monastic literature.[16] Even Chaucer's, Lydgate's, and Hoccleve's examples show that this is true: Chaucer connected his to a prioress who presents her tale as an act of intense devotion; Lydgate, himself a monk of Bury St Edmunds, introduced his Marian miracle as one that Mary performed 'in a devoute abbey / Of an hooly monke'; and Hoccleve's story tells how Mary came to 'a monk ... / In th'Abbeye of Seint Gyle' to establish a new devotional practice.[17] More than this, these authors self-consciously connect their tales to a prior monastic narrative tradition: Chaucer, in mentioning 'yonge Hugh of Lyncoln, slayn also / With cursed Jewes', places 'The Prioress's Tale' in the world of thirteenth-century Latin monastic historiography,[18] specifically that of Matthew Paris's *Chronica majora* and the Waverly

---

an edition of the relevant text (pp. 220–3) and argues that it has 'close affinities with kinds of writing more literary and expansive than normal miracles of the Virgin' (p. 225).

12 *Myracles of Oure Lady*, pp. 20–1.

13 Ibid., p. 21.

14 See Ward, *Catalogue of Romances*. The dozens of manuscripts containing Latin collections held at the BL alone span the twelfth through the fifteenth centuries. For continued discussion of the reform decades and the possible evidentiary problems, see Chapter 5.

15 Whiteford, *Myracles of Oure Lady*, p. 23.

16 Ibid.

17 Boyd, *Middle English Miracles*, p. 57, lines 16–17, p. 51, lines 36–7.

18 All citations of Chaucer's works are from Larry D. Benson, ed., *The Riverside Chaucer*, 3rd edn (Boston, 1987), here *CT* VII.684–85.

and Burton Annals;[19] Lydgate claims that he has taken his from 'Vincencius', who 'in hys Speculatyf Historiall / Of this sayde monke maketh full mensioun', and thus connects the tale to the thirteenth-century *Speculum historiale* of Vincent of Beauvais, a Dominican priest with strong Cistercian connections; Hoccleve is less specific but asserts that he reports the story just 'as seith the scripture'.[20] In their own ways, these authors gesture toward the same notional (monastic) book of Miracles of Our Lady that the anonymous authors mentioned above cite. That the vernacular corpus consistently points to a prior 'book' of examples means exactly that it functions in relation to the *idea* of an authoritative whole. Though there may have been no vernacular 'impulse ... to compile a vast collection which would itself form part of the cult of the Virgin, and whose very compilation was a devotional act',[21] knowledge of, and reliance on, a prior vast collection is implied by the vernacular corpus and, indeed, by its popularity.

The fact that English-language Miracles of the Virgin are so often *exempla* – tales used didactically because of their moral and illustrative effectiveness – is why they have been habitually ascribed to the world of medieval 'popular' literature. The idea that *exempla* reflected the general opinion of the medieval clergy that 'one must speak of concrete things' when addressing 'people who for the most part are ... "rural," "lesser," "simple," "unlearned"', is one that creates a definitive separation between clerical and lay life,[22] and by extension between clerical and vernacular literature. But clearly the case is not so simple here (if it ever is). H. Leith Spencer has put *exempla* in the category of 'non-scriptural *auctoritates*' and has warned that separating such tales 'from the texts in which they are embedded' may result in a misunderstanding of their clerical context.[23] The use of an *exemplum* in a sermon must reflect what a preacher perceives about his audience, but, at the same time, it must maintain the authority that makes it persuasive and effective as a teaching tool. This double role has also been discussed by Claire Waters, specifically in relation to the moment that a sermon turns from commentary on the gospel or a feast to its narrative example. It is the moment that Larry Scanlon has called 'a narrative enactment of cultural authority' and which J.-C. Schmitt described as 'the momentary rupture that ... reinforces again the ideological

---

19 The most striking evidence for the argument that Chaucer was familiar with these is the similarity between Chaucer's and the monastic accounts of the punishment of the Jews. See Roger Dahood, 'The Punishment of the Jews, Hugh of Lincoln, and the Question of Satire in Chaucer's Prioress's Tale', *Viator* 36 (2005), pp. 465–91, especially pp. 471–83; and Chapter 5 below, pp. 151–6.

20 Boyd, *Middle English Miracles*, p. 57, lines 22, 29–30, and p. 51, line 22. Notes on the Vincent of Beauvais text can be found on pp. 123–4.

21 Whiteford, *Myracles of Oure Lady*, p. 23.

22 See Claire M. Waters, *Angels and Earthly Creatures: Preaching, Performance, and Gender in the Later Middle Ages*, The Middle Ages Series (Philadelphia, PA, 2004), p. 63. Waters is here quoting and translating J.-C. Schmitt.

23 *English Preaching in the Late Middle Ages* (Oxford, 1993), pp. 79, 81.

function of the sermon, the speech of authority'.[24] But Waters's reading is more subtle:

> As does the preacher, these tales owe a dual allegiance: to the authority that validates them but also to the experience that makes them acceptably 'realistic' examples. The former demonstrates the preacher's participation in the learned culture of books and tradition; the latter demonstrates his participation in the vernacular culture that he shares with his audience.[25]

Though Waters's comments speak specifically to the use of exemplary narratives in medieval sermons, her view of how such texts function is not at odds with theories of exemplarity generally.

A text that claims to be an example must function both through the authority of whatever whole to which it refers and through an audience's receptiveness and potential ability to imitate the example. As Alexander Gelley has explained, this necessity is *not* one that depends on the existence of the whole. Just as Middle English Miracles of the Virgin often display, exemplary texts of all kinds (lives, anecdotes, fables, parables) may reveal no actual source: 'especially when the context of discourse is persuasive or rhetorical, the source may be altogether hypothetical – the speaker's assumption of a body of evidence to support his position'.[26] From here, it is not so difficult to see how a corpus of texts that claim the same source can frustrate attempts to locate that source. If persuasion is successful, it promotes repetition and imitation and thus moves a text progressively further from whatever exemplar it may have itself imitated (but not necessarily copied). As Gelley puts it:

> [I]n a rhetorical sense not only does the example picture, it may also induce an imitative reproduction on the part of the receptor or audience. The mimetic effect here is linked not, as is usual, to techniques of representation but to forms of behavior, to a goal of ethical transformation. The example turns into an exemplar and its function becomes that of propagating itself, creating multiples.[27]

In this scenario, which sounds very much like what is happening in many Middle English Miracles of the Virgin, there is no 'lost' exemplar, but rather one that is fluid and continually recreating itself, one that is dependent on this very mode of reproduction. '[T]he components of the "exemplary imagination"', to use Anthony Bale's phrase, 'are not sealed, static, or authoritative'.[28] They are constantly in motion, shifting with use and context, and the lack of

---

[24] Quoted in Waters, *Angels and Earthly Creatures*, p. 63.
[25] Ibid., p. 64.
[26] 'Introduction', *Unruly Examples: On the Rhetoric of Exemplarity*, ed. Alexander Gelley (Stanford, CA, 1995), pp. 2–3.
[27] Ibid., p. 3.
[28] *The Jew in the Medieval Book*, p. 90.

philologically detectable development, then, becomes not a lack but rather a necessary component of a genre that is wholly dependent on exemplarity. The notional 'book' of miracles has to suggest a discernable source or set of sources not despite the fact that, but because, there are no such sources. Middle English examples may cite or allude to the Latin, monastic *auctoritates* of the genre's origins without developing in any discernible pattern from those origins.

Propagation, however, does not happen spontaneously. Persuasion requires an audience that is receptive and does undergo what Gelley calls 'ethical transformation'. The examples must realistically take part in and seek to affect a shared culture. In the case of Miracles of the Virgin, this means communication of whatever (shifting) cultural concerns are best addressed by the Virgin Mary. Marian miracles, *especially* when disconnected from large collections or codices of exclusively Marian material, must dramatically illustrate what Mary can do and what devotion to her brings about. Their assorted didactic and persuasive functions are visible in the types of power that Mary displays and in the lessons that her intervention teaches. Indeed, the 'gap' that is part of the generic signature of the English corpus of Marian miracles has the double effect of simultaneously giving the impression of a consciousness of origins and establishing new and unique groups of associated narrative concerns. That is, the later vernacular miracles may both maintain (or mimic) a connection to their originary monastic tradition and display various predictable sets of related thematic positions that reproduce themselves depending on the circumstances of composition and/or propagation.

As I have already mentioned by way of introduction, and indeed in the subtitle of this book, one conspicuous subset of English Marian miracles and its development is made more visible and coherent in this light. The related positions of this set are communicated through the implicit claims that the Virgin Mary has special dominion over text (both physical text and the interpretation of text), legal problems (in worldly courts and heavenly), and Jews (whether punishment or conversion is at stake, and occasionally through mediation in legal or disputational conflict).[29] In miracles that demonstrate these claims, Mary's mastery of the theological, textual, and legal becomes a performance of the monastic origins of books of Miracles of the Virgin; her learnedness and legal literacy is instructional, and it can produce a conversion, especially where Jewish characters are involved. Miscellaneity in these cases is advantageous to a goal of ethical transformation. While I will put most emphasis on when and why these related concerns overlap, they may successfully effect their persuasion separately or together, depending on their contexts. To see this, however, a familiarity with certain English Marian

---

[29] These can also pertain in the Anglo-French Latinate tradition. See, for example, my 'Anti-Jewish Parody around Miracles of the Virgin? Thoughts on an Early Nonsense-Cento in Berkeley, Bancroft Library, BANC MS UCB 92', *N&Q* 54.4 (2007), pp. 379–85.

miracles, as they survive in late medieval miscellanies and compilations, is required. And this is best accomplished not by a general description of the 'Miracle of the Virgin' genre or by a summary of common narratives but by attention to the particulars of individual tales and iterations. So let us look at some texts.

The Founding of the Feast of Mary's Conception

The miracle story associated with the founding of the feast of Mary's Conception treats both the history of English Marian devotion and the nature of Marian intercession. It is an unambiguously English story, ostensibly about William the Conqueror's attempt to curtail a Danish invasion shortly after the Norman Conquest. It was often retold, and there are many versions of it, both in Latin collections and in the vernacular.[30] It involves Abbot Ælfsige (Elsinus, or Helsin) of Ramsey, whom William sends to Denmark to stop the anticipated attack. On his return, the abbot quells a storm and avoids near shipwreck by promising an angelic apparition that he will establish the feast of Mary's Conception in England. When Ælfsige asks for instruction, the apparition explains when and how to celebrate the feast, and, accordingly, Ælfsige institutes it upon his return and promotes it throughout the realm.

Despite its status in the corpus of texts called Miracles of the Virgin – Southern deemed it 'the most important of all the stories in the [earliest] collection', partly because of its 'significant place in the controversy about the introduction of the Feast of the Conception in the twelfth century'[31] – this is a somewhat unconventional example. Mary herself does not appear in it, nor is it a story about the reformation of a sinner, as are most others. Marian intervention is indirect in this case, and the sole purpose of the tale seems to be to ascribe divine authority to a liturgical innovation. It is, nonetheless, generically significant. By the time the legend appears in the English language, only after the feast had gained near full acceptance, it displays exactly the disconnect between Latin origins and vernacular afterlives that I have already mentioned. It is no longer a text connected to a larger body of Miracles of the Virgin, as it had been in the early Anglo-Latin collections, but is rather one whose utility is connected to a specific didactic purpose. It begins to appear frequently in sermons and readings for the feast around the end of the fourteenth century, usually in the context of the apocryphal story of Mary's parents Joachim and Anna, and authors or scribes connect it to its

---

[30] For the Latin text, which is remarkably consistent from manuscript to manuscript, see Elise F. Dexter, ed., 'Miracula Sanctae Virginis Mariae', *University of Wisconsin Studies in the Social Sciences and History* 12 (1927), pp. 37–8. English versions can be found in Theodor Erbe, ed., *Mirk's Festial*, EETS, es 96 (London, 1905), p. 17; E. H. Weatherly, ed., *Speculum Sacerdotale*, EETS, os 200 (London, 1936), pp. 250–1; and F. S. Ellis, ed., *Lives of the Saints, as Englished by William Caxton*, II (London, 1900), pp. 126–9.

[31] 'English Origins', p. 194.

Latin origins only by vague pretense to the authority, and the Englishness, of that prior, notional 'book'.[32] In the late fourteenth-century addition to the *South English Legendary* (see Appendix 1), for example, the author claims to record 'Þe Concepcioun of ur lady, *as þe bok us tolde* [my italics]'.[33]

But this miracle must have been in circulation very shortly after the Conquest, in fact before the Anglo-Latin collections.[34] It is widely accepted that the Conception was celebrated in Anglo-Saxon England and encountered Norman opposition after the Conquest. Debates over its validity resurfaced nearly simultaneously with the appearance of the first Latin collections of Miracles of the Virgin. The legend and its circulation, in both its early and late iterations, reflect mainly theological and clerical concerns and suggest that the early collections were consumed and utilized by monastic audiences who understood them as at least marginally authoritative. This is demonstrated first by the fact that the story was not widely known until after clerical debates about the feast had gained some international fame.[35] Neither Eadmer of Canterbury nor Osbert of Clare, both Englishmen working to promote the feast in the first quarter of the twelfth century, knew of the legend when they wrote certain works advocating it,[36] but by the time the first collections of Marian miracles were completed, Bernard of Clairvaux was writing to the canons of Lyon urging them *not* to celebrate the Conception and citing a 'scriptum supernae revelationis' (a text concerning a celestial revelation) that is generally understood as a reference to this legend.[37] Osbert of Clare, in a letter to the younger Anselm, the author of the first collection of Marian miracles to include the story, praised Anselm for his success in promoting the feast internationally, just after his collection had appeared.[38] It is likely that Osbert referred, at least in part, to the recording and circulating of the story of the feast's English founding.

To the younger Anselm, the legend was a piece of propaganda literature, which he probably took from the annals of the Abbey of Ramsey – at the center of which was the historical Abbot Ælfsige[39] – and the story could not at this time have been meant for any other purpose than to persuade those in positions of ecclesiastical power that Mary's Conception should be celebrated. It was a monastic tale, culled from the history of one abbey and its abbot, recorded by the abbot of another, copied and elaborated by other

---

32 An early English-language version, however, does appear in the *Cursor Mundi* (*c*.1300). See *MWME* XXIV, p. 3217 (item 84).

33 Appendix 1, line 2.

34 On the chronology, see Clayton, *Cult of the Virgin*, pp. 47–50, and Southern, 'English Origins', pp. 194–8.

35 For a summary of progression of the debate in the 'Anglo-Norman realm', see Rubin, *Mother of God*, pp. 173–6.

36 Southern, 'English Origins', p. 194.

37 Ibid., p. 198 n. 1.

38 Ibid., pp. 199–200. Southern surmises that Anselm's collection came together sometime between 1120 and 1125. Osbert's letter is quoted in Bishop, *Liturgica*, pp. 243–4.

39 Southern, 'English Origins', pp. 196 n. 2, 197 nn. 1–3.

monks, including William of Malmesbury, and translated into vernaculars,[40] all for the purpose of validating a liturgical practice and a nascent theology of the Immaculate Conception, and increasing devotion to the Virgin Mary in all its aspects. This was successful on many levels. Though the legend did not quickly become a popular vernacular subject, its Latin circulation continued uninterrupted in England throughout the Middle Ages. As the feast gained acceptance, however, the legend behind its founding became both a necessary vernacular teaching tool and a 'historical' tale of the English place in its propagation and in Marian devotion generally.

The late fourteenth-century version found in some manuscripts of the *South English Legendary* is a particularly interesting example of how the later vernacular texts fetishize their monastic (male) historiographical origins. In the *South English Legendary* version, there is a sustained emphasis on English history and its connection to the feast. Much of the brief legend (forty of 114 lines) is an account of the circumstances that brought about Ælfsige's journey: the political dangers and negotiations of the Conquest, the historically poignant threat of Danish invasion, and William the Conqueror's recourse to specific wise counselors, including the Abbot of Ramsey. While this is also a large part of the narrative found in the Latin text, it is exaggerated and dramatized in the *South English Legendary*. There is attention to the Conqueror's questionable status as a leader, to the death ('wiþ treson') of King Harold, and to the reasoning of the Danish, all of which is absent in the Latin text.[41] The legend's connection of the 'rebirth' of the feast to the years shortly after the Conquest, and especially to the overt political maneuverings of interested governments, is of some importance. What is at stake is not only the institution of a feast but also the reclaiming of an English tradition lost during the Conquest and its aftermath. The appropriation of the political circumstances of the Conquest to the goal of reinstituting lost liturgical practice was a subtle way of turning the tables on the Normans, whose reforms could have encountered little real resistance.

Something of this rhetorical game is reflected in the fact that the angelic apparition who appears to Ælfsige in the legend is always *male*. This is an odd feature of a Marian narrative, especially since this figure appears in direct response to prayers to Mary:

> Here steresman þat was ne couþe heom noþing rede
> Bote to ur leuedy 3erne þat hii bede.
> ...
> Iesu Crist godes sone & is moder Marie
> Hii bytoken al & some here schip for to gye.
> A wel briht aungel in þe see þo cam gon þere

---

[40] Wace translated the legend into Anglo-Norman in the 1170s. See William Ray Ashford, ed., *The Conception Nostre Dame of Wace* (Chicago, 1933).

[41] See Appendix 1, lines 3–36 (here 10).

As druȝe auote upon þe watre as he alonde were
Wiþ clene cloþes, & white ycloþed he him hadde.
To þis abbot Elsy wel myldeliche he gradde.[42]

The implication is that the white-clad figure is sent by Mary to do her bidding, and the gender of this apparition is specified in all known versions. In the earliest Latin versions of the legend, the apparition appears as a bishop or archbishop.[43] S. J. P. van Dijk has speculated that this figure may have represented St Augustine of Canterbury,[44] but it may just as well have stood for Archbishop Stigand, who during the time of the Conquest held in plurality Winchester and Canterbury, both of which observed the feast of the Conception.[45] Or, considering that his nephew put the legend into circulation, it could be St Anselm, who would have been a figure of authority for English and Normans alike. The ambiguity is probably intentional: the male apparition is a Marian challenge to the authority of those who did or would oppose the feast, and whatever figure was most effective might be imagined in its place. In the *South English Legendary* version, in which the gender of the ghostly vision is the only remnant of the original bishop figure, the apparition's ability to walk on water connects it also to that figure of unquestionable authority to whom Mary always has special access, Jesus himself. In any case, the male authoritative response to the humble helmsman's advice to pray earnestly to Mary notably imposes a Marian authority on matters liturgical and ecclesiastical, and reinforces the fact that her intercession is focused in this instance on a man who is both the leader of a monastery and reputedly 'þe wyseste man ychosen of þe contreye'.[46]

The liturgical instruction to this wise man, which is built into the legend through the apparition's intervention, is not only the remnant of Latinate clerical concerns in a popular vernacular text, but is also indicative of newer concerns about how Mary's power works. As Mary Clayton has explained, the specific instructions given by the apparition – he tells Ælfsige to use the service for the feast of the Nativity of Mary, with the word *Conceptio* substituted for *Nativitas* – are a great part of why the story 'reads like an attempt to counter objections to the celebration, and [why it] was later used for precisely that purpose'.[47] While the liturgy for Mary's Nativity would be a text of unquestioned validity and remove apocryphal bias from the feast, however, the details are didactic. The legend's simple instructions concerning the liturgy, the date of its celebration (8 December), and its rationale (to teach that '[o]f Anna heo conceyued was, of Ioachim byȝete') make the lesson, by

---

42 Ibid., lines 49–60.
43 See Dexter, 'Miracula Sanctae Virginis Mariae', p. 37: 'Ecce subito quendam conspiciunt, pontificatus infula decoratum proximum naui.'
44 'Origin of the Latin Feast', p. 257.
45 Clayton, *Cult of the Virgin*, pp. 49–50.
46 Appendix 1, line 23.
47 *Cult of the Virgin*, p. 49.

the late fourteenth century, a rather plodding and unnecessary one.[48] But the most important point to be made about the nature of the liturgical instructions in the *South English Legendary* version concerns the alteration of text.

To perform the service, Abbot Ælfsige need only say the liturgy (which he already knows) on the day instructed, but to do this and promulgate the practice he must change the text of the existing liturgy. In the Latin, this change is attached to performance (he must 'say' *Conceptio* instead of *Nativitas*),[49] and any related textual work is therefore only implied. In the *South English Legendary*, however, the fact that the apparition's command is attached to written work is emphatic. Ælfsige's job in the propagation of the feast is the job of altering text:

> 'Bote þe seruyse þou shalt nyme of hire burþetime,
> & riht so hey3e ordre nyme forþ, matynes & prime,
> Bote whare þat þou fyndest Natiuitas ywrite,
> Þere schal Concepcio forþ ben ysmyte.'[50]

The abbot is to find the written word 'Natiuitas' and then 'ysmyte' (set down, overwrite) the word 'Concepcio', thereby expunging the word 'Natiuitas' to create the appropriate service books. This is a clerical job that requires copying or altering existing liturgical texts, and the agreement to do so is prerequisite to Mary's saving intercession: the apparition who appears in response to prayers to Mary tells Ælfsige that he must follow his instructions if he wants to return to England alive.[51]

The *South English Legendary* version of this legend is about devotion to Mary and how to effect it. The implication is that Mary cares primarily about knowledge of her story and her liturgies, and about the transmission of both. What causes the proverbial storm in this iteration of the story of the founding of the feast of the Conception is that both the feast and the narratives that explain Mary's story are 'neuir telle ne fond ... ywrite'.[52] To honor Mary, one must understand how to edit a text, and how to circulate a story.

'Blood on the Penitent Woman's Hand'

The notion that an inability to construe Mary's textual messages can create problems, or can interfere with spiritual health, is especially remarkable in a tale known editorially (and unreasonably dryly) as 'Blood on the Penitent

---

[48] Appendix 1, line 88.

[49] See Dexter, 'Miracula Sanctae Virginis Mariae', p. 37: 'Sic ubi natalicium in natiuitate *dicitur*, conceptio in hac celebratione *dicitur* [my italics].'

[50] Appendix 1, lines 91–4.

[51] Ibid., lines 65–9.

[52] Ibid., lines 76, 80. The repeated use of this same phrase by the apparition and Abbot Ælfsige may be scribal error (eye skip), but it is copied in three of the four surviving manuscripts.

Woman's Hand'. The early fifteenth-century Bodleian Library manuscript from which it comes contains a full *de tempore* sermon cycle, and this tale, designated a *narracio* in the margins of the manuscript, concludes a homily on the benefits of penitence (see Appendix 2). It is the story of a woman, at one time especially devoted to the Virgin Mary, who enjoys an incestuous relationship with her son. She has a child with that son, but kills the baby as soon as it is born, and the blood that falls on her hand during the murder grows into four lines of Latin verse. Unable to understand the Latin, the woman continues her relationship with her son until the Virgin intercedes by advising a priest to seek her confession and read to her the bloody text. The priest does so, and the woman's contrition is such that both her sins and the text are washed away.

In addition to this story's obvious and interesting emphasis on the usefulness of text and literacy, which I will discuss in a moment, this is also one of a frequently encountered type of miracle in which Mary shows a seemingly arbitrary, even perverse, affection for the most horrendous of sinners. It is one of the best examples of her special attention to past devotion, no matter the severity of the crime that interrupts it, and it reflects well the 'caprice' of late medieval Marian miracles.[53] Mary's special attention in this case, of course, is also connected to the fact that the woman who requires her help has created, in her sexualized relationship with her son and in her bearing the child of that son, a horrible parody of the Holy Family, which Mary must correct. The tale, as an *exemplum*, then, is not only about the efficacy of devotion to the Virgin and of penitence; it is also about correct interpretation of scripture and Mary's place within it.

There is in this tale a fast compounding of abominable sin: lechery, incest, murder, and eventually the decision to remain in a fallen state. The incestuous woman's choices leave her isolated from her community and trapped in a chilling domesticity that the author says admits 'no creature but god and sche hyr self hyr sonne & the deuill'.[54] Yet, at the most private and morally wrong moment of her life, this woman finds herself the vehicle of a perplexing miracle:

> in the brekyng of the neke of þis childe ther fell iiii droppis of bloode upon hyr ryȝte hond, the whiche blood grew in to iiii uersis of herd latyn. Sche kowde rede hem but sche kowde not understonde þem.[55]

The Latin text on her hand is evidence both of her crime and of her spiritual health. That she can read it but not understand it tells us little. Perhaps she can pronounce it but not translate it, that is, syllabically read it aloud as one might when performing liturgical Latin; perhaps she can make some but not

---

[53] Southern, *Making of the Middle Ages*, p. 248.
[54] Appendix 2, lines 9–10.
[55] Ibid., lines 11–14.

full sense of it, or has only a student-like literacy.[56] The author introduces her as a 'gentil woman',[57] suggesting at least the possibility of education, and the implication is that if her hand recorded not *hard* Latin, if it recorded easy Latin, the problem of understanding would be solvable.

The ability to read but not to understand, particularly when the story is told to a listening audience, echoes and plays with the biblical caveat that many 'may *hear* and not understand [my italics]' (Mark 4:12), and this is apparent in the pun on 'herd Latin': the incestuous woman cannot understand *hard* text, but the listening congregation is just as likely to misconstrue *heard* text and momentarily misunderstand that the woman's illiteracy is not only literal, but rather, and more importantly, spiritual. The immediate suggestion that she cannot understand the blood on her hand as meaningful in any way underscores this: after futile attempts to wash the text away, she buries her murdered infant, and 'sche contenewid still in synne withe hyr sonne'.[58] She knows that the bloody words are not good – she would wash them away if she could – but, as this is apparently impossible, she goes on with her life, unchanged. Hers is a willful misunderstanding of a miraculous sign.

Once the Latin verses are uncovered, one of the first things to notice is that this is not hard Latin at all. It is remarkably easy Latin, a fact that would be audibly emphasized by a preacher's reciting its unwavering rhyme and alliteration:

> Casu cecidisti carne cecata
> Demoni dedisti dona dicata
> Monstrat maliciam manus immaculata
> Recedit rubigo regina Rogata.[59]
>
> Blinded by flesh, you have fallen into mishap.
> You have given to the Demon consecrated gifts.
> The hand shows the evil deed. The spotless
> Queen having been petitioned, the redness recedes.

This text is hard perhaps in the sense that it is versified, and that it presents a kind of riddle. That the woman clearly understands its meaning later in the tale, however, when her priest finally reads it aloud to her, suggests that this

---

[56] The ability to syllabify was a skill that preceded *grammatica* (the ability to construe grammatically). On this, and especially women's liturgical literacy and Latin education, see Katherine Zieman, *Singing the New Song: Literacy and Liturgy in Late Medieval England*, The Middle Ages (Philadelphia, PA, 2008), especially pp. 73–141; and Zieman's 'Reading, Singing, and Understanding: Constructions of the Literacy of Women Religious in Late Medieval England', *Learning and Literacy in Medieval England and Abroad*, ed. Sarah Rees Jones, Utrecht Studies in Medieval Literacy 3 (Turnhout, 2003), pp. 97–120. My thanks to Anne Middleton for first pointing out the distinctions.

[57] Appendix 2, line 2.

[58] Ibid., lines 16–17.

[59] Ibid., lines 36–8. The line breaks are added here.

is not what is making it hard. Rather, what is finally suggested is that she cannot make *complete* sense of it.

The only thing that might make this Latin difficult to make sense of is a failure to notice the enjambment of the third and fourth lines. If the sinful woman is trying to read 'immaculata' as part of a syntactic unit contained by the third line only, that is, trying to place the adjective with the feminine 'manus' (and this attempt supports the idea that she has a student-like literacy somewhat beyond mere syllabification), then the third line is very hard to understand indeed. It would read, 'The spotless hand shows the evil deed', and how can her bloody hand be spotless? It bears both the stain of blood and the stain of the crimes it has committed. But it is in this error of translation that the woman's spiritual state is revealed: she can neither understand how her hand may become unstained, as is evidenced by her reluctance to make confession, nor does it occur to her that the 'regina' is 'immaculata', a demonstration of how far she has fallen from her previous state of devotion to Mary. Understanding 'regina' and 'immaculata' together, however, not only leads to sincere contrition but resolves the dark parody of the Holy Family that the incestuous woman had unwittingly created. The Latin text seems to record either nonsense or a very difficult lesson, but the distinction between the stained woman and the unstained Mary becomes dramatically clear with correct translation. Mary's intercession is effected, then, both in textual error and textual correction, in the moment of exegetical confusion.

Chaucer's 'Prioress's Tale'

'The Prioress's Tale' is a version of a very common Miracle of the Virgin. The story it tells is known in more than thirty analogues and at least seven languages.[60] A young schoolboy sings a Latin hymn to the Virgin Mary, in this case the *Alma redemptoris mater*, while walking through a Jewish quarter. This prompts Jewish hostility that results in the boy's murder, but Mary miraculously preserves the child until his body can be found and the Jews suffer the consequences. Chaucer's little chorister, however, who could sing his Latin hymn to the Virgin Mary 'by rote', does not understand the Latin he recites, and in this there is some thematic overlap with 'Blood on the Penitent Woman's Hand'.[61]

---

[60] See Carleton Brown, 'The Prioress's Tale', *Sources and Analogues of Chaucer's Canterbury Tales*, ed. W. F. Bryan and Germaine Dempster (New York, 1958), pp. 477–85. Much new work has been done on the analogues (including new identifications), and particularly on the liturgical context and the Tale's status as a Miracle of the Virgin, in the updated work by Laurel Broughton, 'The Prioress's Prologue and Tale', *Sources and Analogues of the Canterbury Tales*, II, ed. Robert M. Correale and Mary Hamel (Cambridge, 2005), pp. 583–647. See also Bale, *The Jew in the Medieval Book*, Chapter 3 and Appendix 1.

[61] Benson, *Riverside*, CT VII.545.

In 'The Prioress's Tale', Chaucer emphasizes that the central conflict stems from a problem with literate understanding and translation:

> Noght wiste he what this Latyn was to seye,
> For he so yong and tendre was of age,
> But on a day his felawe gan he preye
> T'expounden hym this song in his langage,
> Or telle hym why this song was in usage.
> This preyde he hym to construe and declare
> Ful often tyme upon hise knowes bare.
>
> His felawe, which that elder was than he,
> Answerde hym thus: 'This song, I have herd seye,
> Was maked of our blissful Lady free,
> Hire to salue, and eek hire for to preye
> To been oure helpe and socour whan we deye.
> I kan namoore expounde in this mateere.
> I lerne song: I kan but smal grammeere.'[62]

It is clear that the boy's inability to construe the Latin is due to lack of knowledge of the language, to his only fledgling education, but the idea that textual illiteracy can stand in for spiritual health is still functioning: it is key to the young boy's sanctity and innocence that his understanding of the hymn has no bearing on the strength of his faith or on his understanding of the act of devotion. Moreover, it is crucial that the Jews in this tale, before they react, both understand *and* misunderstand the recited text.[63] In Chaucer's version and in some analogues, the Jews maintain the same spiritual illiteracy as the incestuous woman discussed above, and this creates a similar brand of violence. Chaucer makes it clear that it is not only annoyance that provokes violence; it is also (and maybe rather) that the Jews understand the song:

> Oure first foo, the serpent Sathanas,
> That hath in Jewes herte his waspes nest,
> Up swal and seyde, 'O Hebrayk peple, allas,
> Is this to yow a thing that is honest,
> That swich a boy shal walken as hym lest
> In your despit and singe of swich sentence
> Which is agayns oure lawes reverence?'[64]

The problem is not just that the boy trespasses and sings in the Jewish quarter; it is that his actions are not 'honest' (truthful, but also halakhically pure);[65]

---

62   Ibid., VII.516–29.
63   Lisa Lampert, *Gender and Jewish Difference from Paul to Shakespeare*, The Middle Ages Series (Philadelphia, PA, 2004), pp. 81–2, argues the point very similarly: the 'Jews understand the literal meaning of the *Alma* but fail to understand its spiritual importance, a circumstance that leads to the boy's death in a literal enactment of "the letter kills but the spirit gives life"' (p. 82).
64   Benson, *Riverside*, CT VII.558–64.
65   See *MED*, s.v. 'honeste' (adj.), 4d.

it is the particular 'sentence' (meaning) of his song, which Satan encourages the Jews to *understand* as an attack on their own beliefs. In Chaucer's tale, the affront of the Marian hymn *Alma redemptoris mater* (the first verse of which is a kind of catechism of Incarnation theology) depends on an understanding of its Latin words – and on a fundamental misunderstanding of the mystery of the Incarnation.[66]

It is important to note that the Christian boy's inquiry into the meaning of the hymn is very likely a Chaucerian innovation. In two of the three analogues most closely related to Chaucer's version of the story – the only two that include any dialogue about translation – it is the Jews who ask the question. In one of these (found in Cambridge, Trinity College MS 0.9.38), the answer comes from a Latin-literate Jewish youth, who explains it about as well as Chaucer's Christian schoolboy does:

> Affuit inter eos quidam adolescens de pueris hebreorum in lingua latina parumper eruditus quia latinum intelligens ydeoma. Audiunt cantilenam & mirantur & quia fuit sathan inter eos ecce vnus ex illis inquirit ab hebreo qui literas nouit latinorum, quid puer concineret christianus. Respondit hebreus puerum Antiphonam in laudem matris virginis confectam decantare vt ipsius melliflua suauitas ad marie memoriam animis accenderet auditores. Audito virginis nomine iudeus exclamauit et ecce sathanas misit in cor eius vt puerum traderet & interficeret innocentem.[67]

> A certain one of the Hebrew youths had been enough trained in the Latin language to understand some Latin expression. They heard the song and wondered and, because Satan was among them, behold, one of them asked the Hebrew who was literate in Latin what the Christian boy sang about. The Hebrew responded that the boy was repeating an antiphon made in praise of the Virgin Mother, that its sweet charm might kindle the hearers in their souls to remembrance of Mary. When he heard the name of the Virgin, the Jew cried out, and, behold, Satan sent it into his heart to betray the boy and murder him, though innocent.

Understanding the text's meaning is once again disconnected from the ability to understand the faith. Textual literacy is different from spiritual literacy and proper exegesis, which for sinners and Jews, in a Marian context, requires miraculous intercession.[68] While the little chorister's inability to understand is innocent, neutral and therefore holy, those who should know better are

---

[66] See Beverly Boyd, ed., *The Prioress's Tale*, A Variorum Edition of the Works of Geoffrey Chaucer (Norman, OK, 1987), p. 16: 'Alma redemptoris mater, quae peruia caeli porta manes, et stella maris, sucurre cadenti surgere qui curat populo: Tu quae genuisti, natura mirante, tuum sanctum genitorum: virgo prius ac posterius, Gabrielis ab ore, sumens illud Aue, peccatorum miserere.' For discussion of how different hymns are used in different versions of the story, and for a related but contrasting reading of Chaucer's use of the *Alma*, see Bale, *The Jew in the Medieval Book*, pp. 67–72.

[67] Brown, 'The Prioress's Tale', p. 481. The full text is also printed, with a (different) translation, in Broughton, 'The Prioress's Prologue and Tale', pp. 639–47.

[68] On this, see also Rubin, *Mother of God*, pp. 161–8, 228–36.

culpable. It is only where the construal of meaning might reasonably be expected of a reader – an adult, a cleric, a *literatus*, and, prominently enough in many Miracles of the Virgin, a Jew – that illiteracy is conspicuously insufficient and its absence blameworthy.[69] Chaucer's decision to make complementary, or rather causal, the *spiritual* illiteracy of the Jews and the *textual* illiteracy of the young boy only makes this more poignant.[70]

'The Merchant's Surety'

The meeting of anti-Jewish rhetoric with anxieties over text and interpretation is visible also in the story known as 'The Merchant's Surety', another common and long-lived example of a Marian miracle.[71] The English verse version, one of the surviving Marian miracles found in the Vernon manuscript (Bodleian Library MS Eng. poet. a. 1), is the only one that, through its Christian and Jewish characters, emphasizes the use and misuse of text.[72] The tale concerns a Christian merchant, Theodore, who falls on hard times and takes a loan from a Jewish moneylender called Abraham. Having nothing material to offer, Theodore swears surety on an image (probably a statue) of the Virgin, and then travels abroad on business and forgets about his debt until the night repayment is due. Because he cannot get to Abraham in time, he puts the money into a small chest, prays for Mary's intercession, and throws the chest into the sea. Abraham miraculously discovers the money on time, but he hides it and later demands a second payment from Theodore. When the two return to the Virgin's image to settle their dispute, the image speaks and reveals Abraham's dishonesty, and Abraham converts to Christianity.

The Vernon manuscript author takes great care to establish a sympathetic characterization of both Theodore and Abraham: he dwells on the plight of Theodore, the good name of Abraham, and their affection for each other. Passages of speech and dialogue are notable features of this version of the story, as is the detail with which the author represents the thoughts and actions of the two men (we even get to see Abraham in a private domestic moment, walking quietly at sunrise by the seaside, which, the author tells us, is near

---

[69] Cf. *St Erkenwald*, wherein the saint retrieves information despite the fact that gathered clergy cannot construe the inscription on the heathen tomb. See Henry L. Savage, ed., *St Erkenwald: A Middle English Poem*, rpt (Hamden, CT, 1972), p. 5, lines 5–56, pp. 10–11, lines 155–77.

[70] For a more complete discussion of 'The Prioress's Tale' and its place in the corpus of English Marian miracles, see Chapter 5, pp. 149–64.

[71] See Wilson, *The Stella Maris*, pp. 157–9; Boyd, *Middle English Miracles*, pp. 118–19; and Appendix 4, 'The Merchant's Surety'.

[72] The Vernon version of the tale has been edited by Carl Horstmann, *The Minor Poems of the Vernon MS*, EETS, os 98 (London, 1892), pp. 157–61; and Boyd, *Middle English Miracles*, pp. 44–9 (I use the latter here). On the Vernon's once uniquely large group of Middle English Marian miracles, see Chapter 5, pp. 146–9.

the home that he shares with his wife).[73] The Jew in this story is a good man, but he is misguided both in his greed and his Judaism, and he is not unlike his Christian counterpart, whom the author sets on parallel moral, intellectual, and social planes. The anti-Jewish sentiment of the Vernon version of this story is of a less acerbic tone than much medieval anti-Semitism. It has to do with a disregard for legal text and textual resources, and with the essential misunderstandings of both Christianity and Judaism that that disregard effects.

To make this point, the author characterizes Abraham and Theodore as men of similar economic standing and social status:[74] Theodore is 'of herte fre' and 'lovede God and Ure Ladi', just as Abraham 'in his lay [community, but also law] ... hedde good name' and 'lovede wele' Theodore.[75] The two call each other 'fere' (brother), and we are told that Abraham's response to Theodore's plea for financial assistance is one of 'gret honour'.[76] Abraham understands Christian faith in the Virgin Mary's power, and he tells Theodore that he is willing to take her as surety because he has

> herd oftesithe
> That ladi is corteis and blithe,
> Men seith heo wol hem never fayle
> That in hire servise wol travayle.[77]

Abraham, in other words, believes in Christian belief, as far as it goes, without making any concession to Mary's status as a virgin or mother of God. He also shows his knowledge of the Christian landscape when he suggests that the contract of debt be sealed in a particular church with a particular image:

> we go into your chirche,
> And ther this forward we wol worche.
> Ther is an ymage of hire iliche
> Arayed wel with juweles riche.
> Tac thou hire me ther bi the hond;
> Of the kep i non othur bond.[78]

---

[73] Boyd, *Middle English Miracles*, p. 47, lines 101–6.

[74] This is substantiated by the illustration that accompanies the narrative (fol. 126r), which shows Abraham and Theodore in three different positions: making their pledge before the image of Mary (clearly a statue in the illustration), making and retrieving the payment at the seashore, and praying before the image of Mary. In each case, they are closely juxtaposed, drawn so that they are the same height and size, and making the same gestures. Where they make their pledge, Abraham clasps the hand of the Mary statue and seems to embrace Theodore as he does so. For a color reproduction, see A. I. Doyle, *The Vernon Manuscript: A Facsimile of Bodleian Library, Oxford, MS Eng. Poet. a. 1* (Cambridge and Wolfeboro, NH, 1987), plate 10.

[75] Boyd, *Middle English Miracles*, p. 44, lines 2, 7, 11, 13.

[76] Ibid., pp. 44–5, lines 29, 35, p. 44, line 23.

[77] Ibid., p. 45, lines 37–40.

[78] Ibid., lines 41–6.

Abraham eventually errs in his dishonesty, but this author ties his dishonesty to his greed – not to his Judaism – and makes sure that Theodore is similarly guilty. Theodore, we are told, 'thouhte so muche on his wynnyng' that he 'foryat the day of his payyng'.[79] That is, his focus on money is such that he neglects time, obligations, and friendships. It may be his Christianity that earns Theodore a miracle, but greed and its consequence are not here Jewish attributes. Furthermore, it is exactly the balance struck between the Christian and the Jewish characters that allows a reading of this narrative as a series of mistakes that relies on the misuse of text.

When Theodore commits his money to the sea, he is careful to include written record of the transaction: 'This to Abraham Ieuh sent Theodorus.'[80] It is not enough to pray to Mary and trust in her ability to intercede; a record of the transaction is also required, and Theodore's care for this is part of the miracle formula. It is offset, however, by Abraham's ignoring the binding legal effects of that written record. When he first sees the chest floating in the sea, he has no sense of its meaning or content, but, when he opens it and knows well what it is, precisely because of the document he finds ('beo the lettre he wuste also / From what mon that hit com fro'),[81] he intentionally dismisses the note. His choice to do so reflects his misunderstanding of the miracle: he perceives the communication of a man, not of Mary, and he proceeds to manipulate what Mary has already manipulated by hiding the money and feigning ignorance.

Where Abraham hides the payment is a detail unique to this version of the story, and it is worth special attention. He secretly and deliberately deposits the money in an 'ark':

> He caste it thenne in to an ark,
> That was bothe styf and stark.
> To telle therof no wiht him luste,
> But wente him forth as no wiht wuste.[82]

'Ark' can mean 'box' or 'chest', but the author nowhere else uses the word this way. Though he uses 'cofre' and 'kyst' several times,[83] he uses 'ark' only twice and only to name Abraham's hiding place. But 'ark' can, and frequently does, refer to the Ark of the Covenant or the Holy Ark of the synagogue, and, in this case, there are several reasons to read it this way.[84] In almost every other version, authors are explicit about Abraham's putting the money in an empty box that he finds in his home and hiding it under his bed. The English author pointedly avoids this detail, and instead vaguely sets the 'ark' some-

---

79 Ibid., p. 46, lines 74–6.
80 Ibid., line 94.
81 Ibid., p. 47, lines 115–16.
82 Ibid., lines 117–20.
83 Ibid., pp. 46–8, lines 89, 108, 150.
84 See *MED*, *s.v.* 'arke', 2.

where other than where the money appears and tells us that Abraham must access it in secret. This covert Jewish access to an ark that is somewhere away from his seaside home suggests two possibilities. In the context of money-lending and in the English milieu, it might imply – even a century after the 1290 expulsion – access to the Jewish *archae* that once held the legal and financial records of Jewish communities, and which were protected by the king in various important Jewish cities across the country.[85] It is difficult not to think of the *archae* in connection to the fictional business activities of a prominent Anglo-Jewish moneylender who accesses an 'ark'. Still, the other possibility, that Abraham goes in secret to the synagogue to hide the money, rings truer. The system of balances set up between Theodore and Abraham all but forces a Jewish counterpart to the church's statue of Mary. And only through reading Abraham's 'ark' as the counterpart to Theodore's statue can we understand how both characters have grossly misinterpreted and misused their respective religious objects: for Theodore, Mary's image has become not an object of veneration but an economic tool, just as Abraham's misuse of the Ark turns economic and worldly what should be holy.

The Jewish character here becomes a narrative construct that, as a symbol of the 'old' misunderstanding of the Christian mystery and especially of the denial of the virginity of Mary, is an appropriate foil on which to focus anxieties about text and law. Abraham functions as a symbol of the 'letter of the law', and this is narratively reflected in all of his actions. 'The Merchant's Surety' is on one level a story about a contract, a contract negotiated between Abraham and Theodore that Abraham seeks to collect on twice, since no one other than Abraham has legal proof that Theodore has fulfilled his obligation. This too-literal understanding of what is *legally* acceptable and provable, however, is a large part of Abraham's *spiritual* failure: he considers only how to capitalize on the contract and cannot see its miraculous fulfillment. That Mary is recognized by both parties as an appropriate guarantor of the contract, and that she can resolve the legal dispute, becomes a commentary on both her role in the correction of Jewish readings of law and in salvation generally – as one who can intercede in matters of judgment.

'A Scholar at the Scales of Justice'

The notion that Mary is a legal intercessor for those in spiritual danger is frequently functioning in Marian tales, and her connection to written text and her ability to understand the law (whether 'law' is construed as civil or spiritual) are often related in English examples. A very short tale from British Library MS Additional 37049, a fifteenth-century miscellany that

---

[85] See Robin R. Mundill, *England's Jewish Solution: Experiment and Expulsion, 1262–1290*, Cambridge Studies in Medieval Life and Thought (Cambridge, 1998), especially Chapters 5 and 6 on the locations, contents, and scrutinies of the *archae*.

contains several prose miracles thematically linked by their shared emphasis on Mary's ability to intercede in legal matters earthly and heavenly,[86] offers a succinct example:

> Also in þe same boke, it tells how þer was a clerke in ane unyversite synfully lyfyng. He was raueschyd to þe dome. And he sawe fewe gode deds of his belayd in þe to weyscale. Þe fende held a rolle wrytten full of synnes & layd it in þe toþer party of þe weyscale þat bowed downe. Wherfore sentence suld hafe gone agayn þe synful man. He was ferd & beheld to Saynt Mary þat stode nerhande & sche toke þe rolle offe þe weyscale & gaf þe clerk it in hys hande & he red it. & sone he went to confession to schryfe hym, & chawnged his abet & mendyd his lyfe. & fro þen forth seruyd Saynt Mary deuoutely.[87]

The university clerk's powerful vision of Mary and the Devil at the scales of justice shows concisely Mary's imagined role on Judgment Day, which is here actively connected to her authority as a legal advocate and to her (performative) command of written text. Though the sinner deserves punishment, Mary is able to save him because she can retrieve the 'wrytten rolle' from the Devil and return it for reading. Though this sinner is a university man, his own implied ability to handle text is rendered useless at his moment of judgment, and Mary's privileged ability to do so in such circumstances is the emphasis. She is the master and the advocate. Her maneuverings over the fate of the soul and facility with legal mediation – as displayed here and in 'The Merchant's Surety', in different ways – are consistent elements of the legends I will discuss in the following chapters.

Text, Law, and Jews as Problems and Motifs in English Examples

The most salient features of my readings – the bloody Latin inscription, the young chorister's inquiry, the Jewish merchant's ark, the retrieval of the written roll from the scales of justice – are unique to English-language versions of these tales. The visible line of development I am beginning to sketch, and which I will examine in a significant number of examples, raises some crucial questions: what is it about the English situation that promotes this combination of concerns within this body of literature? And why is the Virgin Mary an appropriate vessel for such concerns? Scholars have certainly noted the medieval tendency to link Mary, as the bearer of the Word, to Wisdom and to Latin literacy, to the disruption of 'hellish bureaucracy' and

---

[86] For extensive discussion of this manuscript and its Marian miracles (printed in Appendix 3), see Chapter 4, pp. 115–37.

[87] See Appendix 3, Charter Group, lines 22–31.

to medieval legal *Latinitas*.[88] Many have devoted pages to Mary's association with 'Jewish difference' and to her variously antagonistic and evangelical relationship to Jewish characters in apocrypha and legend.[89] Reflection on how and in what contexts these features of Marian literature and assortments meet, however, is rare, and while I am not suggesting that *all* English Miracles of the Virgin display this set of concerns (they do not), I am interested in why they do when they do. Here we have an exemplary corpus that – through readings of this set of peculiarities within it – may yield some answers to questions not only about medieval ideas of the Virgin Mary, but also about the nature of some medieval anti-Semitic sentiment, about an available model of feminine legality and piety, about lay ideas of monasticism and monastic ideas of the laity, about social and religious communities, and about medieval ideas of textual interpretation and literacy.

The fitful anti-Semitic content of these texts is certainly not a defining feature of the broadly conceived 'Miracle of the Virgin' genre,[90] but it is in many ways the most interesting component. This is not simply because there is something inherently fascinating and important about the discourse of religious conflict and the real and narrative violence that it engenders (how can one not look?), but primarily because it is through this particular content that the Virgin Mary is frequently defined in the examples I will treat, and in which my three dominant thematic concerns very often meet. Somewhere in Mary's legendary contacts with Jewish characters is a key to understanding both the range of her intercessory dominion and the complexity of her Christian and maternal identities. Over and over again in various English contexts (and this will become relentlessly clear) such content is the site

---

[88] See Barbara Newman, *God and the Goddesses: Vision, Poetry, and Belief in the Middle Ages*, The Middle Ages Series (Philadelphia, PA, 2003), especially Chapter 5; Christopher Baswell, 'Latinitas', *The Cambridge History of Medieval English Literature*, ed. David Wallace (Cambridge, 1999), pp. 143–4; Clanchy, *From Memory to Written Record*, pp. 189, 255–6; and Richard Firth Green, *A Crisis of Truth: Literature and Law in Ricardian England*, The Middle Ages Series (Philadelphia, PA, 1999), pp. 276–7.

[89] I refer here to Lisa Lampert's important discussion in *Gender and Jewish Difference*, especially pp. 47–56, where she asserts that none of the analogies in her argument (nor indeed in my book!) 'makes sense without the aid of another Jewish body, that of Mary, who clothes in flesh the Word itself, giving the exegetical relationships [between Jew and Christian, letter and spirit, or secular and religious law] … a corporeal reality' (p. 48). To the others who have been and will be mentioned in these notes, I should add Joan Young Gregg, *Devils, Women, and Jews: Reflections of the Other in Medieval Sermon Stories*, SUNY Series in Medieval Studies (Albany, NY, 1997), especially pp. 193–203.

[90] Both R. W. Frank, Jr. and Lee Patterson have concluded that approximately 7.5% of the legends in the Middle English corpus are unambiguously anti-Semitic. Putting aside the real problem of defining 'anti-Semitic', however, counting surviving tales and calculating the percentage of those with a certain content does not take into account the ubiquity or popularity of certain individual tales, nor the fact that anti-Semitic tales were in fact among the most frequently repeated and long-lived of the Miracles of the Virgin. See R. W. Frank, Jr., 'Miracles of the Virgin, Medieval Anti-Semitism, and the "Prioress's Tale"', *The Wisdom of Poetry: Essays in Early English Literature in Honor of Morton W. Bloomfield*, ed. Larry D. Benson and Siegfried Wenzel (Kalamazoo, MI, 1982), p. 179; and Lee Patterson, '"Living Witnesses of our Redemption": Martyrdom and Imitation in Chaucer's Prioress's Tale', *JMEMS* 21 (2001), p. 519.

of a widening both of Mary's character and of Christian–Jewish dialogue. Keeping in mind the textual and legal intercessions above, then, and especially 'The Merchant's Surety' and the Latin-literate Jew of 'The Prioress's Tale' and its close analogue, it is worth examining briefly the nature of Jewish presence in England before the 1290 expulsion and the narrative place of Jews in the centuries that followed.

The post-expulsion Jew has, from a literary perspective, frequently been interpreted as a symbol, a sign that was not connected in any way to 'real' Jews but rather to Old Testament Jews (Hebrews) and fantasies of Jewish otherness. The Jewish character that allows this distinction has been variously called the 'hermeneutical Jew', the 'notional Jew', the 'theological Jew', the 'virtual Jew', or 'the *image* of the Jew',[91] and the implication of all of these terms is that Jewish characters take on a literary presence in Christian literature, and sometimes in the absence of Jews, that depends not on their Judaism *per se* but on their relationship to the Christian book. It is not so much physical absence that matters, as Anthony Bale has laudably pointed out: 'The *punctum* of 1290 is of little importance in terms of representation; with the forced departure of Jews from England there is no sudden shift to the fantastical, no immediate change of emphasis.'[92] Rather, we might consider here that the history of Christian thinking and invective against Jews, particularly those on the edge of the diaspora, works in combination with the English historical situation to produce certain brands of anti-Semitic discourse. Jeremy Cohen's explication of Augustine's 'doctrine of Jewish witness' – in which Jews not only must survive as the proof of Christian history and prophecy but also 'serve Christians as guardians (*custodes*) of their books, librarians (*librarii*), desks (*scriniaria*), and servants who carry the books of their master's children to school (*capsarii*) but must wait outside during class' – shows how the link between Jews and religious knowledge and law worked from very early dates.[93]

Sylvia Tomasch has emphasized the crucial role of this book-bearing characterization in the English treatment of Jews both before *and* after the expulsion:

> Jews were expelled not merely because they first possessed (English) lands and goods from which they needed to be displaced, but because they first possessed the (Christian) book – from which they needed to be displaced.

---

[91] See Jeremy Cohen, *Living Letters of the Law: Ideas of the Jew in Medieval Christianity* (Berkeley and Los Angeles, 1999), p. 65; Lampert, *Gender and Jewish Difference*, p. 29 and *passim*; Sylvia Tomasch, 'Post-Colonial Chaucer and the Virtual Jew', *Chaucer and the Jews: Sources, Contexts, Meanings*, ed. Sheila Delany (New York and London, 2002), p. 77 n. 27; and Bale, *The Jew in the Medieval Book*, p. 18.

[92] *Jew in the Medieval Book*, p. 16. Nancy L. Turner, through a comparative study, reaches a different conclusion in her essay on Robert Holcot's theological works: see 'Robert Holcot on the Jews', *Chaucer and the Jews: Sources, Contexts, Meanings*, ed. Sheila Delany (New York and London, 2002), pp. 133–44.

[93] *Living Letters of Law*, p. 36.

In their priority lay the rationale for their alterity, the justification for their abuse, and the roots of their destruction. The Christian dilemma set the stage for the English action: the 'dreadful secondariness' (to use Edward Said's phrase) of medieval Jews was thus a consequence of their intolerable primariness.[94]

This religious-allegorical understanding of the Jew must have been underscored, and maintained in cultural memory, by the professional roles of pre-expulsion Anglo-Jews, many of the most prominent of whom worked in finance and so in legal and literate capacities.[95] Many had to be, and were, literate in Latin, French, and English, in addition to Hebrew, and it is through documents pertaining to debt and the collection of debts that many English Christians would have encountered Jews and the Hebrew language.[96] Hebrew was used on bonds, seals, receipts, tallage sticks, and title-deeds, and such were often recorded as bilingual documents (in Hebrew and Latin, or Hebrew and French).[97] Anyone doing business with Jews would likely have encountered it frequently. As Michael Clanchy has suggested, 'all large propertyowners, particularly lay barons and monasteries, must have seen ... Hebrew writings when they borrowed money. Some indebted magnates of the thirteenth century would probably have come across more writing in Hebrew than in English.'[98]

The antagonism towards Jews and their texts that this situation fostered can probably not be overestimated. It certainly influenced the violence that followed Richard I's coronation in 1189 and the related York riots of March 1190, in which the York Jewish community was brutally attacked and eventually committed mass suicide by immolating themselves. The Augustinian canon William of Newburgh describes the York event as an attack led by those most financially indebted to the Jews, and he reveals that the real object of hostility became clear only after the Jewish community had died for it:

[94] 'Post-Colonial Chaucer', p. 77.
[95] For wide-ranging discussion of the roles of Jews in pre-expulsion England, see Mundill, *England's Jewish Solution*. Bale, *The Jew in the Medieval Book*, p. 14, emphasizes the likely variety of Jewish professions, but the percentage of the Anglo-Jewish population that was involved in moneylending is a matter of continuing dispute, with estimates ranging from 1% to 100%. See also Suzanne Bartlet, 'Three Jewish Businesswomen in Thirteenth-Century Winchester', *Jewish Culture and History* 3.2 (2000), pp. 31–54; and Victoria Hoyle, 'The Bonds that Bind: Money Lending between Anglo-Jewish and Christian Women in the Plea Rolls of the Exchequer of the Jews, 1218–1280', *Journal of Medieval History* 34 (2008), pp. 119–29.
[96] Bale, *The Jew in the Medieval Book*, p. 14, delineates 'English, Anglo-Norman, French, Yiddish, Hebrew and possibly Arabic, Spanish and even Slavic dialects, as well as ... written Latin for business purposes'.
[97] Clanchy, *From Memory to Written Record*, pp. 201–2. The Plea Rolls of the Exchequer of the Jews might also occasionally contain Hebrew. Amidst Christian Latin (and occasionally Anglo-Norman) records of Jewish transactions and suits, one surviving roll has a Hebrew note of quittance of debt in a damaged lower margin, suggesting perhaps some collaboration between Christian and Jewish scribes. See J. M. Rigg, ed., *Calendar of the Plea Rolls of the Exchequer of the Jews Preserved in the Public Record Office, Henry III 1218–1272*, I (London, 1905), p. 110. The Hebrew note is on membrane 6 of roll E9/4 in the British National Archives in Kew.
[98] *From Memory to Written Record*, p. 202.

Caede ... completa, conjurati continuo cathedralem ecclesiam adeuntes, monumenta debitorum, quibus Christiani premebantur, a Judæis fœneratoribus regiis ibidem reposita, ab exterritis custodibus violenta instantia resignari fecerent, et tam pro sua quam et aliorum multorum liberatione eadem profanæ avaritiæ instrumenta in medio ecclesiæ flammis solemnibus absumpserunt.[99]

[W]hen the slaughter was over, the conspirators immediately went to the Cathedral and caused the terrified guardians, with violent threats, to hand over the records of the debts placed there by which the Christians were oppressed by the royal Jewish usurers. Thereupon they destroyed these records of profane avarice in the middle of the church with the sacred fires to release both themselves and many others.

The destruction of Jews and Jewish texts become almost indistinguishable motivating factors in this case, as they were to be later in the Barons' War of 1264–67, when attacks on Jews in Canterbury, London, and Worcester included the destruction of the *archae* that contained the debt records and forced Simon de Montfort to offer cancellation of Jewish debts to alleviate the raiding.[100] Pre-expulsion hostility toward Jews themselves was inextricably linked to their control of the legal texts that so powerfully controlled the lives of their debtors and business associates.[101]

Power over Hebrew (Jewish) texts, and the struggle for that power, then, functioned in narrative, legal, and sacred contexts. For the handful of Christian scholars and theologians who did understand Hebrew, the primary motive behind their learning was the conversion of the Jews. Friars in England and on the continent had made a point of learning Hebrew in the thirteenth century for the express purpose of preaching to, and disputing with, Jews.[102] The study of Hebrew was established at Oxford around the same time that the Dominicans opened a priory in the Jewish quarter of the town and began aggressive conversion campaigns. These attempts to influence Jewish communities were

---

[99] Hans Claude Hamilton, ed., *Historia rerum Anglicarum Willelmi Parvi*, Publications of the English Historical Society, II, rpt (Vaduz, 1964), p. 28. The translation here is from Jacob Rader Marcus, ed. and comp., *The Jew in the Medieval World: A Source Book, 315–1791*, rev. Marc Saperstein (Cincinnati, 1999), p. 150.

[100] The connection between the burning Jew and the burning Jewish text is exploited in Marian miracles too, specifically in the 'Legend of Theophilus' and in the story known as the 'Jewish Boy' (and wherever these two narratives are connected). See below, pp. 61–2, 68, 73, 87.

[101] J. R. Madicott, *Simon de Montfort* (Cambridge, 1996), pp. 315–16; and Mundill, *England's Jewish Solution*, p. 259. See also my essay on related transactions between women, 'Inscribed Bodies: The Virgin Mary, Jewish Women, and Feminine Legal Authority', *Law and Sovereignty in the Middle Ages and Renaissance*, ed. Robert Sturges, Arizona Studies in the Middle Ages and Renaissance 28 (Turnhout, forthcoming 2010). It might be argued that the most prominent issue in the riotous destruction of texts is the struggle for cultural power; compare the York riot to the actions of the rebels in the 1381 Peasant's Revolt as discussed by Steven Justice, *Writing and Rebellion: England in 1381*, The New Historicism: Studies in Cultural Poetics 27 (Berkeley and Los Angeles, 1994).

[102] On Dominican and Franciscan conversion campaigns, see Jeremy Cohen, *The Friars and the Jews: The Evolution of Medieval Anti-Judaism* (Ithaca, NY, and London, 1982).

supported by the government, especially by Edward I, who would eventually expel the Jews but first ordered the mandatory attendance of Jews at Dominican sermons by upholding the papal bull *Vineam sorec* in 1280.[103] The idea that Jews would convert if only they would listen to reasonable and learned testimony of those familiar with their own scriptures, however, proved undeniably false in all but exemplary (and especially Marian) literatures. It is even likely that it prompted one Northampton Jewish man to mock the attempt by disguising himself as a friar and preaching false Christian teachings before he was caught and sentenced to parade naked through certain towns, presumably to prove that he was in fact Jewish.[104]

Symbolic of the letter and not the spirit, spiritually connected to law and not to grace, Jews were symbolically and actually connected to textual and legal domains in the Christian mind. In England, this was nowhere more emphatically demonstrated than through Jewish identification badges. In accordance with the Fourth Lateran Council decision that all Jews wear a distinguishing badge of shame, English kings continually reissued and refined their demands concerning the badge.[105] Where Jews all over the continent were forced to wear yellow circles, English Jews were prescribed a distinct *tabula*: large representations of the two tablets of Mosaic law, which in practice looked like an open book.[106] In England, Jews were literally marked with, and as, a book.

What is perhaps surprising – and the reason for the summary I have just given – is that the Virgin Mary could be construed very similarly. As the bearer of the Word, she was both connected to Christian (English) notions of the Jew and the symbol of exactly what Jews rejected. Miracles of the Virgin in which Jewish belief in the Incarnation is at stake (and it could be argued that *all* Miracles of the Virgin enact the truth of the Incarnation) are at once the most volatile and the most complex, for it is precisely in the figure of Mary that Judaism meets Christianity, that Judaism turns into Christianity. She is, at the moment of the Annunciation, both wholly Jewish and wholly Christian, and medieval English authors were certainly interested in maintaining her Jewishness. Langland, for instance, reminds us that 'Jhesu Cryste on Jewes doughter alyghte'; the *South English Legendary* makes sure that

---

[103]   Cohen, *The Friars and the Jews*, p. 82; Mundill, *England's Jewish Solution*, pp. 48, 69.

[104]   See Hilary Jenkinson, ed., *Calendar of the Plea Rolls of the Exchequer of the Jews Preserved in the Public Record Office, Edward I 1275–1277*, III (London, 1929), pp. 311–12. The episode is briefly mentioned in Mundill, *England's Jewish Solution*, p. 275, though there is no speculation on the reason for the punishment. My essay, 'Desire for Religion: Mary, a Murder Libel, a Jewish Friar, and Me', *'Something Fearful': Medievalist Scholars on the Religious Turn in Literary Criticism*, ed. Kathryn Kerby-Fulton, special issue of *Religion and Literature* (forthcoming 2010) discusses the case further and expands on some of the material in these few pages.

[105]   Mundill, *England's Jewish Solution*, pp. 49–50.

[106]   The 1275 Statute of the Jewry, printed in Mundill, *England's Jewish Solution*, p. 292, specifies that 'each Jew after he shall be Seven Years old, shall wear a Badge on his outer Garment; that is to say, in the Form of Two Tables joined, of yellow Felt, of the Length of Six Inches, and of the Breadth of Three Inches'. For medieval illustrations of the English badge, see Heinz Schreckenberg, *The Jews in Christian Art* (New York, 1996), p. 305.

readers understand that Christ was circumcised because the family 'nolde noȝt aȝen þe olde lauwe beo'; and a preacher might be careful to specify that Mary appeared before the Assumption not in a church but 'in þe sinagoge', or lament that 'þe Iewes had hure, but þei wold not beleue in hure'.[107] The fact of her Jewishness is absolutely unremarkable in a gospel context, but in medieval accretions it can be read as a response to Christian recognition and internalizing of Mary's Jewishness in light of a developing theological focus on the Incarnation as the historical moment at which Judaism and Christianity part ways.[108] All Marian narratives have the potential outcome of conversion, and Mary, inhabiting a liminal space between Judaism and Christianity, is in fact an unsurprising intercessor for such purposes.

It is exactly this that is highlighted by the only extant Marian miracles in which Christian–Jewish disputation is an organizing feature. In both of these tales, which are appended to homilies in John Mirk's early fifteenth-century *Festial*, argument over the plausibility of the Incarnation seems to foreshadow and make necessary Mary's appearance. A learned Christian debates with a learned Jew, and only at the moment of stalemate, when the Jew flatly refuses to accept that Jesus's birth is a virgin one, does Mary intercede to force a conversion. In one, a monk and gifted scribe who visits Jerusalem debates Mary's virginity with 'a Iew þat was a grete mastur of þat contre', until the Jewish master asks him to paint an image of the Virgin. Once painted, the image of the Virgin and Child comes to life, the Christ-child begins to nurse at his mother's breast, and the Jewish master converts and teaches others of his newfound faith.[109] The more extraordinary example, however, comes at the end of a sermon on the Annunciation, in a little *narracio* said to be a response to those who have asked 'why þer stondyth a wyne-potte and a lyly bytwyx our lady and Gabyrell at hur salutacyon'.[110] That is, the conceit is that the preacher has had inquiries about the meaning of a commonplace feature of Annunciation iconography.[111] Why is there so often a pot of lilies in such images? Well, answers this text, consider this: it happened once that a Christian and a Jew sat together, a wine pot between them, and they discussed the incarnation of Christ. After the Christian had explained that belief in it is similar to the easy belief that lilies grow without human intervention, the Jew responded, 'When I se a lyly spryng out of þys potte, I wyll leue (believe),

---

107 See respectively A. V. C. Schmidt, ed., *The Vision of Piers Plowman: A Complete Edition of the B-Text* (London, 1987), XI.246; Charlotte D'Evelyn and Anna J. Mill, eds, *The South English Legendary*, I, EETS, os 235 (London, 1956), p. 4; and Woodburn Ross, ed., *Middle English Sermons*, EETS, os 209 (London, 1940), pp. 247, 329.

108 This is a consequence of the medieval movement to emphasize Christ's humanity and can be seen first in scholastic ideas about Jewish disbelief. See Gavin I. Langmuir, *Towards a Definition of Antisemitism* (Berkeley and Los Angeles, 1990), pp. 115ff. Cohen, also, discusses disputation texts on the subject in *Friars and the Jews*, pp. 116–17, 155–6.

109 Erbe, *Mirk's Festial*, pp. 302–3.

110 Ibid., p. 108.

111 On this *exemplum*, see also Nancy E. Atkinson, 'John Mirk's Holy Women', *Papers on Language & Literature* 43 (2007), pp. 346–8.

and er not.'[112] Of course, a lily immediately sprang from the pot, and the Jew consequently converted. What is striking, however, is Mirk's commentary:

> For þis skyll, þe potte and þe lyly ys sette bytwyx our lady and Gabryell. For right as þys Iewe dysputeþe with þys crysten man of þe maner of þe conceyte of our lady; ryght soo oure lady sputyd with þe angel of þe maner, and how scho shuld conceyue, and be mayden er and aftyr. þen scho asentyd þerto.[113]

The physical closeness of Christian and Jew in this *exemplum* – side by side, talking, debating scripture, apparently drinking together – happens only in an effort to recreate the image of Gabriel and Mary as a figure of Christian and Jew. Mirk suggests superimposing this image of Jewish conversion on Annunciation images, with the lily pot as the cue for emphatic identification of Mary with 'Jew'. The Annunciation lilies, then, are not symbolic of Mary's purity but are rather the visual residue of a Jewish conversion. The imposition of continued Jewish doubt on the scene is correct and perpetually defensible so long as the doubting Jew is the figure of Mary and not of himself: he becomes the figure of Mary; his doubt mimics scripture about her; she too disputed before she assented; she too had required a miracle to shift her belief. The vacillation between the biblical moment of Jewish assent and post-biblical Jewish denial is an insidious encouragement to view Mary as the 'correct' Jew. Implicitly cast as the learned disputing Jew – and this sermon argues that the ubiquitous iconography of the Annunciation should continually prompt us to cast her this way – Mary's Jewish identity comes to complement her legal advocacy and textual (interpretive) acumen.

To make the case that this is relevant to a significant portion of English Marian miracles without more than a little doubt, however, it is necessary to move away from the work of this chapter – from what has been essentially the work of definition and orientation. It is finally necessary to roll back the centuries and return to origins, though not only the ones that R. W. Southern outlined. His notion of the English origins of the Miracles of the Virgin, though correct and compelling in its particulars, cannot lead to the fourteenth- and fifteenth-century vernacular Marian examples I have just discussed, primarily because of the strict divisions into which he separated the corpus.[114] When he separated '*collections* of stories which had an independent literary existence [my italics]' from what he called 'individual stories', or from those used

---

[112] Erbe, *Mirk's Festial*, pp. 108–9.

[113] Ibid., p. 109.

[114] In this he followed the divisions of Adolfo Mussafia, who did the foundational work on the genre, surveying over 200 manuscripts primarily of German and Austrian provenance. See *Studien zu den mittelalterlichen Marienlegenden*, Sitzungsberichte der kaiserlichen Akademie der Wissenschaften zu Wien, Phil.-hist Klasse (Vienna, 1886–98). This major study appeared in five parts in the following volumes: 113 (1886), 115 (1887), 119 (1889), 123 (1891), and 139 (1898).

solely for 'illustrations of … argument' in theological tracts or sermons,[115] he effectively dismissed the earlier and later mechanisms of this genre's development in England. He insisted on categorical divisions understandably, because their conflation complicated the history of the large Latin collections that seemed almost spontaneously to appear in twelfth-century England, but the individual stories that predate the Middle Ages and circulated independently in sermons or legendaries look much more like the Marian miracles that did in fact go on to thrive in England than do the Latin collections.

It is 'independent literary' tales that create a fascinating amalgam of the Marian character as Jew and Christian, lawyer and doctor, theologian and disputant, merciful mother and punishing *domina*, Empress of Heaven and Hell and humble young girl. These tales also tell a story of English origins. In as much as those early monastic collections were compilations as well as compositions, they incorporated preexisting narratives, and they were shaped by, and modeled on, those narratives. The history of an individual Marian miracle in England may be part of the confusion that Southern wanted to avoid, but it is crucial to remember that many legends had a life before the moment that he discussed, and that those early compositions and compilations came from 'monasteries with strong old English traditions … [and] men united in admiration for the forms of Anglo-Saxon piety'.[116] In the next chapter, I will turn to one of the most important of those individual legends, one which deeply influenced Anglo-Saxon conceptions of Mary's intercession and which unquestionably created a type of tale and a type of Mary that would endure in England. There are visible lines of development in *English Miracles of the Virgin*, but we need to reach back further than the twelfth century to see them.

---

[115] Southern, 'English Origins', pp. 177–8.
[116] Ibid., p. 197.

2

The Theophilus Legend in England
Mary the Advocate, Mary the Jew

> Ingens documentum futurum, quantum in cognatae gentis
> conuersione laboret industria Mariae.

> It would take a massive book to tell how energetically
> Mary labors to convert her own people.

> William of Malmesbury,
> *Miracula Sanctae Mariae Virginae*[1]

The legend of Theophilus 'circulated in both the East and West for a long time before the beginning of the twelfth century',[2] but it is so emblematic of English Miracles of the Virgin that the earliest groupings of Marian miracle stories in England, whether Latin or vernacular, are addenda to the Theophilus story.[3] Though it did not originate in England, it was prominently positioned in two of the early Anglo-Latin collections that were important to R. W. Southern, and its long popularity in England played a significant role in the creation of the Marian miracle genre. It is the story of a sixth-century *vicedominus* (Theophilus) who contracts his soul to the Devil with the help of a Jewish sorcerer, and then successfully prays for Mary's help to undo the contract. Theophilus is the archetypal sinner of Marian literature, and Mary is, in this story, a powerful legal advocate with particular power over the written word, and with a special ability to intercede where Jews are concerned.

The usual summary of the origins and dissemination of the legend says that it was written in Greek in the sixth century; that it was first recorded by one Eutychian, who claimed to be a member of Theophilus's household and an eyewitness to the events; that it was translated into Latin in the ninth century by Paul, a deacon of Naples; and that Paul's translation became the

---

[1] Canal, *El libro de laudibus*, p. 136.
[2] Southern, 'English Origins', p. 177.
[3] This is the case in the mid-twelfth-century Latin collections of Dominic of Evesham and William of Malmesbury, in the late twelfth-century anonymous Anglo-Norman collection in MS BL Royal 20 B. XIV, in Adgar's early thirteenth-century Anglo-Norman collection, and in the Marian miracle cycle of the *SEL*. I will discuss Dominic and William's use of the legend below, pp. 62–74, and the *SEL* cycle in Chapter 3, pp. 82–93.

basis for all later Western versions of the story. There is good evidence for this summary, but it is also true that the repetition of these basic elements has obscured the case and its implications.[4] Though the legend is certainly of Byzantine origin, the authorship and dating of the original composition are not really discernible, and the Greek text survives in only three medieval manuscripts, two dating roughly to the eleventh century and one to the fifteenth.[5] It is in one of these eleventh-century codices that an 'authorial' colophon first appears and the supposed eyewitness 'Eutychianos' makes his claims, but it is probable, of course, that the colophon is the work of a later scribe who copied or reworked the story. E. F. Sommer's assertion that 'Eutychianos' is 'a mere man of straw invented by the author or copyist to give the story an air of truth' is surely not far off.[6] There is no evidence that the colophon existed, nor indeed that any Theophilus legend existed, before the late ninth century when the Latin work of the deacon called Paul appeared.

'Paulus Diaconus' was working in Naples during the last quarter of the ninth century.[7] He was an important member of a small school of translators whose project included making Byzantine hagiography accessible to the West.[8] The theological problems that had been specially addressed by

---

4   The scholarly iteration of this account of the legend's origins can be found, for example, in Southern, *Making of the Middle Ages*, pp. 247–8; Boyd, *Middle English Miracles*, pp. 127–8; and Philip Palmer and Robert More, *The Sources of the Faust Tradition from Simon Magus to Lessing* (New York, 1965), pp. 58–9.

5   The date usually assigned to the miracle (the year 537) was not used until the thirteenth century, in the *Legenda Aurea*, though 'from the mention of the "Persian invasions" [in the first lines of the legend] it is possible that this date is approximately correct' (see Palmer and More, *Sources of the Faust Tradition*, p. 59). The earliest Greek text is in Bibliothèque Nationale MS Coislin 283, and several scholars feel definitely that the other known early Greek example is significantly later (Vienna, Nationalbibliothek MS palat. gr. 3), though Boyd in *Middle English Miracles*, p. 128, says that the Paris manuscript is 'possibly as late as the eleventh century' and claims that the Vienna manuscript is older. For more detail, see George Webbe Dasent, *Theophilus in Icelandic, Low German, and Other Tongues* (London, 1845), pp. ix–x, pp. 94–6; Karl Plenzat, *Die Theophiluslegende in den Dichtungen des Mittelalters* (Berlin, 1926), pp. 16–19; Ludwig Radermacher, *Griechische Quellen zur Faustsage*, Akademie der Wissenschaften zu Wien, Phil.-hist Klasse (Vienna and Leipzig, 1927); and G. G. Meersseman, *Kritische Glossen op de Griekse Theophilus-legende (7ᵉ eeuw) en haar Latijnse vertaling (9ᵉ eeuw)* (Brussels, 1963), pp. 15–16.

6   Quoted in Dasent, *Theophilus in Icelandic*, p. 94.

7   This Paul is not to be confused with Paul the Deacon, author of the *Historia Langobardum*, though there is some evidence that he has been. Marina Warner, *Alone of All Her Sex: The Myth and the Cult of the Virgin Mary* (New York, 1976), p. 323, for example, is obviously confused when she claims that 'Paul the Deacon (d. *c.*799), a monk of Monte Cassino, translated the *Miracle of Theophilus* into Latin and from then on it circulated throughout Christendom'. J. C. Jennings, 'The Origins of the Elements Series of the Miracles of the Virgin', *Mediaeval and Renaissance Studies* 6 (1968), p. 86, also incorrectly ascribes the text, assuming that the Theophilus translator had sent his work to Charlemagne rather than Charles the Bald. It is unclear whether Malcolm Godden has made the mistake in 'Experiments in Genre: The Saints' Lives in Ælfric's *Catholic Homilies*', *Holy Men and Holy Women: Old English Prose Saints' Lives and Their Contexts*, ed. Paul Szarmach (Albany, NY, 1996), pp. 263–76, but his discussion of the *other* Paul the Deacon's contributions to the Cotton-Corpus Legendary does not ease the confusion.

8   The influence of Eastern Christianity on Neapolitan culture, especially in the eighth and ninth centuries, has been ably discussed by Michele Fuiano, *La cultura a Napoli nell'alto medioevo*, Storia e pensiero (Naples, 1961), pp. 131–52. Fuiano discusses the historical and cultural back-

Byzantine thinkers by this time included the efficacy and necessity of penitence in response to the Augustinian notion of grace, and the importance of the role of the Virgin Mary in Christian salvation.[9] The translation of certain legendary accounts, specifically the lives of Mary of Egypt and Theophilus, seems to have introduced these discussions into the popular imagination of the West, as did the gradual Western acceptance of Marian feasts with apocryphal bases, and all that survives of the work of Paul the Deacon of Naples indicates that he had a special interest in the translation of texts that spoke exactly to these issues.[10]

The only work other than 'Theophilus' that can be ascribed to him with certainty, in fact, is a Latin translation of the life of Mary of Egypt, which likewise tells of an extreme but penitent sinner who benefits from Marian intercession at the moment of contrition. Paul's translation of this *vita* includes a preface that survives only in one tenth-century manuscript, wherein he writes that he had done the translation 'cum tomulo de cujusdam vicedomini poenitentia' (with a little book concerning a certain penitent *vicedominus*). He had already presented both texts to Charles the Bald, he says, but since the texts had gone missing, he was sending them again.[11] His second edition was evidently successful, as the two translations appear together in a group of four early manuscripts,[12] and they are widely acknowledged to be among the earliest texts to show the Virgin Mary in her role as intercessor for sinners.[13] But they are, together, more than this. They are elaborate hagiographical narratives, and in them the Virgin Mary intercedes not just for the quotidian sinner but for a hardened prostitute (Mary of Egypt) and for a man who has systematically rejected her and her son and contracted his soul to Satan (Theophilus). As these companion pieces traveled together in referential relationship to each other, they began to define Mary's intercessory personality, and they marked the beginning of a certain collectability of Marian legends that the Theophilus story seems to have begged, and which Paul the Deacon of Naples clearly recognized.

Paul's translation of the Theophilus legend was the first version of the story known in England. There are four English survivals from the eleventh

ground of the Neapolitan school and the work of Paul the Deacon of Naples specifically. There is evidence that the iconoclastic controversy and subsequent immigration of Greek-speaking religious to Naples and Monte Cassino encouraged a certain amount of bilingual cultural exchange, especially with regard to hagiography.

9   Ibid., pp. 143–7.
10 On Paul's interests and motivations, see Paolo Chiesa, 'Le tradizioni del Greco: l'evoluzione della scuola Napoletana ne X secolo', *Mittellateinisches Jarbuch* 24/25 (1989/90), pp. 71–2.
11 See Albert Siegmund, *Die Überlieferung der griechischen Christlichen Literatur*, Abhandlungen der bayerischen Benediktiner-Akademie (Munich, 1949), p. 269. Siegmund confidently dates Paul's Mary of Egypt to 876 or 877, presumably because of this dedication.
12 Ibid., pp. 269–70. In the single tenth-century survival that contains Paul's preface to his *vita Mariae Aegyptiacae*, however, the legend lacks its companion piece.
13 See Fuiano, *La cultura a Napoli*, p. 131; Chiesa, 'Le tradizioni del Greco', pp. 71–2 n. 10; and Clayton, *Cult of the Virgin*, pp. 257–8.

century and earlier, and dozens of later medieval copies.[14] In all probability, it is this Neapolitan 'translation' that was exclusively known and accessible in England for at least two centuries after it was done, and its influence on English Marian devotion was such that Mary Clayton has labeled it 'one of the most important texts inspiring devotion to Mary in Anglo-Saxon England'.[15] So let us begin with a summary of its content:

> Theophilus, *vicedominus* (archdeacon or secular deputy) of the church at Adana, near Tarsus in Cilicia, is a charitable and pious man. When he is elected to succeed as bishop of his church, he humbly declines. The man who does become bishop expels him from his office, and Theophilus quickly loses his fame and possessions. He decides to seek the help of a well-known Jewish sorcerer, and the Jew summons the Devil. With the sorcerer's guidance, Theophilus enters into a written contract with Satan to restore his power and wealth. This contract requires him to renounce Christ and his mother – which he does – and Theophilus seals it with his own seal. He prospers for a time, but later repents of his action. For forty days, he fasts and prays fervently for the help of the Virgin Mary, who finally appears before him. At first she chastises him for his error and refuses to help, but she promises to discuss the case with her son. After three more days, she returns to report that she has obtained his forgiveness. Theophilus, however, worries that the charter he sealed is nevertheless binding, and he asks that Mary retrieve the document from the Devil. Mary does this, and she then leaves the document on Theophilus's breast as he sleeps. Theophilus goes to mass to confess his sins, bear witness to his miraculous salvation, and take communion. The bishop celebrating mass gives an impromptu sermon urging the congregation to pray to Mary as Theophilus did, and Theophilus burns the Devil's charter before all. He dies three days later, and his soul travels 'in manu Filii Dei & immaculatæ semper Virginis Mariæ' (into the hands of the son of God and the immaculate ever Virgin Mary).[16]

Anglo-Saxon liturgical texts confirm that this account of Theophilus's miracle was well known in England by at least the beginning of the eleventh century. It was used in English Offices of the Virgin that pre-date the earliest survivals

---

14 These are MS BL Harley 3020 (late tenth-century), MS BL Cotton Nero E. I (late tenth-century), MS BL Cotton Vespasian D. II (eleventh-century), and Salisbury Cathedral Library MS 221 (eleventh-century). For a full list of manuscripts containing this version of the Theophilus legend, see Ward, *Catalogue of Romances*, pp. 586–740. Paul's life of Mary of Egypt also appears in Cotton Nero E. I and the Salisbury Cathedral MS. See Patrick H. Zettel, 'Saints' Lives in Old English: Latin Manuscripts and Vernacular Accounts: Ælfric', *Peritia* 1 (1982), pp. 19–20.

15 Clayton, *Cult of the Virgin*, p. 118.

16 All citations of the Latin are from the *Acta Sanctorum* edition of Paul the Deacon of Naples's 'Miraculum S. Mariæ de Theophilo Poenitente', IV February (Feb., I, *BHL* 8121), pp. 483–7 (here p. 487, col. a) and have been checked against the more recent critical edition in Meersseman, *Kritische glossen op de Griekse Theophilus-legende* (there are no significant differences between what I will quote here and what Meersseman prints). An English translation is also available in Palmer and More, *Sources of the Faust Tradition*, pp. 60–75.

of the full text, in readings excerpted verbatim or nearly verbatim from Paul's text, or in prayers that echo Paul's account of Theophilus's penitential prayers to Mary during his forty days of fasting.[17] Clayton has even suggested that 'the use of the Theophilus legend is … compatible with an English origin' for liturgical compositions.[18]

Mary's advocacy for sinners and her ability to save them from hell was recognized in England from as early as the ninth century. In both the Book of Cerne and the Book of Nunnaminster, for example, are expressions of absolute trust that Mary will be granted anything she requests from her son and, in particular, that she can help penitents 'inferni tenebras euadere' (to escape the darkness of hell).[19] Henri Barré has remarked that there are 'very few other explicit witnesses to recourse to the intercession of the Virgin Mary' that exist as early as these,[20] and this historically premature confidence in Mary's intercessory powers seems in England to have led to a detailed imagination of her ferocity in matters of judgment. By the eleventh century Mary might, as a patroness, ensure 'ut non gaudeat inimicus qui non timuit [s]uam inuadere possessionem' (that the enemy may not rejoice who feared not to seize [her] possession), or repay an enemy 'secundum opera malitie sue' (according to the works of his malice). It was acceptable to pray that all adversaries 'ultionis [s]ue uindictam sentiant' (realize the punishment of [her] vengeance), or to ask that she 'inimicorum nostrorum praua consilia ad perpetuam … dampnationem commutetis' (change the evil plans of our enemies into perpetual damnation).[21]

In this context, the Theophilus legend enhanced an already developing characterization of a Mary with significant physical, demonic, and, most importantly, legal influence. It provided narrative excerpts that established for Mary, even in practical prayer, an ability to contend with the Devil, to descend into hell, and to nullify contractual agreements. The appropriation of Theophilus-specific content to general prayers of supplication created an everyman sinner identified with the apostate legally bound to the Devil, and a Virgin Mary with a regnal and legal dominion matched only, perhaps, by her son. Prayers that used the Theophilus text but decontextualized the apostate's desperation could claim that Mary 'sola intulisti salutem' (alone brought salvation), or call her 'omnium potentissima' (the most powerful of all) and wish that 'sentiat serpens at draco malignus uirtutem [s]uam' (the

---

17 See Clayton, *Cult of the Virgin*, pp. 71–2, 109, 114–18.
18 Ibid., p. 109.
19 Ibid., pp. 98–9. The Book of Nunnaminster dates to the late eighth century and the Book of Cerne to the early ninth. Clayton quotes several Marian compositions from the two codices and discusses their originality on pp. 96–103.
20 Quoted in Clayton, *Cult of the Virgin*, p. 103.
21 Quoted and translated in Clayton, *Cult of the Virgin*, pp. 74–5. These petitions are from a prefatory prayer to a mid-eleventh-century Office of the Virgin in MS BL Royal 2. B and seem to be the response of a religious house to dispossession of lands.

serpent and wicked dragon feel [her] power).[22] She could be, as one mid-eleventh-century English lection concludes, 'uirgo quae antiquum diabolicae perditionis cyrographum aboluit totoque seculo subuenit' (the virgin who destroyed the old signed document of diabolical surrender and came to the assistance of the entire world).[23]

Mary's unparalleled power and the belief that she could contend with the Devil, win back a damned soul, and undo a bad contract became part of what defined her role in Christian salvation in Anglo-Saxon England. Her position in these liturgical compositions is as one who maintains the theological bureaucracy between heaven, earth, and hell. For any reader who knows the Theophilus legend, however, these are also reflections of Theophilus's confidence in her unique ability to save him, and they allude to her retrieval of his document from hell. The eternalizing of the abrogated diabolical 'cyrographum' (cited just above) echoes Paul the Deacon's text quite unmistakably: Paul six times uses the word 'chirographum' to describe the charter with which Theophilus renounces Christ and Mary.[24] In liturgical use, this ability to annihilate the hellish charter and solve even the most profound contractual dispute is of utmost importance.[25] It becomes a general, if figuratively specific, statement of Mary's role as advocate for sinners and facilitator of salvation.

'Theophilus' in Ælfric's *Catholic Homilies*

An accretion of Mary's legendary power may be what the Anglo-Saxon homilist Ælfric responded to in the sermon on Mary's Assumption in his first series of homilies (*Catholic Homilies I*). Ælfric wrote two sermons explaining Mary's death and subsequent bodily assumption into heaven, and in one he included a brief summary of the Theophilus legend – in fact, the first vernacular rendering of the story.[26] In the same sermon, however, he was (and not uncharacteristically so) concerned to limit the impact of apocryphal Marian material circulating in England. Mary's death had been a favorite topic of increasingly fantastic apocrypha, and Ælfric emphasized the need for

---

[22] Ibid., pp. 114–16. These come from a lengthy Theophilus-inspired prayer in a pre-Conquest Winchester psalter (MS BL Arundel 60).

[23] Ibid., p. 78. This is from a short Saturday Office of the Virgin in the Portiforium of St Wulstan (Cambridge, Corpus Christi College MS 391). The same prayer is extant in three other English manuscripts from the twelfth through fifteenth centuries and makes its way to a group of French manuscripts as well, though Clayton (*Cult of the Virgin*) argues convincingly for the precedence of the English examples on pp. 79–80.

[24] See Paul the Deacon of Naples, 'Miraculum S. Mariæ de Theophilo', p. 484, col. b (twice); p. 486, col. a (twice); p. 486, col. b; p. 487, col. a. He elsewhere uses *chartula*.

[25] The 'Devil's Charter' or 'Devil's Letter' is a document that takes on a life of its own in later figurative development. See Morton Bloomfield, *Piers Plowman as a Fourteenth Century Apocalypse* (New Brunswick, NJ, 1961), p. 80.

[26] Both sermons are discussed at length in Clayton, *Cult of the Virgin*, pp. 235–44.

47

caution in assessment of the ultimate fate of her body. To this end, he voiced the pseudo-Jerome letter known as *Cogitus me*:

> witodlice ge neadiað me þæt ic eow recce hu seo eadige maria on þysum dæigþerlicum dæge to heofonlicere wununge genumen wæs ... hu ðes mæra freolsdæig geond æighwylces geares ymbryne beo aspend mid heofonlicum lofe 7 mid gastlicere blisse gemærsod sy; þy læs ðe eow on hand becume. seo lease gesetnyss. þe ðurh gedwolmannum wide tosawen is. 7 ge ðonne þa gehiwedan leasunge for soðre race underfoð.[27]

> Certainly you want me to tell you how the blessed Mary, on this very day was taken to a heavenly dwelling, ... how this great feast day is spent with heavenly praise in the course of every year and is celebrated with spiritual bliss, lest false narrative, which through heretics is widely spread, should come to your hand and you then take feigned lies for a true account.

Ælfric's inclusion of this passage (he used only twenty-six of the pseudo-Jerome letter's 117 paragraphs) allows him to introduce the topic of the Assumption by calling those who circulate apocryphal narratives 'gedwolmannum' and such narrative itself 'lease gesetnyss', vocabulary that in his other works (the Preface to Genesis, for example) applies to the irresponsibly unlearned and to false or even mendacious texts.[28] The homily that follows from this expression of distaste for the merely legendary is for the most part unsurprising. Ælfric pieces together scriptural evidence for Mary's post-Crucifixion biography, explains the location and situation of her grave near Mount Olivet in Jerusalem, and discusses the theological appropriateness of a miraculous assumption for the mother of Christ. That is, the sermon gives a relatively balanced account that follows quite naturally from a general denunciation of apocryphal material.

In this context, however, Ælfric also includes two legendary accounts of Marian intercession. The homily concludes with a very brief description of the fall and penitence of Theophilus, and then with an elaborate account of Mary's punishment of Julian the Apostate, a story taken from a tenth-century *Vita Basilii* that Ælfric also translated for his life of St Basil in the *Lives of Saints*.[29] Clearly apocryphal accounts of Mary's life, which require some basis in scripture, are separate from accounts of Mary's intercession in a sinner's life. Should the distinction confuse a congregant or reader, there

---

[27] All citations of Ælfric's Assumption homily (Sermon 30) are from Peter Clemoes, ed., *Ælfric's Catholic Homilies, The First Series*, EETS, ss 17 (Oxford and New York, 1997), pp. 427–38, here pp. 429–30.

[28] The quoted passage is a fairly strict translation from the pseudo-Jerome text (the 'ge' addressed is Eustochium), though other parts of the sermon are less faithful and include interpolations. See Malcolm Godden, *Ælfric's Catholic Homilies, Series I and II: Commentary*, EETS, ss 18 (Oxford and New York, 2000), pp. 248–9.

[29] This Latin version of the life of St Basil is conjectural (see Clayton, *Cult of the Virgin*, p. 241). For Ælfric's St Basil, see W. W. Skeat, ed. and trans., *Ælfric's Lives of Saints*, EETS, os 76 (London, 1881), pp. 51–91.

is more at stake for Ælfric than mere differentiation between apocrypha and canon anyway: what is at stake is the very nature of Marian tradition and transmission.

What Ælfric wants to communicate about Mary is not dissimilar from what he wants to communicate about Jerome, whose authority he leans on. He introduces the topic of Mary's Assumption with an explanation of Jerome's willingness to share his theological knowledge. In particular, Jerome's ability to translate Hebrew and Greek makes him more than a good reader in Ælfric's eyes. He is a cultural go-between, sensitive to the nuances of multilingual and multicultural interplay. Ælfric describes him in this way:

> ðes hieronimus wæs halig sacerd 7 getogen on hebreiscum gereorde. 7 on greciscum. 7 on ledenum fulfremedlice 7 he awende ure bibliothecan of hebreiscum bocum to ledenspræce; He is se fyrmesta wealgstod betwux hebreiscum. 7 grecum. 7 ledenwarum.[30]

> This Jerome was a holy priest and very learned in the Hebrew language, and in Greek, and very comfortable with Latin. And he translated our Bible from Hebrew books into Latin speech. He is the foremost intermediary between Hebrew and the Greeks and the Latin people.

Ælfric praises Jerome first for the extent of his learning and his efforts to share it, and then for his ability to make the transmission and translation of texts a conversation between peoples and not only between books. He is an intermediary, a 'wealgstod', and *this* gives him his authority.

Of course, it must be said that Hebrew is the emphatically bookish starting place in this exchange. Of the three languages Ælfric discusses here, Hebrew is the only one that is not connected to people or conversation. In this commendation of the translation process, Hebrew is language and books ('hebreiscum gereorde' and 'hebreiscum bocum'), while Greek is both language and people ('greciscum' and 'grecum'), and Latin lives as speech and people ('ledenspæce' and 'ledenwarum'). The exchange begins from a system that is closed and therefore stable – not Hebrews, but Hebrew books – and it extends forward to living languages and peoples. This is important to what Ælfric has to say about Mary's Assumption. First, apocryphal narratives about Mary's death are not reliable because they are not part of the closed system of Hebrew scripture and therefore become unstable. Second, his own translation project, in which this sermon is involved, requires sensitivity to the problems of living and unstable traditions of language. Third, and most important to my point, he values in Jerome the same attributes he values in Mary. This last will also be crucial to why he might choose to use the 'Legend of Theophilus' in this context.

Ælfric emphasizes Mary's post-Crucifixion role as a teacher and authoritative transmitter of knowledge. She is the grieving mother for whom the

---

[30] Clemoes, *Catholic Homilies*, p. 429.

apostles care, of course, but she is also the educator and spiritual guide of the apostles, the pedagogical source of Christianity, in whom the Holy Spirit placed not only Christ himself but also the power to know and to teach. As Ælfric puts it,

> heo him cuðlice ealle þing ymbe cristes menniscnysse gewissode; for þan ðe heo fram frymþe gewislice þurh ðone halgan gast hi ealle geleornode 7 mid agenre gesihðe geseah. þeah ðe þa apostoli þurh ðone ylcan gast ealle þing undergeaton. 7 on ealre soðfæstnysse gelærede wurdon; Se heahengel gabrihel hi ungewemmede geheold 7 heo wunode on iohannes 7 on ealra þæra apostola gymene on þære heofenlican scole ymbe godes æ smea-gende.[31]

> she openly taught them everything about Christ's incarnation, because she, from the beginning, had certainly learned all through the Holy Spirit and had seen with her own sight. But the apostles understood everything through the same Holy Spirit. And in all truthfulness they were taught. The archangel Gabriel kept her unblemished, and she dwelled in the care of John and of all the apostles, meditating on God's law in their heavenly school.

Mary had learned through revelation ('þurh ðone halgan gast'), and, in Ælfric's rendering, she bore the responsibility of translating that revelation for others. He is emphatic about the manner of transmission here: as a school-master she taught ('gewissode', 'gelærede') and ran the 'heofenlican scole' in which the sole curriculum was the law ('godes æ'). In Ælfric's estimation, the purpose of Mary's continued existence after the death of her son, and the reason that the apostles are charged to care for her, is her ability to transmit the new law of God. This is her foundational role in the Church. If Ælfric in part seeks to rationalize why the elect god-bearer was not assumed into heaven with her son, or why she needed to continue to live and to die after the fulfillment of her maternal role, this is much of his explanation: so that she could share her knowledge and establish the 'scole' – the yeshiva really – of the new law.

After characterizing Mary in this way, however, and after explaining the nature of her death and justifying her assumption, Ælfric simply echoes the pseudo-Jerome exhortation to confession – confess, because Mary will hear and understand no matter what your sin – and he abruptly leaves off his selective translation of the letter before moving on to the legends of Theophilus and Julian the Apostate, which he calls 'sume oþre trymminge be þære mæran godes meder' (some other supporting texts about the glorious mother of God).[32] Certainly any exhortation to confession, especially one that expresses confidence in Mary's intercessory role, is not unrelated to

---

[31] Ibid., p. 431.
[32] Ibid., p. 435.

Theophilus's situation as one who commits grievous sin and yet finds salvation upon his willingness to repent; however, the topic of Marian intercession is new to this homily, and the shift is abrupt. Initially, the legends seem related only by their general praise of Mary and perhaps by Ælfric's recourse to 'bocum', the tools of transmission elsewhere so critical and unstable. He submits by way of transition that Mary's 'frofer and fultum cristenra manna' (comfort and aid of Christians) is 'oft geswutelod, swa swa we on bocum rædað' (often manifested, just as we read in books),[33] and then he tells the poorly developed story of '[s]um man' whom Mary helped despite his sinfulness, that is, Theophilus:

> Sum man wæs mid drycræfte bepæht swa ðæt he criste wiðsoc. 7 awrat his handgewrit þam awyrigedan deofle. 7 him manrædene befæste; his nama wæs þeofilus; He þa eft syððan hine beþohte. 7 þa hellican pinunge on his mode weolc; 7 ferde þa to sumere cyrcan þe wæs to lofe þære eadigan marian gehalgod. 7 þærbinnon swa lange mid wope 7 fæstenum hire fultumes 7 þingunge bæd. oð þæt heo sylf mid micclum wuldre him to com. 7 cwæð ðæt heo him geþingod hæfde. wið þam heofenlican deman hire agenne sunu.[34]

> A certain man was so deceived by sorcery that he renounced Christ and wrote his charter to the accursed devil, and pledged homage to him. His name was Theophilus. Afterwards he returned to himself and considered in his mind the punishment of hell; and he went then to a certain church that was consecrated to the praise of the blessed Mary, and therein he prayed so long for her assistance and advocacy with weeping and fasts, until she herself with great glory came to him and said that she had mediated for him with the heavenly judge, her own son.

This very brief synopsis admits no clues to its source, and Ælfric moves on immediately to the story of Julian the Apostate, which he develops elaborately and with such lack of symmetry that one must wonder why Theophilus is here at all. How does this relate to what precedes and follows it? How much did Ælfric know of the story? And what did he expect his audience to know?

We can be sure that Ælfric knew the Latin legend of Paul the Deacon of Naples, which, as I discussed above, had already seeped into the English liturgy. The text was collected among the works that have been firmly established as Ælfric's main hagiographical sources.[35] The Cotton-Corpus Legendary (*c.*1000) contained Paul's versions of 'Theophilus' and 'Mary of

---

33 Ibid.
34 Ibid., pp. 435–6.
35 These included the homiliaries of Haymo of Auxerre and of the more famous Paul the Deacon (see n. 7 above), and the collection of anonymous hagiographical materials known as the Cotton-Corpus Legendary (MS BL Cotton Nero E. I and Cambridge, Corpus Christi College MS 9), believed to be his most used source. See Godden, *Ælfric's Catholic Homilies*, pp. xli–xliv.

Egypt', both of which had been subsumed into it and lost their authorial attributions. These legends are separated by several folios in the surviving manuscripts,[36] but it is possible that their proximity and general similarity of content suggested to Ælfric the kind of Marian collectability that Paul himself had foreseen when he placed them together, and that Ælfric attached to the Theophilus legend in England by compiling it with a different miracle story from another source. This Latin version of the legend is the one that Ælfric knew and would reasonably have expected that many others knew.

But Ælfric does not keep much of Paul's version of the legend. An argument from absence might claim that the story was already so well known in England at this time that he needed to say very little to bring its particulars to the mind of his audience, and this may be the case. The telescopic version of Theophilus's downfall and the delayed and dramatic sentence, 'his nama wæs þeofilus', certainly suggests this possibility, as does the liturgical ubiquity of the legend. By itself, however, such an argument detracts from examination of Ælfric's methods of compilation and discernible choices. He seems entirely unconcerned with the details of Theophilus's diabolical surrender, and he expunges the role of the Jewish sorcerer (though I will argue below that it cannot be far from his mind). He sees little need to speak of Theophilus's tortured contrition and confession, or of his death. These omissions highlight, however, that he is absolutely concerned – almost to the exclusion of all other elements of the story – to communicate Mary's legal abilities, and thus the great benefit of Mary's presence in the English landscape.

What is important to him is not the manner of Theophilus's fall but rather how Theophilus literally seals his fate. Theophilus was deceived by magic ('mid drycræfte bepæht'), but what Ælfric emphasizes is that the result of this deception is a legally binding contract. All of the language that describes Theophilus's action is legal. He writes a text symbolic of legal transaction, a 'handgewrit' (a charter, chirograph, or deed, probably a translation of Paul the Deacon's 'chirographum' or 'chartula'), and he completes the ritual with performance of tribute: 'him manrædene befæste', that is, he made the legal act of homage to the Devil. Likewise, the language that describes Mary's action is legal. Theophilus prays for Mary's 'þingunge' (intercession, but also mediation or advocacy), and when Mary appears to Theophilus she reports that she has seen the 'deman' (judge) and managed to mediate for him against that judge, her son ('him geþingod hæfde'). Ælfric evokes the image of the Court of Heaven, before which Mary has pleaded her case, advocating for a defendant who is at a considerable disadvantage, as he has signed a contract against himself. Mary's extraordinary legal power, however, is such that she can nullify both the performative and the written act of bondage.

---

[36] See Peter Jackson and Michael Lapidge, 'The Contents of the Cotton-Corpus Legendary', *Holy Men and Holy Women: Old English Prose Saints' Lives and Their Contexts*, ed. Paul Szarmach (Albany, NY, 1996), pp. 136–7.

Ælfric implies that she can do this for anyone. All Theophilus needs is fear of hell and a church consecrated to Mary, and many such churches existed in Anglo-Saxon England. According to Clayton, Ælfric's special inclusion of Marian church consecrations in the Theophilus story is also an important point of connection with the legend of Julian the Apostate that follows it and likewise includes a church dedicated to Mary. By bringing together the legends of Theophilus and Julian, and by presenting the two as collectively appropriate to praise of Mary, not only was Ælfric powerfully localizing Marian intercession but, by lifting miracle stories from other saints' lives and situating them so as to emphasize Mary's role, he was also 'anticipating the twelfth-century collections of miracles of the Virgin which follow the same procedure on a larger scale'.[37] He would have found in the *Vita Basilii* another tale of a soul contracted to the Devil paired with Julian the Apostate, one not about Marian intercession (it is Basil who intervenes) but generally similar to Theophilus, enough so that Ælfric used very similar vocabulary when he translated it for the *Lives of Saints*. It is the tale of a young man who seeks a sorcerer, in this case for the love of a woman; the sorcerer leads him to the Devil, who promises to help him so long as he will put their agreement in writing; the young man must forsake Christ, and he writes a charter in his own hand to that effect, until later the woman he loves seeks St Basil's assistance.[38] While the context may have been different, the Theophilus legend, with its lawyerly Mary handling otherworldly documents, provided an expression of saintly intercessory power still appropriate to a pairing with the Julian story. It complemented the Marian character that Ælfric created through his use of the pseudo-Jerome *Cogitus me*, and it balanced the ferocity of Marian judgment in the case of Julian's death.

The legend of Julian the Apostate is a negative miracle that tells how Julian's execution was orchestrated by the Virgin Mary herself, through the martyr Mercurius and St Basil. As Ælfric relates it, just after his Theophilus *exemplum*, St Basil prays for Mary's help in a church consecrated to her, and, as a result, he is privileged to see a vision of Mary as a warrior queen: 'geseah se biscop mic heofonlic werod on ælcere healfe þæs temples 7 onmiddan ðam werode sæt seo heofonlice cwen maria' (the bishop saw a great heavenly troop on each side of the temple, and in the middle of the troop sat the heavenly Queen Mary).[39] Mary, amidst her troop, calls her servants to arms and issues a death sentence: she summons the martyr Mercurius 'þæt he gewende wið ðæs arleasan wiðersacan Iulianes, and hine acwelle, se ðe mid toðundenum mode God mine Sunu forsihð' (so that he may go against the wicked apostate Julian and kill him, he who with an arrogant spirit denied God, my son).[40]

---

[37] Clayton, *Cult of the Virgin*, p. 240. Clayton also discusses the very similar compilation of Fulbert of Chartres here (*c.1028*), but Ælfric's work is 'almost certainly' earlier.

[38] See Skeat, *Ælfric's Lives of Saints*, pp. 72–9.

[39] Clemoes, *Catholic Homilies*, p. 437.

[40] Ibid.

After Julian's death, the evidence that remains of his execution is a bloody spear, returned to Mercurius's burial place as testament to the holiness and miraculousness of the act. The returned spear is reminiscent of the negated charter returned to Theophilus's sleeping body after Mary's retrieval of it from hell, just as the violent punishment of Julian might have happened to the apostate Theophilus had he not been penitent. Both are powerful images of Marian judgment.

Ælfric's choice of compilation reflects a foundational estimate of Mary's intercessory roles. The pseudo-Jerome letter established for him an authoritative account of Mary as a learned teacher and intermediary (matched by Jerome himself), while the framework of the Assumption narrative emphasized her position in the Court of Heaven. The legend of Theophilus, as it existed in Paul's Latin translation, would have provided an image of Mary as a powerful advocate with particular power over written law, and the legend of Julian the Apostate offered a story about the terror of any Marian judgment that is not merciful, one that had already (serendipitously) been paired with a diabolical-charter tale in the *Vita Basilii*. Though Ælfric habitually followed an orthodox line on Marian doctrine by denying apocryphal accounts of her early life and death, what he emphasizes about Mary's character through the pairing of Theophilus and Julian is momentous. His notion of how the Virgin manifests herself as 'se mæsta frofer 7 fultum cristenra manna' (the greatest comfort and aid of Christians), as he had said these legends would show, includes her abrogation of contracts and her ability to punish violently those who go against the faith.

The Latin 'Theophilus' of Paul the Deacon of Naples

The link between Ælfric's Jeromian characterization of Mary and his use of Theophilus is more appropriate the more one knows of his Latin source. The homiletic unit to which Ælfric attached the legend, as I have argued, set Hebrew scripture as a closed system stable only when treated as such (which helped justify his denunciation of Marian apocrypha), and then described Mary meditating on exactly that scripture, 'godes æ'. In the school for the apostles, she taught the new revelation: 'heo him cuðlice ealle þing ymbe cristes menniscnyesse gewissode' (she openly taught them everything about Christ's incarnation), which she knew through experience and special dispensation.[41] What Ælfric described, in other words, was an evangelizer of Jews, a Mary who taught the truth of Christ through the established scripture, and who was well equipped to do so: she was the Jew who closed the Hebrew scriptures at the moment of her conversion (through her acceptance of the Annunciation) and made way for the new and living tradition that Jerome

---

[41] Ibid., p. 431.

and Ælfric were continuing in their transmission of non-apocryphal, authoritative narratives. It is this Mary who is connected to the Theophilus legend that Ælfric knew, wherein the apostate is led astray by a Jew and led back to Christ by Mary.

Paul the Deacon's 'Theophilus', the Latin text to which Ælfric had access, offers a complex and structured exhibition of the Jewish 'character', one which not only encompasses its Jewish sorcerer but also influences its portrayal of the Christian protagonist, and of Mary herself. In terms of plot, every element of the story pivots on Jewish identity: the initial conflict, the rising action, the crisis, climax, and resolution, all occur as a result of an engagement with the Jewish sorcerer or with Jewish identity that is clearly marked by the protagonist or the narrator. The author carefully sets the three main characters – the sorcerer, Theophilus, and Mary – as shifting reflections of, and foils for, one another. The structural similarities of 'Jewish' and Marian intercession, and of the courts in which those intercessions happen, mean that Theophilus is moving not only through diabolical and heavenly realms in his conflicting desires for wealth and salvation, but also through stylized Jewish and Christian spaces that only Mary seems to mediate successfully.

Fundamental to an understanding of Paul's influential text, then, is the introduction of the Jewish sorcerer early in the legend and the description of his role in Theophilus's downfall at the court of the Devil. While the sorcerer is undoubtedly evil – he is 'infelix', 'Deo odibilis', 'execrabilis' (unhappy, hateful to God, accursed) – he is also the first advocate for Theophilus.[42] He is 'hebræus nefandissimus et omnino diabolice artis operator, qui jam multos, infidelitatis argumentis, in foueæ perditionis immerserat barathrum' (a Hebrew, most wicked and a practitioner of altogether diabolical arts, who had already, through heretical arguments, drowned many in the abyss of the pit of perdition),[43] but Theophilus consistently remakes himself through his identification and disidentification with this 'Hebrew'; and Mary will later both mimic and reject his actions as well. The Jew is the direct agent of Theophilus's downfall, but it is important to the way Paul's text works that he accomplishes no more than Theophilus himself understands and allows, for his self-consciousness and anxiety about his decision and resulting spiritual state dictate his interactions with both the sorcerer and Mary.

In the description of Theophilus's fall – which I will quote at some length, as the text is not well known – the Jew ends up little more than a guide, and he is eventually indistinguishable from the Christian:

> Quippe inani gloria succensus Vice-dominus incurrit miserrimus in ruminationem indigestæ cupiditatis hujus seculi, & urebatur ambitionis desiderio. Unde festinus perrexit noctu ad præfatum Hebræum, pulsansque januam, aditum pandi precabatur. Videns igitur eum Deo odibilis ille Hebræus ita

---

[42] Paul the Deacon of Naples, 'Miraculum S. Mariæ de Theophilo', p. 484, col. a.
[43] Ibid.

corde contritum, vocauit intra domum, & dixit ei: Cujus rei caussa ad me
venisti? At ille corruens provolutus pedibus ejus, dicebat: Quæso te, adjuva
me, quoniam Episcopus meus opprobrium in me exercuit, & hoc operatus
est in me. Respondit ei execrabilis ille Hebræus: Crastina nocte hora ista
veni ad me, & ducam te ad patronum meum, & subveniet tibi, in quo
volueris. Ille autem hæc audiens gratulatus fecit ita, medioque noctis venit
ad eum. Nefandus vero Hebræus duxit illum ad Circum civitatis, & dixit
ei: Quodcumque videris, aut qualemcumque audieris sonum, ne terrearis,
nec signum Crucis tibi facias. Illo autem spondente, subito ostendit ei
albos chlamydatos cum multitudine candelabrorum clamantes, & in medio
Principem sedentem. Erat enim diabolus, & ministri ejus. Tenens autem
infelix ille Hebræus manum Vice-domini, duxit illum ad flagitiosum illud
concilium; & ait ad eum diabolus: Quid nobis hunc hominem adduxisti?
Respondit: Ab Episcopo suo præiudicatum, vestramque adjutorium postu-
lantem, Domine mi, perduxi eum. Dixit autem ille: Quale illi adjutorium
dabo, homini seruienti Deo suo? Sed si meus famulus esse cupit, & inter
nostros milites reputari, ego illi subuenio, ita vt plus quam prius facere
possit, & imperare omnibus, etiam Episcopo. Conversus Hebræus dicit
illi misero Vice-domino: Audisti quid dixit tibi? Respondit: Audivi, &
quæcumque dixerit mihi faciam: tantum subueniat mihi. Et cœpit osculari
pedes ipsius Principis & rogare eum. Dicit diabolus illi Hebræo: Abneget
filium Mariæ, & ipsa quæ odio sunt mihi, faciatque in scriptis, quia abnegat
per omnia; & quæcumque voluerit impetrabit a me: tantum abneget. Tunc
introivit in Vice-dominum illum satanas, & ait: Abnego Christum & ejus
Genitricem, faciensque chirographum, imposita cera signavit annulo
proprio; & abscesserunt utrique cum nimio perditionis suæ gaudio.[44]

Since the wretched *vicedominus* burned for vainglory, he rushed into rumi-
nation of the indigestible greed of this world, and he was inflamed with the
desire of ambition. Whence he went, hasty, at night, straight to the aforementioned Hebrew, and, knocking at his door, he prayed for the door to
be opened. And seeing him so weary at heart, the Hebrew, hateful to God,
called from inside the house, and said to him: For what reason do you come
to me? And he, falling down humbled at his feet, said: I beg you, help me,
for my bishop has committed an injustice against me, and this deed works
against me. The accursed Hebrew responded to him: Come to me tomorrow
night at this hour, and I will lead you to my patron, and he will help you
with what you want. And so, hearing these things, he gave thanks, and he
went to him in the middle of the night. But the wicked Hebrew led him
to the center of the city and said to him: Whatever you see, or whatever
sound you hear, do not be afraid, and do not make the sign of the cross on
yourself. And after he promised this, there immediately appeared before
him white-caped figures, chanting, with a multitude of candelabras, and
in the middle the sitting Prince. For this was the Devil and his ministers.
And the unhappy Hebrew, holding the hand of the *vicedominus*, led him to
that disgraceful counsel, and the Devil said to him: Why have you led this
man to us? He responded: Unfairly judged by his bishop, and expecting an

---

[44] Ibid., p. 484, cols a–b.

audience with you, my Lord, I have guided him. And he said: How will I give counsel to a man subservient to his God? But if he wishes to be my servant, to be considered among our army, I will aid him such that he will have more than he had before and will be able to have dominion over all, even the bishop. Turning, the Hebrew spoke to the wretched *vicedominus*: Have you heard what he says to you? He answered: I have heard, and what he has said for me I will do, so long as he will help me. And he began to kiss the feet of the Prince himself and to beg him. The Devil said to the Jew: He should deny the son of Mary, and all those who are hateful to me, and he should put in writing that he denies them forever, and whatever he wants he should obtain from me; he should wholly deny them. Then Satan entered into the *vicedominus*, and he said: I deny Christ and his mother. And, making a chirograph, he sealed the set wax with his own signet, and both vanished with too much joy in his perdition.

Theophilus seeks the Jew because he has a public reputation as a practitioner of a dark magic, and it is Theophilus's knowledge of, and consent to, the Jew's practices that facilitate his fall. In this version of the legend, Theophilus is certainly not 'bepæht' (deceived), as he was in Ælfric's text, when he chooses to seek 'Jewish' intercession. Theophilus knows what the Jew can accomplish, and he knows exactly where to find him: 'festinus perrexit noctu ad præfatum Hebræum, pulsansque januam, aditum pandi precabatur' (he went, hasty, at night, straight to the aforementioned Hebrew, and, knocking at his door, he prayed for the door to be opened). The Jew teaches Theophilus how to effect the Devil's presence – 'nec signum Crucis tibi facias' (do not make the sign of the cross on yourself) – and he can locate the Devil at the 'Circum civitatis' (center of the city), but the entire arrangement depends on Theophilus's desire and willingness.

Once the court of the Devil has appeared, the Jew's role is temporarily intensified. He is no longer only the guide known by reputation; he becomes also the demonic interlocutor. In the court of the Devil, Theophilus is perfectly capable of understanding what is going on around him: 'Hebræus dicit illi misero Vice-domino: Audisti quid dixit tibi? Respondit: Audivi' (The Hebrew said to the wretched *vicedominus*: Have you heard what he says to you? He responded: I have heard). The Jew, however, must act as the intermediary, since the Devil refuses to speak directly to Theophilus. The Jew approaches the diabolical tribunal 'tenens manum Vice-domini' (holding the hand of the *vicedominus*), and yet the Devil questions the Jew rather than Theophilus: 'Quid nobis hunc hominem adduxisti?' (Why have you led this man to us?). That is, the Devil recognizes the Jew as Theophilus's attorney. The sorcerer must speak for Theophilus and plead his case with sincerity before the 'Princeps sedens' (sitting Prince), and, even when Theophilus acknowledges what is required of him and performs his submission by kissing the Devil's feet, the Devil plainly ignores him. Instead, he speaks over him, directing his instructions to the Jew: 'dicit diabolus illi Hebraeo: Abneget filium Mariae' (the Devil said to the Hebrew: He should deny the son of Mary). The Devil has no interest in speaking to Theophilus, nor does he take note of his answers or physical gestures of homage. Until the contract has been negotiated to his satisfaction, the Devil's business is with the Jew.[45]

It cannot be overemphasized, however, that Theophilus makes his own choice in this transaction and is under the influence of no delusion. He consents emphatically and repetitively even before the Devil exerts influence by speaking through him: he is 'urbatur ambitionis desiderio' (urged on by the desire of ambition); 'aditum pandi precabatur' (he prayed for the door to be opened); he announces, 'Audivi, & quæcumque dixerit mihi faciam: tantum subueniat mihi' (I have heard, and what he has said for me I will do, so long as he will help me); 'et cœpit … rogare eum (and he began … to beg him); and, finally, 'signavit annulo proprio' (he sealed with his own signet). Theophilus's contract requires his willing participation, and the role of the Jew as the advocate who accompanies him to court and speaks for him, combined with the emphasis on Theophilus's awareness and consent, produces a leveling. Both characters are equally implicated in, and necessary for, the contract of renunciation, and both Theophilus and the Jew end up with the same social and religious status before the tribunal: by denying Christ and Mary, Theophilus effectively becomes Jewish. He returns to a pre-Christian state, and thereby stands in for the Jew who 'converted' him. After the sealing of the charter, the sorcerer seems to have disappeared from the scene, and it is an ambiguous 'utrique' (both) that retreats from the court. As the scene concludes with Theophilus and the Devil acting without need of an intermediary, it is logical that 'abscesserunt utrique' (both vanished) refers not to the Jew and Theophilus but rather to the Devil and Theophilus.

Later in the text, the parallel between the two men is more explicit. After his fall, Theophilus continues to interact with the sorcerer, who often comes to him in secret to affirm their relationship and remind him that he has benefited through their association only in as much as he prayed for it ('beneficium & celer remedium ex me & patrono meo, in quibus deprecatus es, invenisti'), which Theophilus freely admits.[46] When the Jew is eventually condemned and put to death (for reasons not revealed), however, Theophilus begins to understand the association differently:

> Ubi vadam infelix ego peccator, qui negavi Christum meum & sanctam ejus Genitricem, & feci me servum diaboli per nefandæ cautionis chirographum? Quis putas hominum poterit illam abstrahere de manu vastatoris diaboli & adjuvare me? Quæ mihi fuit necessitas cognoscendi nefandissimum & comburendum illum Hebræum? Erat enim ante paul-

---

45   I am not the first to notice this. In 'Theophilus: Servant of Two Masters. The Pre-Faustian Theme of Despair and Revolt', *MLN* 87.6 (1972), pp. 33–4, Moshe Lazar, for different reasons, observes this back-and-forth and comments that 'Theophilus needs the Jewish intermediary not only in order to find the Devil but also in order to speak with him'.

46   Paul the Deacon of Naples, 'Miraculum S. Mariæ de Theophilo', p. 484, col. b.

lulum Hebræus ille a lege & judice condemnatus. Quid enim sic honorantur qui Deum & Dominum derelinquentes accurrunt diabolo?[47]

Where will I go, I who, unhappy sinner, denied my Christ and his holy mother, and made myself a servant of the Devil through a chirograph of wicked bond? What sort of men do you think will be able to pull that away from the hand of the Devil, the devastator, and help me? Why was it necessary for me to know that most wicked and burned-up Hebrew? (For this Hebrew was, a short time before, condemned by law and judge.) Is this how they are honored who, abandoning God and Lord, run to the Devil?

It is the sentencing of the Jewish sorcerer that causes Theophilus's awareness of his own demise, and his contrition. He compares himself to the Jew who has been legally put to death and considers the judgment simply the fate of those who reject God and go to the Devil, as both he and the sorcerer had done. It is only after this self-identification with the Jew that he regrets his abnegation and seeks a new advocate in the Virgin Mary, whom he expects may be unique in her ability to undo the condemnation facilitated and suffered by the Jew. Despite his rejection of her, he resolves, 'ibo ad eamdem matrem Domini sanctam ... & ipsam solam interpellabo ... donec per eam inveniam in die judicii misericordiam' (I will go to the same holy mother of the Lord ... and her alone I will entreat ... until I may find mercy through her on the Day of Judgment).[48]

Additional parallels between the Jewish sorcerer and Mary, and between the court of the Devil and the heavenly court presided over by her son, now become starkly clear. When Mary finally appears to Theophilus and rebukes him for his renunciation, she asks him to picture her having to make difficult arguments before the 'nimis justus & pius ... judex' (too just and pious judge). 'Quali fiducia possim postulare eum', she demands, 'cum tu apostataveris ab eo? Quove modo adstabo tribunali illi terribili, & præsumam aperire os meum, & petere clementissimam illius bonitatem?' (With what security can I apply to him, when you have renounced him? How will I stand before that terrible tribunal and presume to open my mouth and request the great clemency of his goodness?)[49] Her language is legal ('fiducia', 'clementissimam'), and, as she describes the *tribunal terribilis* of her son, one is reminded both of the Jew's advocating for Theophilus before the Devil and his condemnation 'a lege et judice' (by law and judge). Not only does the court of the Devil now become a parody of Christ's tribunal, but the advocate Jew becomes a parody of the advocate Mary. Christ and the Devil, Theophilus and the Jew, the Virgin Mary and the Jew, are not simply contrasting figures of good and evil; they are mirror images, clearly separate, but playing perversely similar roles.

---

[47] Ibid.
[48] Ibid., p. 485, col. a.
[49] Ibid., p. 485, col. b.

Theophilus cannot presume upon his Christianity in this situation. Instead, he responds to Mary's rebuke with scriptural examples of penitence and forgiveness that perform his spiritual problem and make plain that the issue is not only penitence but also the seemingly fragile boundary between Judaism and Christianity. His series of Old Testament examples – the Ninevites (Jonah, also cited in Matt. 12:41, Luke 11:32), the prostitute Rahab (Josh. 2, Josh. 6:17–25, also cited in Heb. 11:31, James 2:25), and King David – are ambiguous portrayals of his position in relation to the 'Hebrew' with whom he feared to be judged.[50] The Ninevites were not Israelites (only aided by a prophet of Israel), nor was the prostitute Rahab (only a woman who aided the Israelites), and David, king of the Jews and the Lord's anointed, is an image of Christ despite his many sins. Theophilus, in other words, crafts an argument that addresses his liminal spiritual state from all angles. Whether Mary reads him as someone influenced by a Jew (like the Ninevites), as someone allied with Jews (as Rahab), or as someone who does not yet understand his role in the Christian scheme (as David), he provides precedent for his forgiveness. And when he comes to use Paul in his New Testament examples – 'quomodo B. Paulus ex persecutore vas electionis effectus est?' (how was the Blessed Paul changed from a persecutor into a vessel of the chosen?)[51] – he makes his pleadings partly about conversion, about what divides Jew and Christian, even within the same man.

In this context, it is not incidental that Theophilus's charter becomes the focus of his worry and the material evidence of Marian intercession. The uncomfortable distinction between the 'letter of the law' and the spirit of the Word makes Theophilus resistant to any forgiveness not confirmed by the document's physical destruction. When he reminds Mary that his apostasy was sealed 'per inscriptum amarissimæ abnegationis chirographum' (through a written chirograph of most bitter abnegation), Mary responds, 'Intantum accede et confitere' (only approach and confess).[52] The parodic presence of the Jew and the Devil are once again exposed as perversions – they require written law, while Christ and Mary require only a confession of faith – but Theophilus does not at first seem to understand the contrast. It is a stubborn refusal to accept that Mary has obtained his pardon that makes Theophilus insist on the retrieval of 'execrabilem illam abnegationis chartulam atque nefandam cautionem signatam' (that accursed charter of abnegation and sealed wicked bond), which remains the thing that 'titillat miserrimam animam [su]am' (troubles [his] miserable soul), even after Mary's successful intercession.[53] The fact of Theophilus's unflagging concern obviates the need for verbal response and prompts Mary simply to demonstrate that the charter is irrelevant: 'exhibuit ei S. Maria chartulam cautionis habentem sigillum de

---

[50] Ibid.
[51] Ibid.
[52] Ibid., p. 486, col. a.
[53] Ibid., p. 486, col. b.

cera, sicut dederat illam apostaticam cautionem' (St Mary appeared to him holding the charter of bond, that bond of apostasy, sealed with wax, just as he had given it).[54] Her quick retrieval creates a new and persistent Marian paradigm that reifies the fundamental difference between law and spirit by displaying her literal and figurative power as the one who undoes written law.

Mary has swiftly and easily answered the previous despairing question, 'Quis putas hominum poterit illam abstrahere de manu ... diaboli?' (What sort of men do you think will be able to pull that away from the hand of the Devil?).[55] Of course, it is not men at all. This is the miraculous response, and it is finally punctuated with a paraliturgical performance by Theophilus's bishop, who gives a spontaneous sermon on the subject when Theophilus returns to the Church. Whereas Theophilus had gained his self-awareness through identification with the condemned Jew, the bishop preaches to the gathered congregation about Theophilus and the righteous Jew:

> quadraginta diebus legislator Moyses jejunans, a Deo conscriptas tabulas suscepit, & hic frater noster quadraginta diebus permanens in venerabili templo immaculatæ & gloriosæ semper Virginis Mariæ, priorem gratiam, quam negando perdiderat, jejunando & orando a Deo recepit.[56]

> after fasting forty days, the law-bearer Moses received the written tablets from God, and this, our brother, having remained forty days in the venerable temple of the immaculate and glorious ever Virgin Mary, has received from God, after fasting and praying, the former grace that he had lost through negation.

Through his penitence, Theophilus becomes a Christianized image of Moses, fasting and praying and receiving the law. Likewise, Moses, as the 'legislator' (law-bearer) carrying the 'conscriptas tabulas a Deo' (written tablets from God), becomes an anticipation of Mary, who now may appear before God and return what is written but no longer legal.[57] The bishop's comparison of Theophilus and Moses is a correction of Theophilus's previous misguided preoccupation with written law and associated self-identification with the 'wicked' Jew, a clarification that the post-Crucifixion Jew is distinct from the Old Testament righteous who do, in fact, provide acceptable Christian models for *imitatio*.

Ultimately, the material evidence of this correction is the charter itself, which dramatically meets the same fate as the Jew who negotiated it:

> rogavit eum Episcopus, ut combureret illam nefandissimam chartulam. Quod & factum est, & videntes populi execrabile chirographum, & nega-

---

[54] Ibid.
[55] Ibid., p. 484, col. b.
[56] Ibid., p. 487, col. a.
[57] For further discussion of connections between Moses and Mary in some Miracles of the Virgin, see my discussion of MS BL Additional 37049 in Chapter 4, pp. 129–33.

toriam cautionem combustam igni, cœperunt cum multitudine lacrymarum clamare: Kyrie eleyson.[58]

> the bishop asked that he [Theophilus] burn up that most wicked charter. And that was done, and, watching the accursed chirograph and renouncer's bond burn up in flame, the people began to cry out with a multitude of tears: *Kyrie eleison*.

Described with the same adjectives previously applied to the Jewish sorcerer ('nefandissimus', 'execrabilis'), the document burns in Theophilus's hands and so provides corresponding images of burning Jew and burning charter ('nefandissimum & comburendum illum Hebræum' and 'combure[ndam] illam nefandissimam chartulam'). If Theophilus had not understood that Mary herself is the symbol of the end of the letter of the law, her ease in revoking the charter that had caused his anxiety, and this new parallel between the charter and the Jew, demonstrate precisely her role in the economy of salvation.

And this is the Latin legend that Ælfric knew when he chose to include the Theophilus story in his sermon on Mary's Assumption. It fits very well in a sermon that begins with a distinction between Hebrew books and Greek and Latinate conversation and includes a characterization of Mary meditating on 'godes æ', very much the intermediary between Jewish and Christian law. In both his compilation of legends and his emphasis on Marian legality and intercession, Ælfric was using the Theophilus legend proleptically, anticipating distinctly inflected themes in English examples of the Marian miracle genre and engaging a Marian character that began with Paul's Latin text and continued to circulate in England for centuries. In the next appearances of the Theophilus legend in England, in the twelfth-century Latin collections of Miracles of the Virgin discussed by R. W. Southern, Mary's legal/textual mediation, especially as viewed through the lens of her relationship to Jews and Jewish law, would become essential to the idea of her continuing interaction with the world.

'Theophilus' in Early Anglo-Latin Collections

For Dominic of Evesham and William of Malmesbury, two of the first three English monastics to bring together collections of Marian miracles, 'Theophilus' held a gathering magic. Both men used the Marian characteristics exploited in Paul the Deacon's text to organize their work, and both were clearly struck by its engagement with Jewish 'problems'. While 'Theophilus' was never a story about a Jew – the sorcerer's appearance does not take up very much space in it – complex anti-Semitic rhetoric was part of the legend's

---

[58] Paul the Deacon of Naples, 'Miraculum S. Mariæ de Theophilo', p. 487, col. a.

pedagogy in its early circulation in post-Conquest England, where a developing Jewish community had become a fact of English culture.[59] This new presence made anxieties about Jewish–Christian interactions more pressing, and the 'Jewish' contract of the Theophilus legend could become a paradigmatic case of the perceived danger of Jewish text (both scriptural and documentary), of the perceived danger of Jews themselves, and of Mary's ability to intercede in such matters.

Dominic of Evesham *(fl. c.*1125) used Paul's text to organize his compilation of Miracles of the Virgin and to address just such concerns.[60] He saw in Marian stories an all-encompassing intercessory power, and he began his work with four miracles that, as he explained in his preface, he thought illustrated Mary's power over all of the elements (fire, air, water, and earth).[61] These included the legends of Theophilus and of Julian the Apostate, both of which Dominic found in the same hagiographical codex that Ælfric used, and both of which Anselm of Bury had *not* used in his collection (compiled shortly before Dominic's).[62] The legend of Theophilus was situated second in this series, even though it strained the bounds of the 'elemental' organization.[63] In Anselm of Bury's collection, however, Dominic had encountered the tale of a young Jewish boy who took communion with Christian friends and was thrown into an oven by his angry father, only to be preserved unharmed by

---

[59] On the chronology of Jewish presence in medieval England, see Bale, *The Jew in the Medieval Book*, pp. 14–15, and Mundill, *England's Jewish Solution*, pp. 16–44.

[60] Dominic was prior of Evesham Abbey by 1125 and was primarily a writer of hagiography. For information on Dominic's background and body of work, see J. C. Jennings, 'The Writings of Prior Dominic of Evesham', *The English Historical Review* 77 (1962), pp. 298–304.

[61] To these four, Dominic added ten other tales, several of them contemporary narratives authenticated by the names of their tellers or local affiliations, including a final narrative connected to Evesham Abbey. See Southern, 'English Origins', pp. 178–83. For the order and content of the entire collection, see Jennings, 'Origins of the Elements Series', pp. 84–93.

[62] Dominic, like Ælfric, used what is now MS BL Cotton Nero E. I. (the first part of the Cotton-Corpus Legendary), where he also found (and used later in his collection) Paul the Deacon of Naples's life of Mary of Egypt. Of the four earliest manuscripts in which Dominic's collection appears in near-original form, the one that is likely the earliest of these (MS BL Cotton Cleopatra C. X) inserts Paul's Theophilus nearly verbatim. The other three (Oxford, Balliol College MS 240; Toulouse, Bibliothèque Municipale MS 482; and Aberdeen, University Library MS 137) include an abbreviated version with a short prologue related to the 'elements' theme. For an edition of the collection as it sits in Cotton Cleopatra C. X, see Carl Neuhaus, ed., *Die lateinischen Vorlagen zu den alt-franzosischen Adgar'schen Marien-Legenden*, Part I (Aschersleben, 1886). For a collated edition that privileges Balliol College MS 240, see José Canal, 'El libro "De Miraculis Sanctae Mariae" de Domingo de Evesham (m.*c.*1140)', *Studium Legionense* 39 (1998), pp. 247–83. On Dominic's sources, see Jennings, 'Origins of the Elements Series', pp. 85–6. To compare the organization of Anselm of Bury's collection, see Southern, 'English Origins', much of which argues for the authorship of, and distinct motivations of, Dominic and Anselm (a list of the contents of Anselm's work is on pp. 183–4).

[63] The prologue to the legend of Theophilus in three of the early manuscripts (see n. 62) explains that it exemplifies Mary's dominion over air: 'Satis enim … in aerio gestum constat elemento, quod in ipsis principibus et potestatibus aeris huius, divina pietas, obtentu misericordissimae virginis et matris Mariae violenter ut ita dixerim, gerere visa est' (Canal, 'El libro "De Miraculis"', p. 262). But it is not clear what in the legend substantiates this. The Jewish Boy, however, clearly relates to fire, and the third tale in the series to water (it concerns a woman who gives birth in the sea).

Mary.[64] This, much better suited than 'Theophilus' to the 'elements series', illustrated Mary's dominion over the fire of the oven, and Dominic borrowed it from Anselm, paraphrased it and added his own commentary, and began his compilation with it. Like 'Theophilus', 'The Jewish Boy' 'had circulated in both the East and West for a long time',[65] and likewise it provided a complicated portrait of the liminal spaces between Judaism and Christianity. The decision to place it before 'Theophilus' was not only a decision to make arguments for Mary's elemental sovereignty clearer and stronger but also an emphasis on the importance of Mary's relationship to Jews and Jewish law, and to mercy and judgment.

That Dominic conceived of his first two narratives in this way is reflected in his prologue to the collection, which begins with a discussion of Mary's unparalleled power in heaven. Mary is ranked above all patriarchs, prophets, apostles, martyrs, confessors, and virgins, and from this Dominic concludes that her main role in the lives of sinners is that of legal advocate in the heavenly court, just as she had been portrayed in both Paul the Deacon's 'Theophilus' and in Ælfric's Assumption homily:

> Subsequitur etiam finalis causa qua spes maxime appetenda praecipitur, tam scriptores quam lectores et auditores in die tremendi examinis ab ira iusti iudicis per merita gloriosissimae matris eiusdem iudicis protegi, cuius cognoscimus virtutes, tum scribendo, tum legendo et audiendo venerari.[66]

> And so it follows that in the final trial (hope for which is most eagerly felt), on the day of fearful examination, the writers as much as the readers and listeners will be defended from the wrath of the just judge through the merits of the same judge's most glorious mother, whose virtues we rightly honor both by writing and by reading and listening.

Dominic reasons that all who are involved in the transmission of Mary's miracles can expect her advocacy on Judgment Day. Her ultimate role in the lives of Christians is lawyerly and pedagogical. It is perhaps surprising, then, or simply revealing, that just a few sentences later, when Dominic formally begins the miracle narratives, he chooses to start not with Theophilus's story of Marian advocacy, but instead with a borrowed tale more explicitly about the punishment and the salvation of Jews.

The legend of the Jewish Boy is of more certain origin than 'Theophilus'. Also of Greek origin, it was preserved in the *Historia ecclesiastica* of Evagrius Scholasticus of Antioch (*c.*536–600) and became known in the West through the *De gloria martyrum* of Gregory of Tours (d.595). It was reworked many times and in many places, with varying degrees of eucharistic and

---

[64] See Southern, 'English Origins', pp. 186–7, 191–2.
[65] Ibid., p. 177.
[66] Canal, 'El libro "De Miraculis"', p. 257. Dominic's preface is also printed in Southern, 'English Origins', pp. 179–81.

christological emphases, but it was Gregory of Tours's version that, in the main, persisted into the twelfth century and in England.[67] That text can be summarized as follows:

> The son of a Jewish glassblower in Constantinople attends school with Christian boys. On Easter Day, he unwittingly goes to church with his schoolmates and thus ends up taking communion. At the church, he sees an image of the Virgin and Child. He rushes home and innocently reports what he has done to his parents, who have been looking for him. His father becomes so enraged that he throws his son into the glassblowing oven. The boy's mother rushes to his rescue but cannot save him, and she begins to wail and call for help. The Christians of the town come to her aid, and, as they approach the fiery oven, the flames subside. They see the boy sitting there, miraculously unhurt. He explains to the gathered crowd that the woman whom he saw in the church cradling her child has covered him with her cloak and protected him from the fire. The boy then converts to Christianity with his mother, as do the other Jews of the town. The crowd throws the Jewish father into the very oven in which he tried to incinerate his own son, and he quickly burns to ashes.

Dominic might have altered the tale to underscore the power of the Eucharist (through emphasis on the boy's taking communion), or the power of 'witness' to convert Jews (through emphasis on the response of the Jewish community to the miraculous sight),[68] but he was more concerned to glorify the judgments facilitated by Marian intercession, and the version of the tale he knew worked well for the purposes. Anselm of Bury had updated the Gregory of Tours text by localizing it to the French town of Bourges and attaching it to a monk, Peter, of St Michael's in Chiusa, whom he claimed witnessed the miracle. Mary's contemporary, immediate, and practical ability to effect salvation, conversion, or punishment, then, seems to have been especially attractive to Dominic.

But why *start* this way? Dominic does not choose to similarly modernize the equally ancient tales of Theophilus or Julian the Apostate, but he does accept Anselm's singular alteration of the story with which he carefully chose to begin his collection. It is of course possible that Dominic did not know it in any other form or with any other setting, and that Anselm had in fact heard it from a monk at Chiusa (he spent much of his youth at the monas-

---

[67] On the tale's dissemination and variety, see Jennings, 'Origins of the Elements Series', pp. 86–7; and Rubin, *Gentile Tales*, pp. 8–11 (Rubin discusses its pan-European influence in the Middle Ages on pp. 7–39).

[68] Rubin, *Gentile Tales*, p. 9, explains that the tale 'is significant as a typical example of the *witness* tale, where a Jew effects the conversion of others through the personal experience of miracle and illumination to Christian truth', and she considers this its primary importance in most pre-twelfth-century versions.

tery there),[69] but even in this case the decision to include a tale concerning contemporary Jewish–Christian interactions spoke to an England that Ælfric had not experienced, one with active Jewish communities. The legend was already more focused on the practical problems of overlap between Jews and Christians than was 'Theophilus': the possibility of Jewish and Christian children playing together, or of Jewish knowledge of Christian holy spaces, is differently troublesome than the Jewish–Christian interaction in the legend of Theophilus, which happens mainly in supernatural and theological realms. But Dominic chooses to start by setting these issues literally closer to home, in space and in time, and in so doing introduces Mary's power as a topic of continuing practical appeal.

This is most evident in the new prologue that he added to 'The Jewish Boy', an addition that is usually set by scribes as the beginning of the miracle narratives (after the general prologue mentioned above) and not distinct from 'The Jewish Boy'.[70] Dominic's worry, as he began his series, was evidently the doctrinal and practical problems of the 'gens Judaeorum'. He began with a commentary on the fate of the 'obstinatissima gens' (most stubborn race), damned and destroyed for the guilt of Christ's death and now 'ubique terrarum pro suis criminibus diffusus' (scattered all over the earth because of its crimes). And after lamenting the fall of this people 'quondam Deo tam dilectum, a cunctis terrarum hominibus electum' (once so loved by God, chosen from all the people of the earth), he considers the situation of the Jews in his own time:

> Ecce enim omnis civitas, quocumque locorum sita, hanc gentem infra se positam sustinet, ubique iudaica perfidia intonat. Et cum inter christianos sit multorum iudaeorum conversatio, iugiter tamen permanet in mente eorum verae fidei dubitatio.[71]

> For behold, every city in every place supports this race within itself. Everywhere Jewish treachery thunders forth. And though many Jews conduct their lives among Christians, doubt of the true faith yet remains continuously in their minds.

The expectation is that Mary's intercession will resolve problems of Jewish misinterpretation of Christian prophecy (the rejection of Christ as the cause of Jewish exile), and of current Jewish–Christian interactions (the daily transactions of those living in close proximity).

---

69 See Southern, 'English Origins', pp. 190–1. Anselm's connection to Chiusa is part of what helps Southern later argue for his authorship of the earliest collection and particularly of the updated version of the legend of the Jewish boy (see pp. 198–200).

70 For example, in MS BL Cotton Cleopatra C. X, it follows immediately on the rubric 'Incipit liber miraculorum Sanctae dei genitricis et perpetuae uirginis Mariae. Quomodo puerum Judaeorum ab incendio clibani liberauit' (see Neuhaus, *Latienischen Vorlagen*, p. 9), and elsewhere after 'Explicit prologus. Incipiunt miracula sanctissimae et misericordissimae Dei genitricis' (see Canal, 'El libro "De Miraculis"', p. 258).

71 Canal, 'El libro "De Miraculis"', p. 259.

In the first lines of the tale proper, moreover, Dominic makes clear that the events he narrates might happen in any town that accommodates a synagogue:

> Nam cum in civitate Bituricensi, ut referre solet quidam monachus de Cusa, Petrus nomine, qui forte eo temporis in ipsa urbe aderat, veluti in plerisque cernitur, synagoga iudaeorum esset, evenit per beatissimam Mariam, matrem domini, res mira.[72]

> Now, in the city of Bourges, as a certain monk of Chiusa named Peter was in the habit of relating (he not too long ago visited that very city), there was a synagogue of the Jews, as is very often the case. A miracle happened, through the most blessed Mary, mother of God.

This is different from the first lines Dominic would have found in Anselm's text, where Anselm's tendency to be 'impatient of unnecessary detail' results in a simple statement of the location and 'source'.[73] Dominic adds the synagogue, and the note about how frequently one encounters a synagogue, and immediately what I have previously called 'liminal' spaces become the real thresholds between living communities. Both the tragic and revelatory events of the Jewish boy story, then, are the potential of every Christian city where there is a synagogue. The juxtaposition of Dominic's comment with his matter-of-fact statement that Mary performed a miracle in this situation also renders Marian intercession the potential of every town with a Jewish community, made necessary by the fear that Jewish presence may become unidentifiable.

From both the Christian and Jewish perspectives offered in the story that follows, the problem is that the Jewish boy passes for Christian. He receives the same education, and, like a normal child, he wants to do what his friends are doing: 'inmaturo sensu dominante, quaecumque videt alios facere, ipse coepit similiter exsequi' (when immature senses rule, whatever one sees others do he will begin to do himself).[74] Once the child is in a church for the Easter mass, to which he has followed his schoolmates and at which much of the Christian community is present, no one recognizes him as Jewish, presumably not even the celebrating priest: the congregation approaches the Eucharist 'sine discretione sexus sive aetatis' (without discrimination of sex or age), and 'iudaicus etiam puer cum reliquis pergit' (even the Jewish boy went ahead with the rest).[75] This suggests that he is – in behavior, speech, and appearance – *like a Christian*. These are Dominic's emphases. His version of

---

[72] Ibid., p. 260.
[73] Southern, 'English Origins', p. 199 (the opening lines of Anselm's and Dominic's versions are printed for comparison on p. 192). For an edition of the version attributed to Anselm, which is considerably shorter and includes less commentary, see Dexter, 'Miracula Sanctae Virginis Mariae', pp. 32–3.
[74] Canal, 'El libro "De Miraculis"', p. 260.
[75] Ibid.

the events turns on the anxiety associated with this passing (the ability of the Jew to present himself as Christian, the inability of the Christian to discern difference), which necessitates miracle and punishment.

Much of the miracle that Mary performs in saving the young boy from the violence of his father is in the fact that she makes obvious to all observers the difference between a righteous Jew and a 'wicked' Jew, just as Theophilus's bishop had done. Here too the overlap of Christian and Jewish characters is acceptable only once interpreted properly, and Dominic emphasizes this in his commentary on the events. Where Theophilus was finally identified with Moses instead of the Jewish sorcerer, so the young Jewish boy is connected to Moses to distinguish him from his father. He becomes the new burning bush, simultaneously symbolic of the experience of the righteous Jew and of Mary's incorruptibility: 'Et ecce res mira', writes Dominic, 'ac post rubum a Moyse visum paene inaudita, oculis omnium comprobata apparet' (and behold a miracle appeared, one scarcely heard of since the bush seen by Moses, veri-fied by the eyes of all).[76] And the Jewish father, who stubbornly refuses to accept the miracle, Dominic interprets as the fulfillment of prophecy against the enemy:

> veridica vo[x] psalmistae terribiliter completur in ipso: 'Foderunt foveam et inciderunt in eam.' Et 'Veniat illi laqueus quem ignorat et captio quam abscondit apprehendat eum, et in laqueum cadat in ipso.'[77]

> The truthful voice of the psalmist is terribly fulfilled in him: 'They dug a pit and are fallen into it.' And: 'Let the snare which he knoweth not come upon him, and let the net which he hath hidden catch him, and into that very snare let him fall.'

Both outcomes are necessary in the Christian scheme: the son and the father together verify Christian interpretation of Hebrew scripture, while the son also holds out the eschatological promise of Jewish conversion. The righteous Jew is saved by Mary (burned but not consumed, like the burning bush), while the evil Jew goes up in flames. As Dominic was focused on Mary's sovereignty over the elements, the images in 'Theophilus' of the condemned burning Jew and the burning contract, in particular, may have suggested a relationship between the two stories. The incineration of the father at the end of 'The Jewish Boy' was a distinction of the most common Western version of the legend (in other versions the father is crucified),[78] and it agreed with the Jewish sorcerer's death by fire. The most compelling evidence that Dominic understood 'The Jewish Boy' as related to the 'Legend of Theophilus', however, is simply his decision to juxtapose them.

---

[76] Ibid.
[77] Ibid., p. 261 (with emendation from Neuhaus, *Latienischen Vorlagen*, p. 11). Dominic cites Psalms 56:7 and 34:8, respectively, and I use the Douay-Rheims translation here.
[78] Jennings, 'The Origins of the Elements Series', p. 86.

The combination was a powerful one. Copyists and compilers frequently used the 'elements series' to begin their own books of Marian miracles, and they quickly understood the contemporary appeal of Mary's ability to intercede in matters of Jewish–Christian interaction. Shortly after Dominic produced his Marian work (before 1143), William of Malmesbury compiled his *Miracula Sanctae Mariae Virginis*, a collection of fifty-three miracles with a lengthy prologue celebrating Mary's virtues, excellence as the mother of God, and Assumption. William was deeply influenced by St Anselm, and the works of the younger Anselm and of Dominic were among his sources.[79] Not unlike Dominic, he had a broad interest in historicizing Mary's intercessory powers, and especially in exploiting her ability to pass judgment on Jews, and he was working through both theological and practical notions of Mary's worthiness and power in his collection. In the process, he was capable of displaying what Peter Carter has called 'rabid anti-Semitism'.[80] He could tell, between Marian miracles, a tale concerning Jews of Toulouse who are ritually beaten on Good Friday even 'ad hanc diem' (to this day) because any revenge for the son's injuries glorifies the mother, and because his readers might find it funny.[81] Between his own versions of 'The Merchant's Surety' (discussed in Chapter 1) and 'The Jewish Boy', in fact, William interjected to apologize for telling so few tales against Jews. It would take 'ingens documentum' (a massive book), he regrets, to tell 'quantum in cognatae gentis conuersione laboret industria Mariae' (how energetically Mary labors to convert her own people).[82] As distasteful as they are, these interjections are central to how he conceived of his project and of Mary. For William, Mary was not only the source of Christianity but also a converted Jew, and she therefore had the privileged ability and personal obligation to resolve problems created by her *cognata gens*.

William's appropriation of the Theophilus story, and what he gathers around it, betrays both the importance of this special intercessory role and the fantasy of an urgent need for it. His collection begins with 'Theophilus', the first substantially new version of the legend in medieval England, not copied or abbreviated but reworked with plot details adjusted and commentary inserted, and he had very carefully given it pride of place. We know

---

[79] See Southern, 'English Origins', pp. 200–1; and Peter Carter's detailed discussion of William's sources in 'The Historical Content of William of Malmesbury's Miracles of the Virgin Mary', *The Writing of History in the Middle Ages: Essays Presented to Richard William Southern*, ed. R. H. C. Davis and J. M. Wallace-Hadrill (Oxford, 1981), pp. 127–65, though Carter is uncertain about how much Dominic influenced the particulars of William's retelling of 'Theophilus' (see p. 133).

[80] Carter, 'Historical Content', p. 152.

[81] All citations of William of Malmesbury's *Miracula Sanctae Mariae Virginis* are from Canal, *El libro de laudibus* (here pp. 74, 76). See Carter for a full discussion of the Jews of Toulouse interpolation, 'Historical Content', pp. 149–52. On ritual Holy Week violence against Iberian Jews, see also David Nirenberg, *Communities of Violence: Persecutions of Minorities in the Middle Ages* (Princeton, NJ, 1996), pp. 200–30 (pp. 202–3 on Toulouse).

[82] Canal, *El libro de laudibus*, p. 136.

that William struggled with the sequence of his compilation, because the two surviving manuscripts provide autograph evidence of his editing and significant rearrangement of texts, but he never considered a different position for 'Theophilus'.[83] It was central to his conception of Mary and to the spiritual benefit of his readers, whom he hoped would profit from what he turned to first, a work he calls 'animae meae maximum' (foremost in my soul).[84] In the first line of his Theophilus story, he is preoccupied with its *auctoritas* and its priority: 'Scriptura tradit antiquior quod primum de Theophilo suggerit mens ponere, quamuis dicturienti multa se certatim tentent ingerere' (ancient record passes down what my mind suggests should go first, [the miracle] concerning Theophilus, although, to someone who is undertaking to write, many things rivalrously clamor for attention).[85] His commitment to organizing his work around Theophilus, despite his awareness that many other stories might have had the first position, begs investigation. *What* exactly was foremost in his soul?

It is perhaps counterintuitive, but William's explicit concern to defend the historical truth of Marian intercession is bound up in this very deliberate use of what he calls an 'ancient record' about her miraculous intercession. Throughout this work, William seems to vacillate between moving contemporary stories backward and placing ancient stories within the contemporary landscape (or at least situating them more precisely). For instance, a tale concerning Jews of Toledo who torture a waxen image of Christ, which was very likely supposed to be an early twelfth-century event, William places in the seventh century; and the tale of the Jewish boy from Bourges (the Bourges setting is what he would have encountered in his sources), William sets in twelfth-century Pisa. It is difficult to puzzle through these alterations, and Carter insists that we have on display in William's collection 'the contrast between the scrupulous historian of the remote past and the contemporary myth-maker', an ostentatious attempt 'to harness hagiography to history' that results in 'sheer guesswork' from a historical perspective.[86] Carter points out William's many historical errors – instances of misdating, the placement of 'anonymous and ancient' tales in the mouths of well-known men, seemingly willful alterations[87] – but even erroneous historical details can render Mary's intercession localizable and real. And William did consider himself a historian; twelve of the miracles he includes were taken from his previous historical works, the *Gesta Regum* and the *Gesta Pontificam*, and he insisted that everything he wrote could be verified and ought not be questioned, since 'nemini necesse sit struere aliquid et concinnare, pro ea magnificenda, commentum' (there is no need for anyone to fabricate anything or concoct

---

83 On the manuscripts, see Carter, 'Historical Content', pp. 127–37.
84 Canal, *El libro de laudibus*, p. 64.
85 Ibid.
86 Carter, 'Historical Content', pp. 141, 163, 162.
87 Ibid., pp. 141ff.

a fallacious story to make her [Mary's] exploits more glorious).[88] As even Carter must concede, despite his evident exasperation with William's disregard for sources and research, William was 'doing what no one had done before to establish these miracles in time and place'.[89] What Dominic of Evesham did on a small scale with his comment about the synagogue of Bourges, William was doing on a large scale to express an ongoing relevance for the 'truth' of Mary's power.

Part of this commitment to a combined historical and spiritual truth is reflected in the fact that much of what William writes in the first part of his collection is punctuated by frank anti-Semitism. What Carter categorizes as errors and commentary inappropriate to historiography are very often associated with stories or interpolations about Jews.[90] While the tale that follows 'Theophilus' is not of this sort – it is the legend of Julian the Apostate which, as discussed above, had its own tradition of being paired with 'Theophilus' and could make its own statement about Marian judgment – the third and fourth tales continue to reflect a concern with the effect of Mary's miracles on Jewish faith and on Jewish wrongdoing. When, for example, William turns to his third tale, concerning the seventh-century Archbishop Hildefonsus of Toledo whom Mary honored with heavenly albs and a throne because of his book in defense of her perpetual virginity (*De perpetua virginitate Mariae contra tres infidels*), William pauses to note that Hildefonsus's work was 'praecipue aduersus iudaeos et Heluidium' (principally against the Jews, and Helvidius). Helvidius was a fourth-century heretic, who argued (against St Jerome) that Mary had other children after the birth of Jesus and therefore did not remain a virgin.[91] The information is superfluous. Since the miracle that follows is about how Mary swiftly puts to death the archbishop's less worthy successor for daring to use the gifts she gave to Hildefonsus, this is a tale that is more concerned with Mary's ferocity in judgment than anything else. By introducing it with his comment on the nature of Hildefonsus's treatise, however, William communicates that it is also a challenge to heretical and particularly Jewish resistance to Christianity.

When William comes to his fourth tale, concerning the Jews of Toledo who were executed after Mary revealed to an archbishop celebrating the Assumption mass that they were torturing a waxen image of Christ, it could hardly be plainer that he is framing his collection in precisely the same way that Dominic did in his prologue to 'The Jewish Boy'. Mary's special usefulness in areas of mixed Christian and Jewish population is contemporary and functional for William, and he is employing Iberian examples, whether

---

88 The miracles taken from the *Gesta Regum* and *Gesta Pontificam* are catalogued by Carter, 'Historical Content', pp. 133–6. The quotation can be found in Canal, *El libro de laudibus*, p. 111, though I am using Carter's translation here (p. 163).

89 Carter, 'Historical Content', p. 165.

90 Ibid., especially pp. 142, 145–54, 160–1.

91 Canal, *El libro de laudibus*, p. 71.

ancient or contemporary, as cases in point.[92] The Toledo story is set in the seventh century and is unambiguously about Mary's judgment against Jews, but William prefaces it with reflection on the significance of its Spanish setting:

> Iudeorum multitudine olim Hispanias grauatas esse fides historiarum assuerat, et nunc quoque non inferius contaminari, rumor non ambiguous pro uero affirmat. Denique non semel auditum est quod apud Narbonam habent summum papam, ad quam a iudaeis ex toto curritur orbe. His xenia cumulantibus, his si quid questionis intra eos ortum fuerit quod solutionem desiderat, illius arbitratu decidentibus.[93]

> Trustworthy histories claim that Spain was once burdened by a multitude of Jews, and reliable opinion confirms that even now it is not less polluted. It is constantly reported that they have at Narbonne a high pope, to whom the Jews run from all over the world and who receives their proffered wealth and arbitrates whenever some issue arises amongst them that calls for a solution.

This is likely the first mention of the so-called Jewish Pope of Narbonne. It is a perversion of the papal court of no real consequence to the tale that follows, but it turns what William (erroneously) claims is a seventh-century event into an ongoing historical 'problem', and it allows for fantasies of international Jewish conspiracy that, within decades of William's composition, had devastating consequences for the Jewish communities in England.[94] The implied historical urgency of Mary's intercessory role and the importance of her ability to inhabit theological spaces both Jewish and Christian are linked to a perceived need to negotiate a (fantasized) Jewish bureaucracy and a system of legal arbitration, both of which were a burgeoning part of William's England.

The legend of Theophilus, set as the head note of his collection, allowed William to foreshadow his interpolations on Jewish 'problems' and suggest a continuous historical development, moving from sixth-century Turkey

---

[92] Though Carter, 'Historical Content', p. 153, argues that William's considerations 'can hardly have been prompted by conditions at Malmesbury, where there was no Jewish community', and that his anti-Semitism was based more on 'bookish fervour' than 'experience', it is not at all unlikely that William had experience with Jewish communities, or at least with the kind of gossip that nearby communities might have occasioned. Malmesbury was situated within easily travelable distance of at least three significant Jewish communities in Marlborough (moved to Devizes in the late thirteenth century by Eleanor of Provence), Gloucester (moved to Bristol in the late thirteenth century), and Oxford. See Mundill, *England's Jewish Solution*, pp. 23, 286–90.

[93] Canal, *El libro de laudibus*, p. 73. I am using Carter's translation of the second part of this passage, 'Historical Content', pp. 146–7.

[94] The decision of the Jewish Pope of Narbonne was used by Thomas of Monmouth as a partial explanation for the 1144 murder of little William of Norwich, whose death was blamed on the Norwich Jews. See Augustus Jessop and M. R. James, ed. and trans., *The Life and Miracles of St William of Norwich* (Cambridge, 1896). On the history and use of this myth, see also Carter, 'Historical Content', pp. 146–9; and Langmuir, 'Thomas of Monmouth: Detector of Ritual Murder', *Toward a Definition of Antisemitism*, pp. 224–6.

(Cilicia, the setting of 'Theophilus') and seventh-century Spain (Toledo), to twelfth-century France (Narbonne), French-Iberian borders (Toulouse), and Italy (Pisa). The Jewish facilitation of Theophilus's charter and his status within the Devil's court is not inconsequentially related to William's imagined Jewish court at Narbonne, nor to his celebration of the ritual punishment of Jews 'to this day'. What he alters in his version of 'Theophilus', in fact, serves only to vilify the Jewish sorcerer further and establish Theophilus's status as an unwilling victim of a Jewish conspiracy with the Devil, even as it maintains the focus on Jewish legal advocacy that was so elaborated in Paul the Deacon's text. In William's appropriation, Theophilus questions himself and fears his downfall from the moment he approaches the home of the sorcerer: he is, from the start, 'incomitatus' (unaccompanied, alone) and 'timida' (fearful).[95] Theophilus is not *choosing* to ally or identify with the Jew in William's account, but is rather pulled toward what he knows is unnatural. William's sorcerer is not skilled in 'infidelitata argumenta', as in Paul's text; rather, he is decidedly otherworldly and supernatural, able to incant and conjure at will.[96] Theophilus is the victim of a man 'uetus animas innocentes uenendi artifex' (long-skilled in the selling of innocent souls), and he is consequently never in danger of seeming to be *un*Christian.[97]

Though the crucial moment of identification between Theophilus and the Jew remains in William's text – it is still the legal condemnation and execution of the sorcerer that prompts Theophilus's repentance – there is no doubt about the spiritual state of either character. The extemporaneous sermon of Theophilus's bishop, which in Paul's text separated the righteous Jew from the wicked by identifying Theophilus with Moses, is absent in William's version, and the parallel between the Jewish sorcerer and his contract, previously condemned to the same fiery fate, is differently inflected. After Theophilus writes and seals the contract, William notes that the Jew was later 'decapitatus' (beheaded) and took his place among those who 'in futuro aeternis incendis ingererent' (will ingest flames into eternity).[98] Both the method of execution and the blatant pronouncement of eternal damnation are William's innovation, and though the Jew's decapitation at first seems to resist comparison with the contract's later burning, his quick consignment to the flames of hell actually ensures an eternal comparison: while Jewish conspiracy can be undone and Jewish text can be retrieved from hell by Mary, in William's estimation, the Jew himself cannot be.

As collections of Marian miracles began to form – Dominic of Evesham's and William of Malmesbury's among the first – the legend of Theophilus gath-

---

[95] Canal, *El libro de laudibus*, p. 65.
[96] Ibid.
[97] Ibid. The increased emphasis on the sorcerer's magic may also reflect William's manifest interest in Iberian tales, since Arab and Jewish science (and magic) was, in William's time, emanating from the region in stronger flow than earlier. For a bibliography of work on Spanish versions of the Theophilus legend, see the *CSMD* (*CSM* no. 3).
[98] Canal, *El libro de laudibus*, p. 66.

ered around it evidence of an incessant preoccupation with Jews and legality. These were issues of paramount importance to these English authors who had urgent practical concerns and soteriological hopes about Jewish conversion when they began to work with Miracles of the Virgin. In the version of the legend that circulated widely in Anglo-Saxon and post-Conquest England, the Jew (as opposed to Mary and the authors who disseminated the miracles) was the model of the bad advocate and the bad contract, and space for Mary's legal mediation was created by the liminal position that her own Jewish identity allowed. The lesson of Marian intercession, in this context, urged each Christian to identify with the Jew in the same way that Theophilus had: as the archetypal sinner who denies Christ through an overly literal attachment to written law. The Theophilus story created a Mary who could appear before sinners as the new symbol of law, correcting (Jewish) attachment to written code and passing judgment on those who maintained that attachment. For many illustrative and vernacular treatments of Marian legends that emerged in the next centuries, this characterization of Mary *mediatrix* was profoundly influential.

3

The Theophilus Legend in England, Again
From the Devil's Charter to a Marian Paradigm

> But now we are loosed from the law of death wherein
> we were detained; so that we should serve in newness of
> spirit, and not in the oldness of the letter.
> > The Epistle of St Paul to the Romans 7:6

In the first known Book of Hours, designed and illuminated by the Oxford Dominican William de Brailes sometime around 1240, illustrations of the 'Legend of Theophilus' complement the Hours of the Little Office of the Virgin. William 'writes' the story in ten historiated initials that run across half of the devotional day, adorning psalms and prayers for prime and terce.[1] The written narrative of the legend is not present, but short Anglo-Norman notations accompany the images. Below an illustration of Theophilus's contractual agreement with the Devil, de Brailes writes, 'Theofle fet humage au deable e lui escrit chartre de sen propre sanc' (Theophilus does homage to the Devil and writes for him a charter in his own blood); a tonsured Theophilus kneels before the hook-nosed Devil, and they grasp between them a charter that bears a cartoonishly large seal and an inscription, in clear capitals, 'CARTA TEOFOLI' (see Plate 1).[2] Claire Donovan has emphasized in her discussion of the de Brailes images that '[t]he importance of the written charter in this transaction, the necessity of the written word to establish the unbreakable nature of this contract, shows how literate and legalistic the world of the thirteenth century was becoming'.[3] It shows also how literate and legalistic the English cult of the Virgin Mary was becoming.

William de Brailes illustrated the Theophilus story twice. He also used it as part of an illustration of fortune and the 'Ages of Man' (in Cambridge, Fitzwilliam Museum MS 330), perhaps because of the story's emphasis on wealth and poverty and associated contractual disputes.[4] William himself was very much a part of the burgeoning thirteenth-century world of profes-

---

[1] See Claire Donovan, *The de Brailes Hours: Shaping the Book of Hours in Thirteenth-Century Oxford* (London, 1991), pp. 69–81 (here p. 69).
[2] Ibid., pp. 70–1.
[3] Ibid., p. 70.
[4] Ibid., p. 75.

Plate 1 Theophilus and the Devil hold their charter. London, British Library MS Additional 49999, fol. 34r. © British Library Board

sional book culture and written law. His many contributions (direct and indirect) to Oxford illuminated manuscripts are well known, and he appears in surviving documents as a witness to several property transfers, as the owner of an Oxford tenement, and as a considerable influence in at least one land dispute.[5] That he chose Theophilus to express the effectiveness of Marian intercession is also evidence of a life spent in bookmaking and legal transaction.

Of the ten images that make up William's Theophilus cycle, four feature the infamous charter, and twice Mary is depicted with the charter in hand. In one instance, she engages in hand-to-hand combat with the Devil, who grips the charter by its exaggerated seal-tag while Mary grasps it in one hand and punches him squarely between the eyes with the other (see Plate 2). The now-cropped Anglo-Norman marginal inscription stresses that Mary has succeeded in retrieving 'tout la chartre' (the whole charter).

The next image in the sequence shows Theophilus kneeling before Mary as she returns the sealed document, which hangs between them. Mary holds the charter while Theophilus extends his hands toward her in prayer, creating what was to become an iconic English representation of the Virgin Mary (see Plate 3).[6] And in the final initial, William shows Theophilus burning the

---

[5] Ibid., pp. 15, 201–7.
[6] For comparison, see also Plate 5 and my discussion of the Lambeth Apocalypse and Lincoln Cathedral window below, pp. 79–82.

Plate 2 The Virgin Mary takes Theophilus's charter from the Devil. London, British Library MS Additional 49999, fol. 40v. © British Library Board

charter, held upside down by its seal-tag and still bearing its label, 'CARTA TEOFOLI', in a large and fiery cauldron (see Plate 4).

The illuminator's special identification with Theophilus is explicit. Directly opposite the burning charter (on the facing page), William includes a self-portrait, in which the tonsured habit-wearing artist looks very similar to his depiction of Theophilus kneeling before Mary in supplication. The hand of God reaches down and touches his head, while a marginal gloss eliminates any confusion there might otherwise be about who is depicted ('w. de brail' qui me depeint').[7] William's self-conscious connection to the sinner whom Mary allows to burn the damning charter shows the significance that her

---

7   Donovan, *The de Brailes Hours*, p. 77, fig. 46 (and cf. p. 74, fig. 43).

Plate 3 The Virgin Mary returns Theophilus's charter. London, British Library MS Additional 49999, fol. 41v. © British Library Board

intercession could have for any devotee immersed in documentary culture. As Donovan remarks, these images would have also impressed themselves powerfully on the woman for whom William made the book: '[T]he putting aside of such a binding legal charter as that entered into by Theophilus would have constituted a miracle indeed: a salvation only possible through the intercession of the Virgin.'[8]

And this was a Marian possibility that developed during a time when the charter was an ambivalent symbol in England, a place that had experienced enormous cultural changes – material, psychological, and spiritual – because

[8] Ibid., p. 81.

Plate 4 Theophilus burns his charter. London, British Library MS Additional 49999, fol. 42v. © British Library Board

of the proliferation of written and especially documentary modes. 'Documents did not immediately inspire trust', as Michael Clanchy puts it,[9] and the Theophilus illustrations are a good reflection of both the social and religious significance of the new common kinds of legal interaction. In discussion of those that accompany the text of Revelation in the mid-thirteenth-century Lambeth Apocalypse (Lambeth Palace Library MS 209), Michael Camille has suggested that the image of Theophilus approaching the court of the Devil, shadowed by his Jewish associate and offering his charter before demon scribes, speaks to a cultural moment at least as much as it does to the popularity of the legend: 'As the scribe's role in administration and law grew in the thirteenth century, it is not difficult to see how the mechanics of individual sin and damnation shift from using external signs ... to representations that stress the act of writing the damning document itself.'[10] Similar

---

[9] *From Memory to Written Record*, p. 294.
[10] 'The Devil's Writing: Diabolic Literacy in Medieval Art', *World Art: Themes of Unity in Diversity: Acts of the XXVIth Congress of the History of Art*, ed. Irving Lavin, II (University Park, PA, 1989), p. 356. Camille's discussion of the style of the Devil's writing is also connected to my

to William de Brailes's illustrations in their focus, the Lambeth artist puts hellish scribal and legal practice on display to communicate a suspicion of 'the oldness of the letter' (Rom. 7:6). The charter as a symbol in this context denotes not only the problem of literal attachment to the law but also the potential for transcendence of the law. Mary's ability to penetrate the world of Jewish and demonic writing, in other words, is consistent with Pauline inversions of religious and spiritual law.[11]

The Christian emphasis on the *Logos* was never necessarily an emphasis on writing, and scenes of devilish bureaucracies could put a fine point on that. As Camille explains,

> [T]he warm, personally interactive power of orality, still theologically essential in the true transmission of the Logos, [is opposed] to the cold apparatus of writing. Plato held that writing constituted a kind of death, and Christ's vociferous curse in Matthew 23:25–28 compared the scribe to the empty cup and the tomb in pronouncing, 'Woe to you scribes and Pharisees.' This antitextual tendency meant that 'emphasis on the word inscribed spiritually on the minds of men, as contrasted with letters written on parchment, retained its strength in the Christian message'... If there is a subtext behind this [Lambeth Theophilus] scene, it is another important Biblical authority on language, Saint Paul, who in his second letter to the Corinthians (3:6) stated, 'Written not with ink but with the spirit of the living God ... the letter killeth, but the spirit giveth life.'[12]

In this light, written text can take on not only a mysterious aura, but also a dangerous one; contractual agreements are both actually and spiritually binding, and the symbolic power of the legal text eerily reflects back on the viewer. In the Lambeth scene, for instance, Theophilus's contractual binding of his soul to Satan while demon scribes furiously record the proceedings bears resemblance to daily scribal activities in the thirteenth century. The artist displays both 'the charter which Theophilus hands over and also the writ in devilish script', and the 'doubling up of record-keeping accurately reflects the English royal court of Henry III or Edward I, where the charter which a litigant proffered might be copied by a royal clerk into a plea roll or Chancery record'.[13]

A Marian intervention that both negotiates and interrupts this system could be construed as simultaneously practical and supernatural. The figure

---

readings of Theophilus's charter as a 'Jewish' law: he notes that 'the devil, while scribbling in the Western left-to-right manner, writes a strange diabolic language' that is vaguely Arabic or, in light of the Jewish sorcerer's presence, 'meant to be a form of "pseudo-Hebrew"' (see n. 15). For a critical study of the Lambeth Apocalypse with color plates, see Nigel J. Morgan, ed., *The Lambeth Apocalypse: Manuscript 209 in the Lambeth Palace Library* (London, 1990).

11   See Daniel Boyarin, *A Radical Jew: Paul and the Politics of Identity* (Berkeley and Los Angeles, 1994), Chapter 4, especially pp. 155–6.

12   'Devil's Writing', pp. 356–7. Camille is here quoting Michael Clanchy's opinion of the 'anti-writing bias' in thirteenth-century England (n. 18).

13   Clanchy, *From Memory to Written Record*, p. 188.

of 'real' scribal practice in the Lambeth cycle is resolved by a complementary image of Mary snatching the charter away from the Devil with the assistance of a spear-bearing angel, a legal settlement of understandable appeal in thirteenth-century England, even (sometimes especially) for the laity, towards whom many of the emerging vernacular Marian *exempla* were aimed. In analysis of such images, Camille has underscored the then growing importance of at least some Latin literacy for the *laicus*, 'for whom it could become a matter of life and death in certain legal situations'.[14] And, considering that both the de Brailes and Lambeth books were made for women, Clanchy has implicated even feminine legal transactions, which might be markedly less quotidian than a male counterpart's: Theophilus's 'concern with written record would have ... appealed particularly to those ladies whose happiness depended on the enforcement or cancellation of written contracts. In 1302, [for instance,] John de Camoys conveyed his wife Margaret to William Paynel by charter.'[15] There is some attractiveness, to say the least, in recourse to a higher power that might undo such a transaction.

The English perception of Mary's ability to intercede in legal dispute and through legal documentation – which bespeaks the influence of the Theophilus story – meant also that she could sometimes grant salvation by similar means, that her ability to undo written damnation could transmute into an ability to authorize worldly transactions, as a witness or a scribe. A remarkable instance survives from St Mary's Priory at Monmouth, where a gift was confirmed by means of a charter granted by Mary herself, apparently in order to inspire more confidence in the text than the usual documentation written and witnessed by mere men. The typical symbolic object of conveyance would be a book of the Gospels, but Mary's document is imagined as similarly powerful in this case: 'The charter rewards [a certain] Richard and Beatrice with divine bliss because they have given tithes ... to Mary the mother of God. She is the ostensible grantor of the charter, though the document was presumably written by a monk of St Mary's priory which was the terrestrial beneficiary.'[16] Though Michael Clanchy places this example under the rubric of 'symbolic documents', the charter itself is real; there is no reason to believe that it was not understood as evidence of an actual conveyance, of the miraculous ability of Mary to transfer spiritual goods through text. We need only think, in any case, of the sheer number of medieval seals that featured the Virgin Mary in her royalty to understand how often her presence was actually and literally connected to a legal document.[17]

---

[14] 'Seeing and Reading: Some Visual Implications of Medieval Literacy and Illiteracy', *Art History* 8.1 (1985), p. 40.

[15] *From Memory to Written Record*, p. 189.

[16] Ibid., p. 255.

[17] This is particularly true of monastic seals and the seals of secular clergy, though personal seals often bore legends including prayers to the Virgin Mary. See the plates in Gale Pedrick, *Monastic Seals of the XIIIth Century* (London, 1902); and P. D. A. Harvey and Andrew McGuinness, *A Guide to British Medieval Seals* (London, 1996), Chapter 4 and Appendix.

Thirteenth-century church windows show that this typical imagination of Mary's intercession had also seeped into prominently placed visual representations of her, outside of bookish settings. We know that windows at Canterbury, York, and Lincoln depicted the Theophilus legend, and it is likely that all of them featured Mary with the charter. The only full surviving cycle, from Lincoln, depicts the unholy document (in this case shown as an unfurled roll) in four of its seven panes.[18] It can still be seen in Lincoln Cathedral's north quire aisle (east window) among other hagiographical legends, and its images and inscriptions are clearly visible from the cathedral floor. The panes closest to the viewer show Theophilus negotiating the contract with the Devil and the Jewish sorcerer, and twice show the name TIOFILVS. Above this, joined panes show Mary seizing the long document from the Devil, with the label S. MARIA beneath, while Theophilus turns over the damning document to his bishop on the left. The impression such images would have had on a congregation is increased by their location close to the central choir (now known as St Hugh's Choir), and by their emphasis on the legal document and Mary's role in retrieving it. The creation and resolution of the contract is nearly the whole of the visually represented narrative in this case – and it is perhaps not merely coincidental that the Jewish population in Lincoln lived literally in the shadow of the great cathedral, which also housed the shrine of little 'St Hugh' of Lincoln, for whose 1255 murder nineteen Jewish men were wrongfully executed. What we see in such cases is that the Theophilan nexus of ideas about sin, law, Jewish apostasy, and Marian intercession was slowly but surely creating a Marian paradigm in England.

The 'Theophilus Group' in the *South English Legendary*

Theophilus and his charter shaped early vernacular English Marian miracles. The story was often added to or imitated, translated or elaborated. The earliest appearance of a group of Middle English Miracles of the Virgin, in the collection of saints' lives and verse homilies known as the *South English Legendary* (composed *c.*1270–85 in its earliest form), appear as a constit-

---

18   There are four Theophilus panels at Lincoln, possibly five (a nearby panel shows the burial of a bishop, which may be part of the story), but three are split into two side-by-side scenes. The entire window is catalogued as EG3 in the cathedral's information binder, and the corresponding information sheet was written in 1983 by Nigel Morgan, who dates the work to the early thirteenth century. The entire east window is devoted to hagiographical legends, though the top quatrefoils once had panels depicting the seasons, which have now been removed. In addition to the Lincoln cycle, a single panel at Canterbury is known to have existed, while two from York survive. See Michael W. Cothren, 'The Iconography of Theophilus Windows in the First Half of the Thirteenth Century', *Speculum* 59.2 (1984), pp. 308–41. Cothren is primarily concerned with French examples, however, which are markedly different from the English. The French windows most commonly featured scenes that are not part of the English tradition and tend to depict the Devil's pact as an act of homage (Theophilus's hands within the Devil's). My thanks to Roger Dahood for originally drawing my attention to the Lincoln window.

uent element of the life of 'St Theophilus'.[19] Six miracles are appended to the *vita* in imitation of the hagiographic commonplace of listing, usually at the end of the narrative proper, the postmortem miracles performed by a saint.[20] As the miracles attest, however, Theophilus is a saint only by virtue of his participation in Marian intercession, since the miracles he produces are none of his own. He is a saint by proxy, authorized by Mary's return of the Devil's charter, his *vita* simply one 'uair miracle oure Leuedy dude ... / As heo monye oþere dude'.[21] What St Theophilus generates, if he is a holy figure worthy of any *imitatio*, is a proliferation of Marian miracles. The *South English Legendary* poet, like William of Malmesbury, uses him as a catalyst that quickly produces related examples.

It is not the focusing of Marian intercession on this legend, then, that is the innovation of this early vernacular use, nor is it the inclusion of the story in a collection of *vitae* and sermons, nor is it the compilation of it with other instances of Marian power. All of this describes exactly how the legend began life in England, and by the time the *South English Legendary* was compiled, it would have been more natural to place 'Theophilus' at the beginning of a group of Marian miracles than to think of it alone, especially if the *South English Legendary* poet knew the insular Latin collections that circulated widely in thirteenth-century England.[22] Any audience that had seen or heard or read the story would have understood it first as a lesson about Marian intercession, not as an independent saint's life. It was, as I have already detailed, the standard stuff of liturgical practice and of visual representations of Marian devotion, and it had been established as common sermon fodder for Marian feast days. Within two generations of the first compilation of the *South English Legendary*, one preacher tells us that the story was 'euery woke songe and rad in holychurch in remembrance of þe good Ladies kyndenes and grace',[23] and the force of this routine veneration

---

[19] On the complex dissemination and evolution of the *SEL*, its manuscripts, and textual traditions, see Manfred Görlach, *The Textual Tradition of the South English Legendary*, Leeds Texts and Monographs (Leeds, 1974).

[20] In the *SEL*, this structure is exactly observed, for example, in the cases of SS Agnes, James the Great, Leonard, Clement, Andrew, Nicholas, and John the Evangelist, and in the Exultation of the Holy Cross (where the miracle worker is the Holy Cross). In the earliest *SEL* manuscript (MS Bodl. Laud misc. 108), there are no Marian miracles attached to 'Theophilus', but the conclusion of the legend nevertheless suggests that the miracles were part of the plan: 'Wel fair Miracle ore leuedi dude: þat brou3te him of þulke wo / Ase heo hath manye oþere i-don: and 3eot heo wole wel mo.' See Carl Horstmann, ed., *The Early South English Legendary*, EETS, os 87 (London, 1887), p. 293, lines 193–4.

[21] D'Evelyn and Mill, *SEL*, I, p. 227, lines 199–200.

[22] Though much has been made of the connection between the *SEL* and the *Legenda aurea* of Jacobus Voragine, there is little evidence that Jacobus's collection influenced this portion of the *SEL*. Jacobus does record all but one of the Marian miracles in the *SEL*, but a common or similar source is more likely than a direct relationship, as similarities between the *SEL* and continental collections are not less striking than those between the *SEL* and extant English collections. See Tryon, 'Miracles of Our Lady in Middle English Verse', p. 309, and Gorläch, *Textual Tradition*, p. 173.

[23] Ross, *Middle English Sermons*, p. 261. I discuss this sermon in more detail below, pp. 93–7.

might be summed up by Barbara Newman's comment that 'the God or gods worshipped within any tradition are not only those that its doctrinal formulas proclaim, but those that its devotees address in prayer, its artists paint or sculpt, its poets celebrate in hymns'.[24] What *is* remarkable about the *South English Legendary* 'Theophilus', however, is how it is embedded in an overarching narrative about Marian intercession that would not be possible to tell in a self-contained collection of solely Marian miracles. Its use in this work constitutes a conscious move away from the generic categorization of Miracles of the Virgin that the twelfth-century Anglo-Latin collections imposed and toward a didactic manipulation of inter-textual relationships.

Anne Thompson has argued that the *South English Legendary* is a work with surprisingly careful narrative complexity in its overall structure. Battling the opinions of critics like Derek Pearsall – who has claimed that '[a]ccumulation is the whole principle' of it and that it 'shows no trace' of 'design'[25] – she posits that the *Legendary* can be read 'like any other book one might pick up and read on impulse' and that a deliberate sequential reading is not unfruitful.[26] Thompson uses the beginnings of the work to show the intention of the poet, who in his prologue describes the project as a single, romantic narrative telling the story of the hard-won kingdom of Christendom, of 'Hardi batailles … / Of apostles & martirs þat hardy kniȝtes were'.[27] In presenting the whole of the work as a romance, wherein many knights defend the honor of a single king, he instructs his readers on how to approach his compilation ideally. He has 'an orderly mind' and frames the collection as 'a narrative that takes place in time', and the metaphor of the battling knights 'leads into the concept of "storytelling" as a conscious practice'. [28] I am convinced by this argument, and though Thompson finds a false start in the *Legendary*'s first festal narrative – it begins with New Year's Day, the feast of the Circumcision, which she finds jarringly 'nonnarrative in character'[29] – her central argument can certainly be extended to the Circumcision, if one considers a subnarrative concerning the warrior king's mother.

The poet's account of why the feast of the Circumcision matters is in fact a striking commentary on the romance's protagonist, whom he fashions in the prologue as the leader behind the epic battle. This is a religious war, and it is not inappropriate that it might include first some mention of what is at stake, in this case a reminder to the reader, even before the stories of Christ's 'hardy kniȝtes' start, that Christ was a Jewish man who followed Jewish law. We should honor the New Year's feast, he explains, because 'oure Louerd was icircumsiced as it fel in þe lay' (law), and 'he nolde noȝt aȝen þe olde lauwe

---

[24]   *God and the Goddesses*, p. 294.
[25]   Quoted in Anne Thompson, *Everyday Saints and the Art of Narrative in the South English Legendary* (Burlington, VT, and Aldershot, 2003), pp. 12–13.
[26]   Thompson, *Everyday Saints*, p. 4.
[27]   D'Evelyn and Mill, *SEL*, I, p. 1, lines 62–3.
[28]   *Everyday Saints*, p. 6.
[29]   Ibid., p. 7.

beo'.[30] Christ was careful to maintain the Jewish covenant with God 'þat þe Giwes ne sede noȝt efsone / Þat he ne toke noȝt on as hore faderes were wont to done / Abraham and is ospring þat icircumsised were echon / & þat oure Louerd ham nere noȝt ilich [was not the same as them] ac wiþsede [denied] here lauwe anon'.[31] The first thing that the *South English Legendary* narrative asserts, in other words, is that the son of Joseph and Mary was not, once upon a time when the overarching story commenced, supposed to be different or separate from Jews, that he followed the 'olde lauwe' and would not violate it. We are admonished not to ignore or dishonor this aspect of Jesus's life: 'þe day is well to holde heiȝe of men þat beoþ wise'.[32] Men who are wise will keep in mind that Christ's Jewishness plays a part in the battle.

Indeed, consciousness of the overlap of Judaism and Christianity makes for more dramatic conflict at several points in the *Legendary*, which frequently describes the conversion or punishment of Jews (in addition to the life of Theophilus, this is true of the lives of SS Nicholas and Leonard, in the stories of the Exultation of the Holy Cross and of Mary's Assumption, and not surprisingly in the life of St Paul). In the story of the struggle for Christendom, it is part of the responsibility of both Jesus and his mother, and the apostles, to be Jews who become Christians and then convert other Jews to Christianity. Such conversions (or refusals to convert) take on a continued drama and intimacy after the frankness of the poet's justification of Christ's circumcision, and this is especially true for the Virgin Mary, who gave her eight-day-old son to be circumcised according to Jewish law, as any sequential reader of the *South English Legendary* is meant to remember. The doubled religious identity of Jesus (and by implication of Mary) that is clear from the outset makes the religious conflict that Mary often meets more personal and affective, for she encounters Jewish conflict in nearly half of the tales of her miraculous intercession that appear in the vast majority of *Legendary* manuscripts, including those that follow the life of Theophilus.[33]

The *Legendary*'s account of her death and Assumption, for instance, which includes the familiar apocryphal story of a Jewish attack on her funeral procession, necessitates consciousness of Mary's Jewishness to make its point. In it, a Jewish leader assails Mary's bier, intending to seize her body and burn it, but his hands become stuck so that he cannot remove them, his arms palsy and wither, he feels agonizing pain, and every Jew in the mob that accompanies him is immediately struck blind. When he pleads for help,

---

[30] D'Evelyn and Mill, *SEL*, I, p. 4, lines 10–16.

[31] Ibid., p. 4, lines 19–22.

[32] Ibid., p. 4, line 28. The same message is present, in abbreviated form, in the misplaced prologue of MS Laud misc. 108. See Horstmann, *Early SEL*, pp. 177–8, lines 7–9: 'Þe furste feste þat in þe ȝere comez we cleopiez ȝeres-dai, / Ase ore louerd was circumiset in þe giwene lay, / For to fulfullen hoere lawe.'

[33] In most *SEL* manuscripts, stories of Marian intercession can be found in: the Assumption narrative, the life of St Mary of Egypt, 'Theophilus', and the six miracles that follow 'Theophilus'. Four of these nine include anti-Semitic material. For a chart showing which legends appear in which manuscripts, see Görlach, *Textual Tradition*, pp. 306–9.

St Peter instructs him to believe in Jesus and Mary and to confess his faith aloud, and, after doing so, he is cured of his ailments – all but the blindness, which remains for every Jew present. Peter further instructs him to touch his companions' eyes with a palm branch that Mary had instructed St John to carry in the procession, and more than thirty thousand Jews ('þritti þousond & mo') then regain their sight.[34] Despite the 'happy' outcome, knowledge of Jewish anger is the emotional thrust of this story: John warns the apostles to avoid open mourning because, he says, 'þe Giwes us wolde scorne ʒif hi it miʒte iseo / And segge þat we þerof lieþ þat oure Louerd wole attenende / After oure deþ murie lif';[35] Mary foresees the attack on her body and instructs John to bear a palm branch 'þat hi me noʒt forsake / Þe Giwes';[36] and the Jews who plan the attack reveal their status as former coreligionists when they refer to Mary as 'þe traitors moder'.[37] The overarching narrative of the *South English Legendary* renders this a painful situation: Jews have either themselves become traitors of their own people, or they are literally blind to their own prophecies. The best villains are those with whom one identifies, and the poet makes this conflict between the Jewish population and the Virgin Mary a very personal one. Mary's foresight about Jewish anger toward her is conceptualized here as her first postmortem miracle, and the additional miracles set with the life of Theophilus preserve more of the type.

In the Latin version of the legend that was circulating in England, Theophilus could easily become a convert saint by virtue of his turning away from Jewish influence – a saint like St Quiriac (the Jew who helped Empress Helena find the True Cross), or like St Paul (who converted on the road to Damascus) – and the *Legendary* poet does exploit these elements of the story. He makes it clear that Theophilus seeks his 'Giwes conseiler' of his own volition and emphasizes that he forsakes both God and Mary and all of 'þi lay / Þi Cristendom'.[38] Theophilus's self-identification with the executed Jew remains, and the parallel between Mary and the Jewish intercessor is considerably more straightforward here than in the Latin text:

> Oure Leuedy he þonkede & hure grace as me þingþ wel he aʒte
> More þanne he dude þe luþer Giu þat to þe deuel him broʒte
> Þis was a betere cheffare [bargain, agreement] þanne he biuore wroʒte.[39]

It is clear that the English poet sees Theophilus as a man who loses his Christian identity by negotiating with a Jew and must return to Christianity by severing Jewish influence. This conversion is central to the narrative, as

---

34 Charlotte D'Evelyn and Anna J. Mill, *The South English Legendary*, II, EETS, os 236 (London, 1956), p. 372, line 213. The complete story summarized here appears on pp. 367–73.
35 Ibid., p. 368, lines 104–6.
36 Ibid., p. 367, lines 80–1.
37 Ibid., p. 371, line 178.
38 Ibid., p. 223, line 88; p. 222, lines 38–58 (here 44–5).
39 Ibid., p. 226, lines 163–5.

it also seems to motivate the poet's organization of the Marian miracles that are appended to it.

Immediately following 'Theophilus' is the story of 'The Jewish Boy of Bourges', with which Dominic of Evesham began his collection, and the final miracle in the group of six is the story of the Jews of Toledo, which William of Malmesbury associated with the Jewish 'Pope of Narbonne'.[40] The framing of this little group with anti-Semitic miracles is striking. That 'The Jewish Boy' follows 'Theophilus' is perhaps not unexpected – the stories were also paired in Dominic and William's collections – but it is notable that this author clearly perceives and exploits the structural parallels and relationships found in the Latin predecessors. Jewish guilt and conversion are succinctly bound together in the Jewish boy's one-line confession of faith – 'Ich biluue on hure sone þat þe Giwes honge on þe treo'[41] – as are the destructions of written law and Jewish obstinacy in the father's death. When the crowd of Christians toss him into his oven '& to douste him forbrende', they are also reenacting the concluding action of the life of Theophilus, wherein the 'Jewish' charter is publicly 'to doust ibarnd'.[42] And had the Bourges Jews not taken this action and believed in Christ and his mother, says the poet, they had all been 'ssrewen' (evil creatures).[43] The verbal connection of Jews to the killing text, the boy's declaration of Jewish guilt, and the poet's interjection stand as stark instances of what the overarching narrative can provoke.

'The Jews of Toledo' likewise prompt a sweeping vitriolic statement about Jewish responses to Mary. 'Gywes hatieþ oure Leuedy muche & hure swete sone also',[44] the poet tells us as he begins the final miracle in the group. The claim is all the more pointed because it is directly juxtaposed to the concluding line of the miracle that precedes it, which emphasizes Mary's unwavering mercy and kindness: 'Wiþ ech þing alday we seoþ oure Leuedi swete & milde.'[45] Though the poet omits any details about the fate of the Jews of Toledo, he uses their story to conclude the entire sequence of Marian miracles with a general curse on Jews: 'God ȝiue ȝam harde stonde [hardship] / And alle þat ȝam louie wel for muche is þe vilte / And þe ssame [shame] þat hi ofte doþ oure Louerd in priuete.'[46] This is almost immediately followed by a brief prayer to Mary that begs intercession for the sake of 'þe grete sor þat þou haddest þo þi sone deide on treo'.[47] This final petition for Mary's continual mercy is not only paired with the notion that living Jews are continually doing harm to Mary and her son (it comes when the poet's curse can be no fresher in the mind of any reader or listener), but it also echoes the Jewish

---

[40] See Chapter 2 above, pp. 71–2.
[41] D'Evelyn and Mill, *SEL*, I, p. 229, line 236.
[42] Ibid., p. 229, line 238; p. 227, line 182–3.
[43] Ibid., p. 229, lines 239–41.
[44] Ibid., p. 237, line 485.
[45] Ibid., p. 237, line 484.
[46] Ibid., p. 238, lines 498–500.
[47] Ibid., p. 238, line 504.

boy's confession that he believes in Mary's son 'þat þe Giwes honge on þe treo'.[48] These assertions, which find their source in Mary's 'historical' relationship to Jews, are only found in the *Legendary*'s Marian tales of Jewish conversion, and it is not just vitriol but also a peculiarly Marian justice that is built into such inter-textual reverberations. If the Jews killed her son, the poet implicitly argues, Mary has a right to retribution. The rhetorical turn to general pronouncements about Jewish crimes, then, shows that Mary does not take full advantage of the retribution she could justly impose. That is, the poet's framing of the Theophilus miracle group draws attention not only to Mary's particularly personal connection to Jews but also to the nature of her mercy and judgment, which is now more impressive for what it eschews.

Mary's singular legal abilities, both in the literal sense of negotiating contract law and in the more abstract sense of meting out justice, continue to function throughout this group. I have discussed previously how this overlapping of legal/textual and Jewish 'problems' is not accidental, and neither is it here. The fact that this poet so explicitly notes the similarity of Mary's role to Theophilus's Jewish counselor's – Mary can negotiate a 'betere cheffare þanne he'[49] – in part answers fears about Jewish writing and its consequences that are found elsewhere in the *Legendary*. The life of St Quiriac, most commonly arranged in the manuscripts just four or five legends before 'Theophilus',[50] tells of the bishop and Jewish convert who discovered the relics of the Holy Cross, and of how a Muslim 'emperor' cut off his hand when he refused to accept Mohammed. When the emperor tells Quiriac, 'Ic do ... þis / For þou hast ofte iwrite þer wiþ aȝen oure lawe iwis',[51] the saint's response is one that tells not of Jewish guilt or Muslim disbelief but of Christian anxiety about Jewish text:

> Þou gidi hound [foolish dog] quaþ sein Quiriak wel hastou do by me
> Of a god dede þou were wel vnderstonde wel aȝte ich blessy þe
> For þou bynome me þulke lyme þat me haueþ ofte to sunne idrawe
> For ich habbe ofte iwrite þerwiþ aȝen Cristes lawe
> Þe wile ich was a luþer Giu and on him biluuede noȝt.[52]

Part of Quiriac's sainthood, marginalized by his former identity as it may be (he can never *not* be a Jew), is his awareness of the gravity and danger of his former compositions. In this sense, the punishment afforded him by the Muslim leader is just. It punishes only the member of the body that has offended in a way that is inexcusable.[53] Writing may be forgiven by baptism

---

48 Ibid., p. 229, line 236.
49 Ibid., p. 226, line 165.
50 See Görlach, *Textual Tradition*, pp. 306–7.
51 D'Evelyn and Mill, *SEL*, I, p. 179, lines 7–8.
52 Ibid., p. 179, lines 9–13.
53 Quiriac's reasoning reflects St Paul's commentary on how individual members of the body work in cooperation with the whole. See 1 Cor. 12:26 ('If one member suffer any thing, all the members suffer with it: or if one member glory, all the members rejoice with it') and Rom. 6:13 ('Neither

and sanctity, but it cannot be unwritten. What is saintly here is that Quiriac perceives its permanence.[54]

This is mimicked and differently inflected in Theophilus's return to Christianity from the realm of Jewish influence, which includes his belief that what was written in his denial of Christ and Mary (the feared content of all Jewish writing) is not unwritable or retrievable. When Theophilus tells Mary that he will fear for his soul so long as the charter exists, even though Mary has already obtained his forgiveness and pronounced the biblical valediction 'nesunege þou namore' (sin no more),[55] his anxiety stems from what the Devil has told him about the enduring nature of the written word. In the *South English Legendary* 'Theophilus', the Devil emphatically insists on the charter precisely because of its permanence, and he succeeds in convincing Theophilus that oral agreement is meaningless against Mary:

> Word nis aȝen hure bote wind for þei a mon hure forsake
> Ȝif he wole turne is herte wel gladlich ȝo [she] wil him take
> Þeruore ichelle of þe beo siker ar ich mengi [deal] wiþ þe
> Gode charter of þis couenant þou sselt make me
> Writ wiþ þin owe honde and acely hure [seal it] also.[56]

This is part of Theophilus's 'Jewish problem' (unlike the one that Quiriac overcomes). He maintains to the end that 'wile þe chartre is ihol euere mo ich drede',[57] though even the Devil privately understands that this adherence to written law is misguided. As he steals away with the document, he admits that he will have to lock it away tightly in hell to alleviate his worries that Mary will simply come and take it away.[58]

In fact, Mary's ability to invalidate the document becomes the focus of the poet's moralizing. In the final estimation, this is all about a contract, and the contract is all about Mary's miracles. As Theophilus, in the conclusion of the story, tells his bishop and his congregation 'eueridel' of what has happened to him, the poet qualifies this by saying only that he told them about the 'uorwarde & þe sikernesse' (the contract and the surety) and how Mary 'broȝte him is chartre þat in helle biloke was so uaste'.[59] The bishop then reads the document 'biuore al þat folk ... þat [so that] folk wolde þe chartre wite for miracles as hi bede'.[60] That is, the bishop (and the poet)

---

yield ye your members as instruments of iniquity unto sin: but present yourselves to God, as those that are alive from the dead; and your members as instruments of justice unto God').

54 On the medieval understanding of the threatening permanence of writing, see Clanchy, *From Memory to Written Record*, p. 254: 'Writing shifted the spotlight away from the transitory actors witnessing a conveyance and onto the perpetual parchment recording it. ... [C]harters were directed to posterity.'

55 D'Evelyn and Mill, *SEL*, I, p. 225, line 150.

56 Ibid., pp. 222–3, lines 60–5.

57 Ibid., p. 227, line 182.

58 Ibid., p. 223, lines 72–3.

59 Ibid., p. 226, lines 173–6.

60 Ibid., pp. 226–7, lines 176–9.

wants each member of his congregation to have Theophilus's charter in mind as they pray for Mary's intercession. While the actual text of the charter remains unknown to the reader or hearer of the *Legendary*, written over it is the story of Mary's ability to nullify it, and this is literally enacted in the text. The poet has Theophilus enter the church to tell his story 'riʒt as þe gospel was irad',[61] that is, at the central point in the celebration of Mass, when the gospel reading would occur. It is then that Theophilus bursts into the church, interrupts the mass to tell his story, and, almost inconceivably, creates a situation in which the reading of the charter takes the place of the reading of the gospel: it is at this moment that 'þe charter ... þe bissop let rede'.[62] This situation not only gives the canceled charter the status of gospel but turns it into a stunning symbolic representation of Mary's power. The Theophilus story itself becomes a reenactment of this moment: every time a reader or listener experiences the story, they are in the position of the congregation that witnessed Theophilus's return and should 'þe chartre wite for miracles as hi bede'.

As for the four Miracles of the Virgin appended to the *South English Legendary* 'Theophilus' that I have not yet discussed – also what a congregation can pray for while meditating on the charter – all are concerned to show Mary's persistent sense of justice and loyalty to anyone devoted to her, even in the least of ways. Each details a transaction through which Mary exchanges good deed for good deed. A murderous feudal lord treats his subjects evilly, for instance, but he obtains protection from the Devil because 'euerich day wiþ Aue Marie to Marie he sede',[63] and if a man 'deþ oure Leuedi eni seruise unʒoulde nessel it noʒt beo' (it will not go unrewarded).[64] In another instance, a misguided knight is saved from another diabolical contract because of his previous devotion to Mary. In another instance, a monk who can say no other prayer than the two words 'Ave Maria' is repaid with a miraculous display of precisely those two words. In another, a sinful Oxford scholar, devoted to Mary in his childhood, is led to heaven by Mary herself. In the simple and just agreement to which Mary adheres in these tales, she recompenses any devotion to her. This is not at all unusual in Miracles of the Virgin, but the examples that the *South English Legendary* poet chooses to sandwich between 'Theophilus' and 'The Jewish Boy' on one side, and 'The Jews of Toledo' on the other, also happen to paint Mary as a trickster lawyer and as a woman committed to (spiritual) learning.

When a knight once devoted to Mary finds himself in a position similar to Theophilus – in the miracle known editorially as 'How Our Lady Came to the Devil Instead of the Victim' – Mary mimics the Devil's tactics to preempt an illegal contract. The Devil had tricked the knight, who was upset about

---

[61] Ibid., p. 226, line 171.
[62] Ibid., p. 226, line 176.
[63] Ibid., p. 230, line 280.
[64] Ibid., p. 231, line 294.

losing his fortune, by coming to him 'in a mannes forme' and promising to make him rich again, so long as he would return with his wife. Like the one in Theophilus, this devil speaks in contractual terms: 'we ssoleþ som forwarde [contract] speke', he promises, 'And þou sselt euere riche beo bote þou uorwarde breke'.[65] But when the despairing man returns to the Devil's trap, Mary discreetly interferes by taking 'mannes forme' herself, accompanying the knight in the form of his wife. When the Devil rages at the deception (to which the knight was not privy), Mary demands, 'wy wostou fawe [be feign] / Þat he þe hadde is wif ibro3t þou wost it ner no3t lawe.'[66] Though the Devil argues that there is a breach of contract, since he has already advanced goods in exchange for the knight's wife, Mary's intercession acts as a preemptive dissolution of the illegal 'forwarde', and it is as much a fulfillment of her own contract with her devotees. She reminds this devil that his proposed transaction 'ner no3t lawe' and, in doing so, satisfies another transaction unwittingly struck by the knight, whose previous devotion had earned him her obligation. While such tales of tit-for-tat mean that Mary, as Richard Firth Green has pointed out, 'assumes [the] traditional role of the trickster on our behalf',[67] her particular awareness of what constitutes lawful agreement is the motivation in this case.

The remaining miracles are similarly oriented. In the tale concerning the unlearned monk who was unable to recite even the simplest of prayers, except for the two words 'Ave Maria', Mary is bound to intercede because he repeats those words 'boþe ni3te and day ... in god entente'.[68] After the monk's death, a white lily grows from his grave:

> In ech lef þer was iwrite wiþ lettres of golde rede
> Þeos to wordes Aue Marie þat he so ofte sede
> Þat folk spak þerof wide and wondrede muche þer uore
> So þat hy nome 3am [betook themselves] to rede to loke wat were the
>   more [root]
> Hi dolue and fond þe lilie weie ri3t out of is mouþe.[69]

Mary's use of text here ('iwrite wiþ letters of golde rede') is an expression of reciprocity: Mary receives the monk's attempts to compensate for his illiteracy as an expression of spiritual literacy, and the textual sign that causes worshippers to dig through the ground to find a source confirms that she understands the words in this way. Mary's final gift to the monk who struggled so mightily with text is the conversion of his verbal devotion to textual

---

[65] Ibid., p. 232, lines 311, 320–1.
[66] Ibid., p. 233, lines 353–4.
[67] *Crisis of Truth*, p. 344.
[68] D'Evelyn and Mill, *SEL*, I, p. 234, lines 393–4.
[69] Ibid., p. 235, lines 401–5. This old miracle formula is not lost on Oscar Wilde. See his 'Ballad of Reading Gaol' (Part IV): 'Out of his mouth a red, red rose! / Out of his heart a white! / For who can say by what strange way, / Christ brings His will to light.'

devotion (when the two memorized words appear as written words), which in turn provides a permanent record of his salvation and of the fulfillment of her obligation to him.

Her appearance for an Oxford scholar, a man once so intensely affected by the idea of Mary sorrowing that he thought of himself and his own mother and could never get the image out of his head, shows Mary performing a special academic compensation despite the fact that the scholar had committed some grievous sin (not revealed to the reader). This miracle, unique to England, emphasizes that strong devotion, if only to a single aspect of Mary's experience, will yield her grace, even as it instructs on the nature of spiritual learning versus clerical learning. When the scholar dies at Oxford, the two schoolmates who attend his body dream that Mary performs his academic *commendatio* by presenting him not for his degree but for his salvation:

> Hare felawe soule þat þer lai ded to heuene lede heie
> Oure Leuedy as to teche þe wey hure sulf ʒeode biuore
> And openede þe dore of heuene þat þe soule were in ibore
> Þo heo biuore oure Louerd com adon heo sat akne
> Sone heo sede lo her mi frend þat wel haþ iserued me.[70]

Mary's introduction of the dead scholar at the door of heaven follows closely the ritual of *commendatio*, in which the scholar is presented for an academic honor or next stage of examination, and the clerical wit of this vignette is probably meant to be noticed.[71] While it also of course mimics a *commendatio animae* (commendation of the soul) at death,[72] the importance of the characterization of this devotee as a scholar is in its rendering Mary once again the pedagogue whose intercession is related to degrees of learning. The scholar's willingness to learn is what allows Mary to 'teche þe wey' and present him for higher honors. At the same time, however, his obsessive (rather unscholarly) devotion to Mary's sorrow is what guarantees her academic sponsorship at the hour of his death, when she can become the master who presents his soul for the final examination.

What is emphasized throughout this group is exactly what was emphasized in the early Latin version of 'Theophilus' that circulated in England, and in related stories in Dominic of Evesham's and William of Malmesbury's collections; in fact, the consistency itself is remarkable. Mary's dominion over Jews, over text (charters, inscriptions), and her legal mediation remain prevalent as Marian miracles enter the vernacular. She intercedes by providing

---

[70] D'Evelyn and Mill, *SEL*, I, p. 237, lines 458–62.

[71] On sermons written for *commendationes* and other academic occasions, see Siegfried Wenzel, *Latin Sermon Collections from Later Medieval England*, Cambridge Studies in Medieval Literature (Cambridge, 2005), pp. 300–4. These ritual occasions often also involved wordplay, as for instance in *Piers Plowman* 8.126 (B-text, as edited by Schmidt, *The Vision of Piers*): 'Here is Wil wolde wite if Wit koude teche.' My thanks to Anne Middleton for suggesting the comparison.

[72] On medieval representations of *commendatio animae*, see Paul Binski, *Medieval Death: Ritual and Representation* (Ithaca, NY, 1996), pp. 40ff.

advocacy and justice, by offering surety for the sinner, so that Theophilus's contract in juxtaposition becomes just one element of her legal apparatus, a prop in the theater of soul-negotiation in which Mary shows otherworldly skill and sensitivity. She returns good deed for good, bad deed for bad, and this is true even of the anti-Semitic miracles of the *South English Legendary* Theophilus group: the young Jewish boy's single deed, an unwitting experience of the paschal communion, is rewarded by Mary's protection, while the Jews of Toledo who reenact the torture of Christ receive Mary's negative attention, and the narrator's curse.

The profound influence of the legend of Theophilus on this characterization of Mary is also part of what makes these miracles appropriate to the overarching narrative of the *Legendary*, to the story of the battle for Christianity waged by Christ's 'hardy kniʒtes'. Not only do certain plot points connect to the pathos that collectively develops through the poet's use of the feast of the Circumcision, his account of Mary's funeral procession and Assumption, and his life of St Quiriac (as well as other conversion narratives I have not detailed), but his iteration of 'Theophilus' also prescribes for Marian miracles the 'miscellany' and homiletic usage that is typical in England. Here, placed in an anthology of *vitae* and sermons, the final scenes of the legend suggest a reading of the narrative (the charter) in place of the gospel and imply that a reenactment of the moment of return and the destruction of the charter is in every paraliturgical reading of the story. Both the organization of Marian miracles in the *South English Legendary* and the peculiarities of the legend that introduce them invite comparison of Mary's miracles to other biblical and hagiographical narratives and suggest that their *correct* situation is among prayers, saints' lives, and gospel stories.

'Theophilus' in Sermon and Romance

I want to turn now to two later medieval uses of the legend that bear out the implications of the *South English Legendary* group. These also begin to manipulate Mary's legal acumen into a necessary element in the very transmission of her miracles, even of other miracles that may not exploit the same attributes. If the persistence of the Theophilus story as a typological example seems oppressive, the impression is not at odds with the case. The legend and its increasingly legalistic iterations were exhaustingly tenacious in medieval England, and just how clearly and constantly the story shaped the personalities of Marian intercession there is most evident in its development and shifting contexts.

Take one anonymous sermon set down sometime between 1378 and 1402 for example.[73] Written for the feast of Mary's Assumption, it is very much

---

[73] Ross, *Middle English Sermons*, pp. 241–61 (Sermon 41). There is another anonymous example in MS Bodl. Hatton 96 (unedited), a manuscript related to John Mirk's *Festial*. See Whiteford, *Myracles of Oure Lady*, pp. 126–7.

like Ælfric's earlier homily on the same occasion. It concludes with the same two Miracles of the Virgin – the legend of Julian the Apostate and a brief account of Theophilus – and it likewise portrays Mary as a powerful and studious woman, a Jewish woman, an advocate for sinners, and a woman with extraordinary power in both heaven and hell. The overall impression is so generally comparable to Ælfric's work that it is wholly extraordinary how little usage of the legend evolves in the approximately 400 years that elapse between the composition of the two sermons (a testament in itself to the resistance of English Marian miracles to the vast literary proliferations seen on the continent). This preacher, however, is more explicitly interested in the charter and Mary's ability to retrieve it from hell. His version is as follows:

> And 3iff þou be a gret synner and drede þe þat she will not here þi prayoure for þi synne, þan pray þou with the most synnefull man Theophile, þe wiche þat forsoke God vponly afore þe dewell, and wrote is forsaykyng and sealed it with is own seall, and tok it þe dewell is own person and becam is man. But afturward he sore repented hym and fled vn-to Oure Ladye for helpe. And aftur fourty daies penauns Oure Ladie apered vn-to hym and blamed hym sore for is synne, but 3itt she gat hym for3euenes and brou3the a3eyn from þe dewell is writynge and is seall, and declared þat God had for3eue hym and resceyved hym to grace. Þis is no fabull þat I sey 3ow. It is euery woke songe and rad in holychurch in remembrance of þe good Ladies kyndenes and grace.[74]

I have already mentioned this passage because it comments on the frequency with which 'Theophilus' was recited, and it is notable that this is a more accurate summary of Paul the Deacon of Naples's version of the legend than was Ælfric's (especially because of its attention to the forty days of penance). But it is also significant that, despite description of the paraliturgical use of the story, the action boils down to only two elements for this preacher: Theophilus 'wrote is forsaykyng and sealed it with is own seall', and Mary 'gat hym for3euenes and brou3the a3eyn from þe dewell is writynge and is seall'. It is presented to the congregation simply, as a story about an ill-conceived charter and the resolution of the legal dispute that arises because of it.

This sermon, as a whole, literally repeats the imagined content of the sermon of Theophilus's bishop, and the reading of the story 'euery woke … in holychurch' is tantamount to the reading of the charter and the public accounting of Mary's intercession that concludes any longer version of the legend, as a congregation who heard it frequently would no doubt know. The offhand comment about weekly repetition allows us to envision the active use of one of the most popular and familiar Marian miracles circulating in medieval England. Constant liturgical retellings of a legend in which Mary is

---

[74] Ross, *Middle English Sermons*, pp. 260–1.

primarily an undoer of bad contracts simultaneously privileges this particular image of Mary and lends validity to the fantasy of reprieve that she offers from an increasingly documentary legal system ('þis is no fabull þat I sey 3ow'). What Ælfric, in *his* sermon on the Assumption, had singled out as a legend separate from suspect apocrypha, this preacher also does by praising very specific elements of Mary's extraordinary power and reifying what is appropriate for 'official' recitation. His anonymous work (from British Library MS Royal 18 B. XXIII) is a long and meandering one that mentions Mary and her Assumption relatively few times. This preacher is primarily concerned to show that 'þe word of God is prophetable and also available to foure occupacions, as to techyng, to vndrenymmynge [doing], to chastizynge, and to convey vs to vertewous lyvynge',[75] and he spends much of the homily explicating each of these four points of access to God, occasionally weaving in aspects of Mary's character and life, along with complaints about schisms in the church and the encroachment of heathens on Christian lands. This density, however, only makes what the author does mention about Mary, all of which relates to her Theophilan abilities, more trenchant.

When he discusses the Annunciation and the Archangel Gabriel, for instance, he chooses to emphasize that Mary was meditating, 'intra cubiculum orante' (inside a room, praying) rather than going about her business in the streets,[76] and he describes the whole of the Annunciation interaction as one that authorizes Mary's body, in much the same way that a charter would be authorized.[77] Gabriel received from God, he says, a 'signet' with which to approach Mary, by which Gabriel immediately understood 'þat she was wondur specially merked with þe signet'. This divine seal that confirmed the mother of God was finely engraved, the preacher tells us, more finely than any Great Seal: 'in þe which signet ben graven succession of dyuers 3eres, þe meritis of angels and man, the begynnyng and þe contynuaunce and þe ende of all ryghtwisse pepull'.[78] This focus on her contemplative nature and her divine authorization (she is like a document herself) allows the preacher to

---

[75] Ibid., p. 242.

[76] Ibid., p. 258.

[77] This is different from 'the sealed body' discussed by Karma Lochrie in *Margery Kempe and Translations of the Flesh*, New Cultural Studies Series (Philadelphia, PA, 1991), pp. 23–7, where the emphasis is not on the allegorical authorization of the female body but rather the 'spiritual *integritas*' and the 'unbroken body' in chastity. It does not seem that Mary's virginity is at issue for this preacher, though both documentary and bodily authorizations may be functioning here in different ways. For further discussion of the 'sealed' female body in medieval religious literature, see my 'Inscribed Bodies' and 'Sealed Flesh, Book-Skin: How to Read the Female Body in the Early Middle English *Seinte Margarete*', *Women and the Divine in Literature before 1700: Essays in Memory of Margot Louis*, ed. Kathryn Kerby-Fulton (Victoria, BC, 2009), pp. 69–88.

[78] Ross, *Middle English Sermons*, pp. 258–9. The kind of crowded and finely wrought seal described here might be compared to the fourteenth-century seal of St Augustine's Abbey at Canterbury. See Harvey and McGuinness, *Guide to British Medieval Seals*, p. 24. The preacher says that the story of Gabriel and the signet comes from 'Seynt Austyn, primo sermone de Anunciacione' (p. 257), but there is no known source. Ross comments that it cannot have come from Augustine in any case, since no Marian feasts were observed in Carthage in Augustine's time (see p. 371).

conclude that it is this aspect of her character that makes her 'oure aduocate, and specially to hure chosen seruauntes'.[79] Moreover, her studiousness and advocacy are once again not separate from her Jewishness: her assumption into heaven, he fastidiously notes, cannot have been in a church: 'Þis Ladi apered in þe churche, oþur [or rather] in þe sinagoge, þis day [my italics].'[80] These details are closely set against his awareness of her supernatural ability to penetrate hell and command demons. Mary is herself a

> gret signe and token [þat] stretcheth don in-to þe depnes of hell, for all þe dewels þer dredys þe name of þis glorious Virgyne and ben subdewed to hur powere. And she letteþ hem to tempte hure seruaundes to þe uttrest entente of here malice, Genesis 2. Þis token also stretcheþ in-to heven, for she is þer emprys.[81]

All of this creates not only a clear portrait of the specific mechanisms of her intercession but also – as her Jewishness is presented in such close juxtaposition to her ability to battle devils – a powerful romantic character.

In the same way that the heavy romance influence in the *South English Legendary* life of St Thomas Becket creates for that saint a Saracen mother,[82] Mary's genealogical 'otherness' could create for her a romance identity. Subtly reinforcing the association of Mary with the Jewish sorcerer of the Theophilus legend that was read weekly in church, this preacher effectively turns her into a romantic figure of otherworldly and mysterious power, indeed a figure that she frequently is in accounts of her miracles. Even in an orthodox sermon, this characterization is crucial to her intercessory role: it is plainly connected to 'Theophilus' and to other Marian miracles that tell of her negotiations for souls (the *South English Legendary* story of Mary appearing in the guise of a knight's wife, for example), but it is also related to her ability to intercede in legal and textual disputes. An increasingly literate, documentary culture had special need of this Mary. There was an 'association between writing and demonic forces ... at precisely the period when the technology of writing, its role in spiritual and secular life, as well as its symbolic value, was undergoing profound and permanent change'.[83] When, as Camille points out in his discussion of the Lambeth Apocalypse, 'devils are *litterati* and can be represented in the art of the period as the sinister scribes of documents',[84]

---

[79] Ross, *Middle English Sermons*, p. 260.

[80] Ibid., p. 247.

[81] Ibid., p. 246. Ross is puzzled by the author's citation of Genesis: 'This must be a wrong reference, but I cannot correct it. There is no passage in the second chapter of Genesis which has any remote connection with the desire of fiends to tempt men, and their restraint by the Virgin' (p. 368). It is not impossible, however, that the scribe has miscopied the reference, or that it is a misremembered allusion to the *third* chapter of Genesis, in which the serpent tempts Eve. This chapter would hold a natural connection to discussion of the temptations of devils, and to the common motif of Mary's undoing of Eve's sin.

[82] See D'Evelyn and Mill, *SEL*, II, pp. 610ff.

[83] Camille, 'Devil's Writing', p. 355.

[84] 'Seeing and Reading', p. 40.

Mary's otherworldly power becomes crucial to her ability convincingly to represent protection from such writing, which could be experienced 'not only as origin, anchor, and explanation but also as the instrument of domination and exclusion'.[85]

In a late iteration of the Theophilus legend that appears in Bodleian Library MS Rawlinson Poetry 225, a mid-fifteenth-century manuscript containing fragments of *South English Legendary* texts, these various elements of the developing Marian paradigm come together.[86] This text survives in a codex that is not a 'good' copy of the *Legendary*. In Manfred Görlach's opinion, it is clear that whoever copied it was not a professional scribe, that he compiled his materials over a significant period of time with many interruptions, and that he compared his texts with multiple variant copies.[87] Many of the standard *Legendary* materials have been altered in meter, and others are unique texts. 'The value of the [Rawlinson] texts', writes Görlach, 'is slight except as a vivid illustration of a collector's activities at the end of the Middle Ages.'[88] But this is just the kind of 'unprofessional' departure that can tell us much about the reception of 'Theophilus' and of other Marian miracles in the later medieval period.

For one thing, the unique version of the legend in the Rawlinson manuscript offers a significant challenge to any notion that Marian tales constituted 'devotional' poetry.[89] This is unquestionably a 'Romance of Theophilus'. In 643 lines of traditional tail-rime, it includes much dialogue, a typical romantic introduction of the hero, an otherworldly creature (the Jewish sorcerer) that lures the hero away from his true path, and an elaborate otherworldly adventure between the Devil and Mary in hell. As Beverly Boyd has commented, this version is strangely disconnected from others: 'In contrast to [the typical] study of spiritual pride and its consequences, the Rawlinson poem seems little concerned with the tragic circumstances of the fall of Theophilus, or with the moral implications of the tale.'[90] Though it is unrelated in form and style to the *South English Legendary*, however, the Rawlinson text may not have seemed to its copier at all disconnected from other Marian tales found there, especially if he had ever come across the *Legendary*'s prologue, which self-consciously fashioned Christian history as an exciting romance narrative.

85 Camille, 'Devil's Writing', p. 355.
86 The Rawlinson Theophilus has been edited by Boyd, *Middle English Miracles*, pp. 68–87 (all citations are from this edition). The manuscript in which it appears, along with commentary on its contents and their place in the *SEL* tradition, is described in Görlach, *Textual Tradition*, pp. 109–11.
87 Görlach, *Textual Tradition*, p. 110.
88 Ibid., p. 111.
89 The text does not fit any traditional definition of 'devotional' literature, but it is possible that the Rawlinson compiler thought that it did, or at least that he found it among devotional texts. It appears in the manuscript near 'conservative' *SEL* versions of the *vitae* of SS Katharine, Clement, and Nicholas, and very close to a unique life of St Barbara and a life of Christ. See Görlach, *Textual Tradition*, p. 110.
90 'The Rawlinson Version of Theophilus', *MLN* 71 (1956), p. 556.

Boyd has compared this 'Theophilus' to those tales 'satirized by Chaucer in *Sir Thopas*' and has cynically posited that 'it is not necessary to look beyond the metrical form for an explanation of the poet's adaptation of the legend … [T]he poet was interested in the adventure, not in the moral, and he edited the traditional miracle of the Virgin to fit popular narrative form.'[91] But the Rawlinson 'Theophilus' is ultimately concerned to communicate the same lessons about Marian intercession that are present in every other version I have discussed. Beyond this, everything implicit about the story in its early Latin form here becomes aggressively explicit. The Jew is now blatantly trying to convert Theophilus to Judaism ('The Jew sey hym so sore mournen / And thought in herte how he myght hym turnen / To beleven on his lawe'[92]), and some of the most compelling episodes, which had always been unwritten, are now elaborately described: the poet reveals the content of the charter and describes at length Mary's descent into hell and her interaction with the Devil as she attempts to retrieve the charter, events that were only hinted at in previous versions.

Each newly elaborated scene intensifies the terms of the contract and the complexity of its language and circumstances. As Theophilus (finally) reveals the content of the charter, after the Devil commands him to read it aloud, it is clear that the narrative function of the charter's text, for this poet, lies in the revelation of the legal trick it contains. The Devil demands of Theophilus, 'Forsac first Jhesu and Marie, / And al hir hool cumpanye, / … And make me a charter with thin hond, / As men don that sellen lond',[93] but when Theophilus reads the charter that he has composed, he reveals to the reader that it does not include exactly what the Devil has requested:

> Alle men knowen that arn and schul ben,
> That this chartre schul herin and sen
> With eris and with eye,
> That I, Tyofle, here forsake
> God only, and to the Devil me take.[94]

The nature of the document is clear enough – it is to be set 'as men doon that sellen land' and its locution records the exact opening formula of any Latin charter (*sciant presentes at futuri quod ego …*) – but Theophilus builds in a loophole.[95] Though the Devil asks that he forsake Jesus and Mary 'and al hir

---

91 Ibid., p. 559.
92 Boyd, *Middle English Miracles*, p. 72, lines 127–9.
93 Ibid., p. 76, lines 265–9.
94 Ibid., pp. 77–8, lines 307–11.
95 On the meaning and utility of the opening formula, as according to Henry de Bracton, see Emily Steiner, *Documentary Culture and the Making of Medieval English Literature*, Cambridge Studies in Medieval Literature (Cambridge, 2003), pp. 28–30. For a critical translation of Bracton's work, with notes, see Samuel E. Thorne. trans., *De legibus et consuetudinibus Angliae* (Cambridge, MA, 1968). The Latin text and translation are accessible (and searchable) online at: http://hlsl. law.harvard.edu/bracton/index.htm.

hool cumpanye', he carefully renounces 'God only'.[96] Because the phrase *can* mean 'the one God' (that is, the Trinitarian God, the denial of whom implies a forsaking of Christianity entirely), the Devil does not notice a problem. It is clear, however, that Theophilus intends 'God only' to mean 'just God and no one else'. When a voice from heaven later warns him, 'Revertere! Revertere!' (Turn back! Turn back!),[97] he reflects on his ability to call on Mary precisely because he has not forsaken her: 'Now I have God forsaken / Mercy I may never taken / But it be thourgh Marie.'[98] It is not good theology, but it is legally not a problem. The loophole depends on an overly literal reading of the contract, and it is this kind of reading that the majority of the Rawlinson text is concerned to explore. The final 400 lines are almost entirely concerned with the legal implications of the charter and Mary's consequent ability to dispute the contractual ownership of Theophilus's soul. Much of what ensues follows quite carefully the legal formulae for scrutinizing the terms of a charter.[99]

The concern is initially Satan's. He is aware that a contract is necessary for the exchange, and his anxiety over ensuring its validity is an eccentric feature of his character. When Theophilus seems to have completed the legal process, which 'Satanas thought a long fare', he asks anxiously, 'Is the chartre good?', and Theophilus readily admits that there is a problem with it: 'Sire, the chartre it has no cel.'[100] That Theophilus himself suggests the sealing of the charter seems counterintuitive. If he has any concern for his soul at this moment, and had the foresight already to manipulate the document's wording, why would he mention it? What overwhelms narrative sense at this point, however, is a preoccupation with the ritual of legal transaction. Satan demands all of the necessary elements of contract-making as he goes on to explain why Theophilus must read the document aloud:

> 'Red here that chartre anon
> Beforn thise men everychon,
> That thei moun bere therof witnesse.
> In chaffaring [negotiations] of myshappe
> Witnesse is good for after-clappe [adverse consequence],
> Be it more or lesse.'[101]

Satan's concern with witness and possible dispute, though it reflects familiarity with medieval law and with each performative element necessary to validate the charter, is merely comical under the circumstances, especially

---

96   It is clear, however, that Theophilus understands 'God' and 'Jesus' to be synonymous, as he later claims that he 'forsok Jhesu so good'. See Boyd, *Middle English Miracles*, p. 81, line 416.
97   Ibid., p. 80, line 409.
98   Ibid., p. 81, lines 424–6.
99   For details on this procedure in land tenure cases specifically (what the Devil invokes as a model in this text), see Green, *Crisis of Truth*, pp. 149–54.
100   Boyd, *Middle English Miracles*, p. 77, lines 286, 291–2.
101   Ibid., p. 77, lines 295–300.

since the medieval audience likely knows well the outcome of the story. His comment that 'in chaffaring' there is commonly 'after-clappe' bespeaks long experience with such barters, especially to an audience also familiar with apocryphal stories of Christ's legal trickery in his harrowing of hell,[102] and the comic nervousness is heightened when the Devil then demands 'manrade' (homage) in addition, and several further verbal assurances from Theophilus.[103] Nearly one hundred lines of dialogue communicate Satan's desperate pleas for confirmation before he will verify that he will keep his side of the bargain. Finally, he warns Theophilus, 'loke thu be trewe ... / Loke thu never forsaken me / For no lord newe.' And Theophilus, with not a glint of self-awareness, comments simply that to forsake his sworn lord in such a way would be neither legal nor moral: 'That were a theves dede.'[104]

Enter the heroine. It is not long before Mary appears to remind Theophilus that in fact the Devil is all 'thefte',[105] and she is direct about the role she must play in his rescue. As this is a contractual dispute, she announces, 'I wil ben thi procatour' (attorney),[106] and the poet makes special effort to display her considerable lawyerly skills.[107] Her trip to hell to retrieve the charter marks in this text an extended on-site legal debate, in which she explains to the Devil that his charter is invalid because, through it, he has tried to purchase what Christ has already purchased. The two argue about the validity of each claim on the property:

> 'Certis, thereagayn I will cleymen [assert my rights]
> …
> I have a chartre trewe and good.
> He wrot it hymself with his owen blod.
> Therfor Tyofle is oure.'
>
> 'Tyofle, that clerk, ys me wel dere;
> Therfore I am now comen here:
> That chartre I wil haven.
> Jhesu, my sone, hath hym wroughtte

---

102 On the theory of the 'Devil's rights' and the popularity of the harrowing of hell story, see Green, *Crisis of Truth*, pp. 344–55.
103 Boyd, *Middle English Miracles*, p. 78, line 336.
104 Ibid., p. 79, lines 369–72, 378.
105 Ibid., p. 82, line 467.
106 Ibid., p. 82, line 479.
107 The Virgin-as-lawyer role made explicit in this text cannot but make one think of Shakespeare's *Merchant of Venice*, in which Portia (in the guise of a man) acts as attorney to Antonio and successfully challenges Shylock's claim on the pound of flesh with an overly literal reading of the bond that allows for the flesh but makes no mention of blood (IV.i). Portia's 'quality of mercy' has often prompted comment that she is a descendant of the medieval Virgin Mary in her role as merciful intercessor (her famous speech begins with the law maxim *Clementia non constringit*, also used by Langland in the C-version of *Piers Plowman* V.61), but Shakespeare's story of a Jewish contract ultimately renegotiated by a chaste (Christian) female lawyer deserves general consideration as a descendant of the legend of Theophilus.

> And sithen on the rode hym boughtte.
> With ryght he wil hym craven [claim].'[108]

Satan responds to Mary's point with the fact that a completed transaction renders the agreement valid, even if the agreement should not have been possible because of Jesus's prior claim, but Mary cleverly retorts that the Devil has not given his own goods, but rather Christ's, since all made things are her 'sones werk'.[109]

Mary's legal tricks, however, are not quite enough to defeat Satan. Ultimately unable to better her argument, the Devil finally tells her that she cannot have the charter because it is locked away within hell. This prompts a display of physical strength, which might be compared to the medieval recourse to combat as a last resort in legal disputes:[110]

> No wondir it was that the fend was wo,
> For sche benom hym the chartre tho,
> Marie, that lady bryght.
> Although he were bothen wroth and grym,
> Sche tok the chartre fro under hym
> And benome hym his myght.[111]

The three times that Mary 'takes' in this stanza ('taken' or 'benomen') emphasize what is at stake. She can take both the charter and the Devil's might, and this verbal association of the Devil with the document is not accidental.

Mary and the Devil are connected to the charter, but their orientation toward the text is radically different. The Devil presides over treacherous transaction (he cannot make a valid purchase using stolen goods), while Mary's relationship to the charter turns on sound principle. Her intercession involves righting what is essentially a misreading. The charter seems valid to the Devil (and to Theophilus) only because it has not been read correctly, and Satan's exasperated exclamation at the end of this interpretive and finally physical struggle bespeaks his essential misunderstanding of the function of law and text for Mary:

> 'Thi myght is bothen in Heven and in Helle
> And overal aboute.
> In Helle ne in erthe is no lawe
> Ne treuthe that is worth an hawe:
> My ryght goth alwithoute.'[112]

---

[108] Boyd, *Middle English Miracles*, pp. 84–5, lines 541–2.
[109] Ibid., p. 85, line 563.
[110] The practice was probably antiquated by the time this text was written, but see Green, *Crisis of Truth*, pp. 82–5, 89–90.
[111] Boyd, *Middle English Miracles*, p. 85, lines 565–70.
[112] Ibid., p. 85, lines 572–6.

From Satan's point of view, there is no meaningful law. He has in this situation struggled to maintain the legal ritual, to provide witnesses and seal, homage and exchange of goods, but his understanding is narrow: he considers only the immediate context. Mary, however, interprets law within the sweeping context of creation, Christianity, and her son's sacrifice. The problem for Satan, and what even Theophilus does not realize in his desperation to retrieve and destroy the charter, is that Mary can argue from the position of 'Christ's charter', the validity and precedent of which cannot be challenged.[113]

This essential lesson of the Rawlinson 'Theophilus' comes when Mary finally suggests different reading material for the struggling hero:

> 'Have now, Tyofle, chartre thin,
> And loke thu be ever trewe servaunt myn,
> Myn miracles to rede.'[114]

In many ways, her demand of Theophilus is similar to Satan's. She asks him to read, and her corresponding admonishment, 'loke thu be ever trewe', echoes Satan's previous instruction upon the first negotiation of the contract, 'loke thu be trewe'.[115] But Mary's command calls for servitude not through reading of a legal document but through wide reading of the Miracles of the Virgin, which are presented here as an antidote to the letter of the law. 'Written not with ink but with the spirit of the living God', Mary's legal code is taught and confirmed in the stories of her legends, and this poet inscribes both the personality and transmission of those lessons in his final voicing of Mary.

This kind of rhetoric – also seen in Dominic of Evesham's prologue to his collection of Marian miracles, in the *South English Legendary*'s instructions to think of the charter while praying for miracles, and in the anonymous Assumption sermon's comment on the frequency of 'Theophilus' readings – shows that the Theophilan model of Marian intercession, as it entered vernacular contexts, was doing more than repeating an already extant notion of Mary's mercy and kindness for one and all. The legend helped to establish

---

[113] This document (from a literary standpoint) actually existed. In *Charter of Christ* poems, the elaborate conceit is that Christ's body stretched on the cross is like animal skin stretched on a frame to create the parchment that bears his contract with humanity. Scourges and thorns are the pens, the blood (and sometimes the spit of Jews) the ink, the wounds the individual alphabetic characters, the pierced heart the seal, and, in shorter versions, the poem itself is nothing but the text of the charter. There are more than a dozen surviving, short and long, dating from *c.*1350 at the earliest. See Mary Caroline Spalding, *The Middle English Charters of Christ*, rpt (Whitefish, MT, 2007). For general information on these texts and their development, see Laura Ashe, 'The "Short Charter of Christ": An Unpublished Longer Version, from Cambridge University Library, MS ADD. 6686', *MÆ* 72 (2003), pp. 32–44; Steiner, *Documentary Culture*, pp. 47–90; Green, *Crisis of Truth*, pp. 26–63, 276–7; and Miri Rubin, *Corpus Christi: The Eucharist in Late Medieval Culture* (Cambridge, 1991), pp. 302–6. See also my discussion of a fifteenth-century iteration of 'The Prioress's Tale' in relation to a *Charter of Christ*, pp. 160–3 below.

[114] Boyd, *Middle English Miracles*, p. 86, lines 601–3.

[115] Ibid., p. 79, line 369.

a particular characterization of Mary: Jew, lawyer, trickster, mighty, learned, able to penetrate hell and battle or outwit demons. This is a characterization that is crucial to a full understanding of medieval devotion to her. It was also dynamically involved in promoting Miracles of the Virgin, setting their tone and possibilities, and, in England, endorsing particular textual and paratextual contexts for Marian miracles. One must continue to imagine 'Theophilus' in the background of many of the homiletic, private devotional, and literary English examples of the later Middle Ages.

4

The Virgin and the Law in Middle English Contexts

> Þys ys þe disposiciun of þe tabyll at our lady auter yn þe
> cathedrall kyrke of yorke. Þat ys for to say þat ower lady
> ys ymagened in v maner of wysys. Þe fyrst ys our lady
> hauyng yn here hand the tabelis offe moyeses and vndir
> here fete þe bernyng buske of moyses and also þe figure
> off þe worlde.
>
> York altar table description, c.1425[1]

The Middle Ages saw the rise of Mary *mediatrix*. As Jaroslav Pelikan has
summarized it, 'the systematic clarification of the title Mediatrix was the
principal objective expression of Mariology and the chief theological contribution to Christian teaching about Mary during this period', but this was
sometimes in tension with the dominant 'literary form and devotional motif
of the Mater Dolorosa'.[2] Nevertheless, both the human suffering of mother
Mary and her superhuman (often aggressive) intercession and advocacy
were internationally recognized. Eastern theologians often addressed her as
'Mediatrix of law and of grace',[3] and this title, as it was reflected in medieval
Marian devotion, was in some ways very logical: 'If Christ is both judge
and mediator, then modest and anxious human sinners may well look for an
advocate who will mediate with Him.'[4] Indeed, the whole legal apparatus of
saintly intercession cannot be called unpredictable within a wide view of the
Judeo-Christian tradition, which always saw the relationship with God as a
matter of covenant. What Richard Firth Green has called 'bargains with God'
or the 'need to believe in a *deus pactor*' is not only common in popular medieval hagiography – an expression of a potent 'covenantal theology' – but also

---

[1] From Oxford, Corpus Christi College MS 132, fol. 69v, edited in Vincent Gillespie, 'Medieval
Hypertext: Image and Text from York Minster', *Of the Making of Books: Medieval Manuscripts,
Their Scribes and Readers: Essays Presented to M. B. Parkes*, ed. P. R. Robinson and Rivkah Zim
(Brookfield, VT, and Aldershot, 1997), pp. 228–9 (here p. 228, lines 1–4).

[2] *Mary Through the Centuries: Her Place in the History of Culture* (New Haven, CT, and London,
1996), pp. 125–6.

[3] Ibid., pp. 130–1.

[4] Rosalind and Christopher Brooke, *Popular Religion in the Middle Ages: Western Europe 1000–
1300* (London, 1984), p. 31.

transcends temporal and cultural divides.[5] Still, such bargains were 'particularly common in England', and where other saints might broker agreements based on symbolic gestures of 'trothplight', such as 'bowed groats' or token rings or monetary payment, the Virgin Mary was very often entrenched in *documentary* modes.[6] She showed special attention to agreements that were expressed in charters or that included written conveyances.

The examples I have discussed in the previous chapters are cases in point. While I have so far concentrated mainly on a particular group of legends (and those organized around responses to a single influential legend to boot), however, I now want to depart from that in order to examine ways in which other English uses of Marian miracles might move from a didactic focus on 'the charter' itself to a broader construal of how Marian intercession negotiates the 'letter of the law' and reveals that crucial difference between words and the Word. To do so, this chapter will treat three specific instances of the miracles in fifteenth-century English homiletic and miscellany contexts. Each reinforces Mary's association with writing and law, but we shall see too that this association could sometimes overlap imaginatively with her motherhood and her Jewish identity.

Mary and the Too-Good Scribe in John Mirk's *Festial*

Mirk's ubiquitous *Festial* is a vast and wholly orthodox sermon cycle. It was 'central to preaching in English in the fifteenth century', though Mirk, an Augustinian canon at Lilleshall Abbey in Shropshire, probably composed most of it in the 1380s.[7] One *Festial* manuscript (British Library MS Harley 2403) records a short sequence of Marian *exempla* that includes the story of Mary's restoration of a writer's severed arm. That tale will be my immediate subject, but let me first say something about the small group of miracles in which it appears. Because *Festial* manuscripts are many (nearly forty survive, in various forms), and the work was printed repeatedly in the fifteenth and sixteenth centuries,[8] it is difficult to say if these miracles are among the oldest or most widely available materials. The sequence is found in some form, however, in two closely related codices, both part of the first recension

---

5   *Crisis of Truth*, Chapter 9 (here pp. 336–8). By way of comparison, Green discusses the motif in certain works of Nigerian authors Chinua Achebe and I. N. C. Aniebo.

6   Ibid., pp. 336–8, 342.

7   On Mirk and the composition of the *Festial*, see Alan J. Fletcher, 'Unnoticed Sermons from John Mirk's *Festial*', *Speculum* 55.3 (1980), pp. 514–15 (here 514); Green, *Crisis of Truth*, pp. 338–9; and Susan Powell, 'John Mirk's *Festial* and the Pastoral Programme', *Leeds Studies in English* 22 (1991), pp. 85–102. On the dating, see Alan J. Fletcher, 'John Mirk and the Lollards', *MÆ* 56 (1987), pp. 217–24.

8   Fletcher, 'Unnoticed Sermons', p. 515, reckons the number of manuscripts at 'thirty-seven, ahead of that of the Wycliffite cycle'. See also Whiteford, *Myracles of Oure Lady*, p. 106; and Beth Allison Barr, *Pastoral Care of Women in Late Medieval England*, Gender in the Middle Ages (Woodbridge, 2008), Appendix I.

'descended from the original *Festial*'.[9] This is a complicated little group. In one manuscript (British Library MS Cotton Claudius A. II), it exists as a piece 'de salutacione beate marie' with a single *narracio* attached (there labeled 'de miraculis beate marie' but *not* a story of Marian intercession), and in the other manuscript (MS Harley 2403), there is the same 'de salutacione' homily with either two or three *narraciones* attached, depending on how the divisions are understood.[10] The 'group', then, might be described as one that contains only a single real Marian miracle, or as one that contains as many as four.

This requires some explanation. The short lesson on the Marian salutation ('de salutacione beate marie') is not so much a sermon as a miracle narrative and should itself be catalogued as a Miracle of the Virgin, as indeed Peter Whiteford has catalogued it.[11] It begins with very brief advice to lay people to say the 'Ave Maria' in English with sincere devotion, and then it turns to a common Marian miracle known as 'Eulalia'. This is the only Middle English version of 'Eulalia', though it appears first in the earliest originary Anglo-Latin collection.[12] Its namesake is a nun of Shaftesbury Abbey who rushes through her *Ave* hundreds of times per day (the number is 150 for Mirk) until Mary appears to her and enjoins her to say her prayers more slowly and sincerely.

In both the Cotton Claudius and the Harley manuscripts, the story of a corrupt moneylender follows 'Eulalia'. In this tale, a vindictive moneylender maliciously compels a debtor to swear falsely 'by þe lawe' and 'on a boke' that he has repaid money owed, and, because of this meanness, he receives a gory and terrifying vision of the crucified Christ, who admonishes him for squandering a soul so dearly bought.[13] The Virgin Mary does not appear in this story, but it is labeled 'de miraculis beate marie' in MS Cotton Claudius A. II nonetheless, and it concludes there with the note 'aliud miraculum de Sancta Maria' (though no more follow). Whether this was construed as a Marian miracle, or its incipit and explicit are simply erroneous, is unclear,[14]

---

9   Barr, *Pastoral Care of Women*, pp. 125–9.

10   Brief descriptions of these two manuscripts are in Barr, *Pastoral Care of Women*, pp. 127–8, and more detailed ones in Carl Horstmann, *Altenglische Legenden, neue Folge* (Heilbronn, 1881), pp. cxiii–cxviii.

11   Whiteford, *Myracles of Oure Lady*, p. 105.

12   Southern, 'English Origins', pp. 184–5. The common Latin versions of 'Eulalia' can be found in Dexter, 'Miracula Sanctae Virginis Mariae', pp. 35–6; and T. F. Crane, ed., *Liber de Miraculis Sanctae Dei Genitricis Mariae* (Ithaca, NY, and London, 1925), pp. 40–1. Crane's work is partially a reprint of the 1731 edition of Bernard Pez.

13   Erbe, *Mirk's Festial*, p. 300.

14   I have not been able to examine the codex, so I cannot comment with certainty on the nature of the Latin notations. Erbe, *Mirk's Festial*, pp. 299–301, includes them in his edition without comment; and Horstmann, *Altenglische Legenden*, p. cxviii n. 1, says only that a section 'de miraculis b. Marie' can be found within the Eulalia 'sermon'. Close examination of *exempla* in *Festial* manuscripts will surely repay the effort for any scholar working on Marian miracles, as catalogues frequently list only the sermon proper, and *exempla* can change from codex to codex. As Peter Whiteford has noted in *Myracles of Oure Lady*, p. 106, 'given the differences in content which occur in *Festial* manuscripts, it is possible that other manuscripts contain additional or

but we might call it 'Marian' in any case, for reasons I will discuss in a moment.

In MS Harley 2403, an additional *narracio* follows the moneylender story. Carl Horstmann describes this as a single addition, but Whiteford lists it as two separate miracles.[15] To be sure, it is set on the page as a continuous narrative: it contains the story of the writer who ends up with a severed arm after a forged document leads to a false accusation of treachery, and then the story of how this same man traveled to Jerusalem and converted 'a Jew þat was a grete mastur of þat contre' by painting a miraculous image of the Virgin and Child.[16] That is, the text added to MS Harley 2403 comprises two discrete stories about the same (unnamed) monk-scribe who is apparently a talented writer *and* painter. The tale of the writer with the severed arm, without the Jerusalem continuation, appears in Middle English also in *Jacob's Well* and the *Alphabet of Tales*, though in each of these instances it is significantly different, attached explicitly to St John of Damascus and his scholarly and liturgical texts.[17] In the *Festial* context, it is about an anonymous monk immediately identified as a skillful teller of 'feyr miracles of our lady'.[18]

The MS Harley 2403 group, then, must grab our attention. It is hard to guess to what kind of sermon it might have been attached, particularly because the tale of the moneylender's vision of Christ seems to interrupt the Marian content.[19] It is perhaps not unexpected, however, that even that vision was so emphatically marked as a Marian miracle by one copyist (in the Cotton Claudius manuscript). It begins very much like the more familiar Marian story of 'The Merchant's Surety' (discussed in Chapter 1),[20] and it focuses on legal dispute and manipulations of the legal system. As the vision of Christ appears at the end of the tale, it is certainly not impossible that a scribe at first thought that the tale was Marian, or that it was understood that Mary might be inserted extemporaneously (standing beside Christ, say, or in the prayers of the wronged man) without any violation whatsoever of a

different miracle stories [than what Erbe edits]'. Barr has catalogued the 110 *exempla* in Erbe's edition in *Pastoral Care of Women*, Appendix II.

15 See respectively *Myracles of Oure Lady*, p. 105, and *Altenglische Legenden*, p. cxvii. Horstmann also notes here that the 'Eulalia' text is longer in MS Harley 2403, and he does not mention whether the Latin notations are also present in the Harley manuscript. Barr, *Pastoral Care of Women*, p. 150, takes the addition as a single *exemplum* (no. 110).

16 Erbe, *Mirk's Festial*, p. 302. I briefly discussed the tale of the miraculous image in Chapter 1, p. 39, as an example of a Christian–Jewish disputation story unique to England.

17 See Arthur Brandeis, ed., *Jacob's Well*, Part I, EETS, os 115 (London, 1900), pp. 277–9; and Mary Macleod Banks, ed., *An Alphabet of Tales*, EETS, os 127 (London, 1904), pp. 262–4. The identification of John of Damascus also means that these versions are more concerned with the 'Saracen' setting than is Mirk's.

18 Erbe, *Mirk's Festial*, p. 301.

19 The sequence (in whole or part) may be appropriate for Marian feast days, though the story of the writer (John of Damascus) is attached to a homily on equity and obedience in Brandeis, *Jacob's Well*, pp. 272–7, and takes Christ's Ascension as its concluding gospel lesson.

20 See pp. 29–32 above.

typical English Marian miracle paradigm. Considered this way, the group is in fact wholly unexceptional. It begins with one of those tit-for-tat tales of the sort included in the *South English Legendary* Theophilus group (Marian instruction is granted to a nun who says her devotions daily), followed by a tale concerning legal dispute, then a tale about a scribe who writes her miracles, and finally a tale of Jewish conversion.

What is in the midst of this, however, is worthy of special notice as another instance of Mary's response to written conveyance and transmission of Marian text. The story of the writer with the severed arm shares with other English Marian tales an emphasis on a particular kind of dissemination (of apocrypha and legend, liturgical and paraliturgical performance), which was also present in the *South English Legendary* Founding of the Feast of Mary's Conception, in Dominic of Evesham's prologue, in the anonymous fourteenth-century Assumption sermon, and in the Rawlinson romance of Theophilus.[21] To the extent that this group and other Marian miracles that can be found in the *Festial* conform to Green's explication of 'bargains with God' and his saints, it also offers an important Marian variation on a theme. Green uses the *Festial* as an extended instance of vernacular covenantal theology, but also as an example of the Virgin Mary's position within that scheme. Mirk's sermons are full of battles between demons and saints and transactions between the living and the holy dead – prayers are offered in exchange for intercession, veneration in exchange for protection – and Mary 'was especially generous in this regard'.[22] Marian *exempla*, in Green's view, reveal the 'formalism' that is 'the most striking aspect of Mirk's view of divine covenants (as with their common-law counterparts)'.[23] This is certainly borne out in the little *Festial* sequence here described, but the story of 'How Our Lady Restored a Scribe's Arm' also pushes beyond the formal structure of the saintly covenant and displays Mary's complementary tendency to reveal distinctions between old law and new.

It is in fact a tale that hinges on scrutiny of 'the letter' and the crucial difference between form and content, which Mary implicitly insists is communicated effectively in all of her miracles. Her scribe is introduced as

> an holy monke þat loued our lady wondur muche. Þe whyche monke was neuer wery to preyse hur, and tell feyr miracles of our lady, and feyre talus of hur nyȝt and day; and so þys monke was þe feyrest wryter þat was knowen in all þe world.[24]

The quality of his writing is dependent on its content (Mary's 'miracles' and 'talus'), which is causally linked to his wide fame; his Miracles of the Virgin

21 See above, pp. 22–3, 64–7, 93–5, 102–3.
22 Green, *Crisis of Truth*, p. 341.
23 Ibid., p. 343.
24 Erbe, *Mirk's Festial*, p. 301.

are set as his 'trothplight', as his contribution to the contractual agreement that later obligates Mary's intercession.

When it follows that the 'Emperour of Rome' sends a young relative to the monk to learn 'to wryte as wel as he did', the young man eventually becomes jealous of his master.[25] To ruin his teacher, the disciple forges a treasonous letter to the 'þe Sowdon' (Sultan) that asks the enemy to attack and destroy the Emperor, and he arranges for this letter to fall into the Emperor's hands. When interrogated, the student claims that only his master could have written the letter, and the Emperor incorrectly agrees:

> þe Emperour send aftur þys monke and apeched hym of þys lettre; and he sayd he knew it not. And þen they schewed him þis lettre, and seyde it was his honde. And he seyde þat he neuer wrote it. And wythoute eny oþer jugement þe Emþerour commaunded to smyte of his arme by the elbowe.[26]

In contrast to the praise of the monk's writing that begins the *exemplum*, this is certainly not an issue of content. The judgment and the sentence are determined by whether the letter is written in 'his honde'. It becomes clear at this point that the monk's reputation is not based solely on his devotional work but also on the shape of his letters, his script, which is as identifiable as a signature in this case. That the monk has shared only his technical expertise is problematic: in sharing only this aspect of his writing, he has not communicated the spirit of it to his disciple.

It is at the point when the Emperor has issued the mistaken judgment and severed the monk's arm that Mary intercedes. Her appearance is prompted by a combination of concern for the transmission of Miracles of the Virgin and for matters of law. She seeks both to rectify the false judgment and to return the monk's ability to disseminate stories of her intercession. Except for his consideration of the physical characteristics of the monk's script, the Emperor had acted 'wythoute eny oþer jugement', and both the author and Mary are critical of so rash a ruling. In response to it, Mary appears to the monk as he lies in prison, his severed arm festering, and she inquires about his wellbeing. When he tells her, 'myn arme is roted awey þat was wont to peynte an ymage of þe wherever I went',[27] she instructs him to retrieve the severed part and reset it at the elbow. If he follows her instructions, she says, 'hit schal be hole'. And, of course, he does: 'so he did as heo bade him, and hit was as hole as euer hit was, and as wel he wrot as euer he did before.'[28]

Though the obvious concern with written transmission and lawfulness securely connects this story to others I have discussed, the most interesting feature is its ambiguity about what 'written' means in the first place. Though

[25] Ibid.
[26] Ibid.
[27] Ibid., p. 302.
[28] Ibid.

the monk begins as someone who can '*tell* feyr miracles of our lady', he is at the same time described as 'þe fayrest *wryter*' (and even the definition of 'wryter' is difficult to pinpoint as the tale progresses, for it variously refers to composition and script), and he later complains that his arm 'was wont *to peynte an ymage* [my italics]'. Not until the prison dialogue between the monk and Mary is there any mention of the monk's ability as a visual artist, and it seems momentarily that painting must be synonymous with writing – or else the sudden change of the protagonist's profession is jarring indeed. To complicate matters further, we learn that after his arm was made whole, 'he *wrot*' again, though, if we include the Jerusalem continuation as part of the same tale, we know that he in fact goes on to convert a Jew by *painting* Mary.[29] In other words, the monk in question is simultaneously a teller, a writer, and a painter, and the implication is that these are not separate abilities. Though the emphasis in the narrative is on his writing – the action that necessitates intercession is the circulation of a letter written in his hand – the circulation of text in this story is simultaneously about voice, letter, and image, about hearing, reading and seeing.

In his 1985 discussion of text and image, Michael Camille cited Gilbert Crispin's *Disputation between a Christian and a Jew* as a good explication of the medieval 'relationship between spoken, written, and pictorial language':

> Answering the Jew's accusation that Christians practice idolatry in worshipping the horrible effigy of a tortured naked man on a cross, the Christian says that, 'Just as letters are shapes and symbols of spoken words, pictures exist as representations and symbols of writing.'[30]

Gilbert's 'Christian' sentence shows neatly how voice, letter, and image can be construed not only as interdependent but also as elements of writing. There is a syllogism here: if letters are symbols, and pictures are symbols, then pictures are letters. The Christianity of the message comes in the interdependence of the three: just as belief in only one person of the Trinity is heresy, dependence on a single element of 'writing' is spiritually dangerous. In the Marian story of 'þe feyrest wryter þat was knowen in all þe world', the apparent confusion between voice, letter, and image teaches this very lesson. The villainy of the monk's disciple and the Roman Emperor is their dependence on the letter alone. The disciple seeks to destroy his master with the 'shapes and symbols' of written script, which he has been taught to imitate and thereby pervert. His inability to see beyond the letter is the source of his jealousy and of his treachery. It is also the source of his damnation: we learn in conclusion that the traitorous student meets the fate originally designed for his master. He who considered the letter alone has the member that betrayed

---

[29] Ibid., pp. 302–3, and p. 107 just above.
[30] 'Seeing and Reading', p. 32.

him severed – though this time without hope of intercession.[31] Similarly, the Emperor's error in judgment stems from the fact that he relies solely on *seeing* the text. He did not inquire beyond the visual evidence of the letter, and his dependence on this single factor is the direct cause of his error. The monk, on the other hand, because his association between voice, letter, and image is so fluid as to be indistinguishable, earns his salvation of Mary.

The Blessed Virgin Mother and *Legislatrix*

One of the more striking English examples of Mary's relationship with text and law comes in a form that offers a complicated relationship between image, text, and interpretation: the plans for the late fourteenth-century Lady Chapel of the Cathedral Church of York included a design for a Marian *tabula* (likely intended for the front of an altar, as many were throughout the period).[32] The piece does not survive, and may never have existed, but a description is extant in the early fifteenth-century Oxford, Corpus Christi College MS 132, where the *tabula*'s series of five interrelated images and texts are described.[33] In its manuscript context, this is the final vernacular piece in a set that includes 'two series of couplets describing the statue in the dream of Nebuchadnezzar, moralized as a mnemonic of the virtues and deadly sins' and a text that 'explores the Augustinian Image of Sin to provide guidance in the examination of conscience so as to facilitate the restoration of the Image of God'.[34] As Vincent Gillespie argues:

> [T]he preservation of this text in its current form, out of its apparently intended architectural context, as the third and final in a series of vernacular discussions of different kinds of images, shows that it was capable of adaptation and function in a context that explores hypertextual links between words and pictures. As a textual artefact rather than a pictorial artefact, the images it describes must be 'ymagened' without the benefit of an actual visual referent ... The scheme of iconography must be performed in the imagination of its reading or listening audience.[35]

And what must be imagined about Mary through these textual images is a powerful woman whose appearance is not unrelated to the characterizations we have so far encountered.

I will repeat what is printed at the head of this chapter, the opening passage of this textual artifact:

---

[31] Cf. St Quiriac's severed hand, and his discussion of fit punishment for heretical (Jewish) writing in the *SEL*, pp. 88–9 above.

[32] See Gillespie, 'Medieval Hypertext', p. 207.

[33] Ibid., p. 206. Throughout his discussion of the manuscript context, Gillespie argues that the *tabula* existed only as a design plan (see especially p. 224).

[34] Ibid., p. 208.

[35] Ibid., p. 224.

Þys ys þe disposiciun of þe tabyll at our lady auter yn þe cathedrall kyrke of yorke. Þat ys for to say þat ower lady ys ymagened in v maner of wysys. Þe fyrst ys our lady hauyng yn here hand the tabelis offe moyeses and vndir here fete þe bernyng buske of moyses and also þe figure off þe worlde. And þer scho ys calde Rubus Moisi et Domina Mundi with vers wretyn vndyr her fete.[36]

Holding the tablets of Mosaic Law, a representation of the open scriptures, Mary is depicted as both the bearer of the law and the 'arke' that contains the law. She stands at once atop Moses's burning bush and the world, and this figure of Mary bestriding the earth and holding above it the tablets of the law (an open book) both links Mary to her Jewish heritage and creates for her a specifically textual *auctoritas*. She is superimposed on the image of Moses bearing the tablets and so becomes a new Moses. Labeled 'Rubus Moisi', however, she also becomes the voice of God, the object of revelation to Moses, and therefore, by implication, simultaneously the giver and bearer of the law, both the enlightener of the new and the connection to the old. She is both the queenly image of Mary *mediatrix*, as the 'Domina Mundi', and the Augustinian image of the Jew, bearing the books of the Christian world.[37]

The Latin verses that are supposed to accompany this image (the 'vers wretyn vndyr her fete'), which the vernacular writer also records, reinforce these relationships between Mary and Mosaic scripture. They cite Exodus, Judges, and Proverbs, with traditional reinterpretations of the burning bush, Gideon's fleece, and the house of Wisdom as prefigurations of the Incarnation. There are five six-line stanzas of Latin verse in the *tabula* description, to be paired with the five images described, and each stanza uses Hebrew scripture to demonstrate Mary's fulfillment of the 'old' law.[38] Her status as a keeper of the law is strikingly maintained, too, in another of the images, in which Mary is figured as a warrior who stands atop the Ark of the Covenant:

> Þe thyrd [ymage] ys our lady with her schilde yn hyr arme and vnþir here fete þe mone and þe arke offe the holde testament. And þer scho ys callyd Dey Genetryx et Arca Testamenti.[39]

Mary stands armored, holding a shield, but what she protects in this instance is not her devotees but the Ark of the Covenant. The moon under her feet comes from the familiar description of the birthing mother in Revelation

---

36 Ibid., p. 228, lines 1–5.
37 See pp. 35–6 above. Jeremy Cohen, *Living Letters of the Law*, pp. 32–6, explains that Augustine used various similes to describe Jews as servants of Christians exactly because they were guardians of their books, for instance in *De civitate dei*: 'they unwillingly provide for us by having and by preserving these books' (here p. 32). It is also worth repeating that medieval Anglo-Jews wore a badge of shame shaped like the tablets of the law. In the first York table image, then, Mary bears the same image that marked English Jews before the 1290 expulsion.
38 Gillespie, 'Medieval Hypertext', pp. 228–9 (here p. 228, lines 6–11).
39 Ibid., p. 228, lines 21–3.

so commonly associated with the Virgin Mary (Rev. 12), a description that immediately follows upon the last appearance of the Ark of the Covenant (Rev. 11:19). The author/artist uses this juxtaposition to bind Mary to the legendary Ark that holds the tablets of the law of God. When the Latin label names her 'Arca Testamenti', she indeed becomes that Ark.

This is not a very complicated leap. As the 'Dei Genetryx', Mary literally contains the Word. But the Latin verses recorded below this image of the 'Arca Testamenti' (and by that I now mean the woman and the ark itself) use Revelation 11:19–12:2 to make the connection more forceful:

> Arca dei visa templo cely reserati
> Et signum grande mulier circumdata sole
> Sub pedibus luna cuius sunt signa beate
> Virginis et matris que sunt a virgine visa.[40]

> The ark of God was seen opened in the temple of heaven, and there was a great sign, a woman encircled by the sun with the moon under her feet, which are the signs of the blessed virgin and mother, which were seen by the virgin.

Mary is allowed a vision of the opened ark (though the position of the woman in relation to the ark is more ambiguous in the biblical verses), and she sees the contents historically lost to all other eyes. She becomes in this *tabula*, then, not only the law-bearer but the one able to access the lost text of God at the time of judgment. Other labels for Mary used in this *tabula* description are 'Templum Salamonys' (a symbol of justice and wisdom) and 'Ymparatryx Ynferny' (Empress of Hell), both of which call up her superhuman control over salvation and punishment.[41] The association of these with Mary's access to law begins to fold in on itself: she is the temple that she sees restored in heaven; she houses the opened ark that she sees outside herself; she is the Ark of the Covenant that contains the tablets of the law; she holds in her hand the tablets of the law.

This kind of thinking about Mary is reflected in the fact that she is a predictable presence in English Judgment iconography from about the mid-thirteenth century on, and it is in this context that her corporeality – her status as the 'Dei Genetrix' and birthing mother, also exploited in the complex nexus of words and images in the York *tabula* – is most strongly linked to her legality. It is common to see her holding her breasts at Judgment, thereby inextricably binding her flesh to her ability to function as a legal authority. This motif of the breast at judgment, however, was in fact quickly conflated with Mary's ability to intercede for sinners in matters of contract law, especially because of the long visual and narrative popularity of the legend of Theophilus in England. Nigel Morgan once expressed skepticism at the idea

---

[40] Ibid., p. 229, lines 26–9.
[41] Ibid., lines 32, 43–4.

that a Last Judgment scene might have shown the Virgin Mary holding a book instead of her breast, describing a Winchester wall painting that survives only in a nineteenth-century watercolor copy this way: 'The copyist misunderstood the motif in showing her holding a book in the position of her breast. The Virgin certainly did not use a book as the instrument of intercession in the Last Judgement, and it was assuredly her breast she was holding.'[42] But, as unlikely as it is that a copyist mistook a breast for a book, it is not impossible that an artist late in the thirteenth century imagined exactly such an instrument of intercession for Mary.

In fact, the manuscript examples that Morgan uses to describe the more common motif of the breast are related to images of the Theophilus legend and so are related to images of the Virgin baring *text*. Morgan cites a Last Judgment scene done by William de Brailes, wherein 'the Virgin is kneeling beside the seated apostles' (whom I would say occupy the position of jury in such a scene).[43] This is fol. 3 of Cambridge, Fitzwilliam Museum MS 330, where de Brailes had depicted Theophilus and the 'Ages of Man' in a Wheel of Fortune. Morgan also cites the Lambeth Apocalypse, where the motif of the Virgin's bared breast is part of the Theophilus cycle and is accompanied by an Anglo-Norman notation of the dialogue between Christ and his mother. This dialogue expressly links the breast and the document: as Mary bares her breast and pleads with her son, he replies, 'Mother, I agree to your request. Go and recover the bond.'[44] In other words, Mary's presentation of her breast, the symbol of her human maternity, leads to Christ's admission that she has control over the document. It is not necessary to imagine that a book (or document) and the breast are at odds. The substitution in a Judgment scene, rather, implies an association between Mary's body and the book that is foreseeable: because Mary bore Christ, she becomes both the container for, and the bearer of, God's law. As the 'Arca Testamenti', she is intuitively linked to apocalyptic imagery, including the rediscovery of the ark and its texts, and the open books of judgment in Revelation 20.

This complex of symbolic modes can resolve any perceived tension between the medieval theological and doctrinal elaborations of Mary's status as a strong *mediatrix* and the more popular devotional appeal of the *mater dolorosa*. The combination of her mediatorship in judgment, her importance as a fulfillment of Hebrew scripture, and her maternity can create of Mary an inscribed body: she contains, she is, and she affects text, because of her status as the Word-maker. The notion that Christ is an inscribed body, an authorized and sealed charter (as evidenced in Middle English *Charters of*

---

42   'Texts and Images of Marian Devotion in Thirteenth-Century England', *England in the Thirteenth Century: Proceedings of the 1989 Harlaxton Symposium*, ed. W. M. Ormrod (Stamford, 1991), pp. 69–103 (here pp. 96–7).

43   Ibid., p. 95.

44   Ibid., p. 96.

Christ) is easily transferred to her, the body that contained him and shares his flesh. As Pierre Bersuire wrote in the fourteenth century, 'Christ is a sort of book written into the skin of the Virgin.'[45]

Miracles of the Virgin in British Library MS Additional 37049

At least one other English artist in the fifteenth century used the association of Mary's maternal body with the book in the context of legality and judgment: in British Library MS Additional 37049, a heavily illustrated, mid- to late fifteenth-century English-language religious miscellany of Yorkshire Carthusian provenance. Many of the texts on the book's ninety-six folios are devotional, and most appear elsewhere in better copies, but the combination of these texts and a large number of colorful and amateurish illustrations make this a striking record of late medieval devotion.[46] Douglas Gray has noted that its most remarkable aspect 'is the overwhelming presence of the illustrations and the way in which most of them are carefully fitted to the texts, often clearly designed to operate in an interactive way'.[47] Jessica Brantley's recent book on the manuscript treats it as a model of English Carthusian devotional reading and writing practices and examines its texts and illustrations as interrelated elements of monastic reading performance. Brantley commendably argues for fuller consideration of 'the striking fact that every reader [of this codex] notices: these texts depend so heavily on the images that accompany them – the two are so closely linked in the structure of the page – that neither can be said to exist in fullness of meaning outside this particular context'.[48] In short, it is 'the combination of words and pictures' that matters most in this book, and this is just as true of its Marian material as of any other part of it.[49]

The majority of the codex's illustrations have to do with death: there is a decisive focus on the Crucifixion, images of Christ covered in wounds, of the bleeding heart of Christ, many of Death as a spear-bearing skeleton, of decom-

---

[45] Quoted in Green, *Crisis of Truth*, p. 418 n. 14.

[46] See Appendix 3, which provides notes on contents and available manuscript descriptions.

[47] 'London, British Library, Additional MS 37049 – A Spiritual Encyclopedia', *Text and Controversy from Wyclif to Bale: Essays in Honour of Anne Hudson*, ed. Helen Barr and Ann M. Hutchison (Turnhout, 2005), p. 100.

[48] See *Reading in the Wilderness: Private Devotion and Public Performance in Late Medieval England* (Chicago and London, 2007), here p. 5.

[49] Ibid., p. 5. Despite the scope of her learned book, Brantley's attention to Marian material happens only incidentally in the course of her larger argument, and she does not treat the series of Miracles of the Virgin at the end of the codex (which I will discuss here). Explicitly Marian elements important to her total conception of the book, however, are the Byzantine-style portrait of Mary on fol. 1v (pp. 170–8), several illustrations of Mary that show her in relationship to the supposed Carthusian reader (pp. 154–66), and 'holy name' meditations that appear on fol. 21r–v (pp. 184–7). I print the latter in Appendix 3.

posing bodies, and monks on their deathbeds.[50] The overall impression is one of gore, and, as Gray writes, 'a "macabre" element is very prominent'.[51] Hope Emily Allen, when she examined the book to study its Rollean texts, clearly found it distasteful, and her words still give good account of a predictable gut response: 'The whole volume is filled with pictures of the crudest and most lurid sort: extremes of sensationalism … alternate with crude representations of a mystical sort.'[52] Accompanying the images of death, however, are Old Testament battles; apocalyptic scenes; multiple Last Judgment scenes; Christ enthroned and sitting in judgment; and a famous illustration of the *Short Charter of Christ*, which shows the charter recording Christ's contract with humanity (sealed by his wounded heart) pinned like a large broadside to his crucified body.[53] That is, the iconographic message is not only about death and mortality, but about apocalyptic hopes, about judgment after death, and about the legal mechanisms of divine judgment.

In this light, a secondary iconography of the manuscript should be considered: there is also a significant interest in the Virgin Mary. The first illustration in the codex is a full-page color bust of the Virgin (fol. 1v), and there are seventeen other images of her throughout.[54] Nine of these show her either enthroned in heaven, in a position of judgment alone or beside Christ, or before sinners who pray to her *in extremis*. Also set in this context is a group of Miracles of the Virgin, and what I am interested in here is not the Marian narratives *per se* but the relationship of this particular compilation of legends to the manuscript's illustrative program. MS Additional 37049 includes nine prose Marian miracles in all (a tenth 'miracle in *tituli*' can be included in the count, though I will take this extra one as an illustration of a narrative rather than a separate representation), and six of them are illustrated. Though none of these have direct sources elsewhere, several are common narratives, and analogues have been catalogued.[55] For the sake of clarity and cross-referencing, then, I will list them, along with editorial titles, related illustrations, and their locations in the manuscript:[56]

---

[50] For plates of all illustrations, see James Hogg, ed., *An Illustrated Yorkshire Carthusian Religious Miscellany, British Library London Additional MS. 37049*, III (all published), Analecta Cartusiana 95 (Salzburg, 1981).

[51] 'London, British Library, Additional MS 37049', p. 101.

[52] *Writings Ascribed to Richard Rolle Hermit of Hampole and Materials for His Biography* (New York and London, 1927), p. 307.

[53] For discussion of this in the context of other *Charters of Christ*, see Steiner, *Documentary Culture*, pp. 75–90, 193–228 (reproduction on p. 86). See also Douglas Gray, *Themes and Images in the Medieval English Religious Lyric* (London and Boston, 1972), p. 130; and Brantley, *Reading in the Wilderness*, pp. 189–91 (fig. 5.13).

[54] This is done on a parchment bifolium (the rest of the codex is paper), with a full-page illustration of Christ as the 'Man of Sorrows', and was possibly a later addition. For discussion of the portraits in the context of processional icons, see Brantley, *Reading in the Wilderness*, pp. 170–8 (fig. 5.1), where these opening images are introduced as a 'response to, or even a commentary on, the book that follows' (p. 170).

[55] See the contents list in Brantley, *Reading in the Wilderness*, pp. 307–25, and Appendix 4 below.

[56] Titles here reflect those catalogued by Brantley, *Reading in the Wilderness*, pp. 303, 312, 325 (her

1 'Debate for the Soul' or 'Miracle in *tituli*', fol. 19r (illustration of no. 9 below, see Plate 6)

2 'Prose Tale of the Lazy Servant of St Anselm' or 'The Servant of St Anselm Carried Off by a Devil', fol. 21v

3 'Marian Miracle of the Clerk of Oxford' or 'The Clerk of Oxford', fol. 27r (illustrated on the same page)[57]

4 'The Drowned Sacristan', fol. 94r–v (illustrated on fol. 27v, see Plate 8)

5 'A Hand on the Scales of Justice' or 'The Wicked Clerk's Vision of Judgment', fol. 94v[58]

6 'A Compact with the Devil Rescinded' or 'The Clerk Who Refused to Forsake the Virgin', fols 94v–95r

7 'A Monk of Cluny Rescued from Despair' or 'The Monk Who Despaired', fol. 95r (illustrated on fol. 30v, see Plate 7)

8 'The Devil and a Young Man Make a Charter' or 'How A Youth Was Rescued from a Pact with the Devil', fol. 95r (illustrated on the same page, see Plate 5)

9 'The Virgin Bares Her Breasts for a Sinner' or 'How Our Lady Pleaded for a Sinner's Soul', fol. 95v (illustrated on fol. 19r, see Plate 6)

10 'The Knight Who Refused to Abjure Our Lady' or 'The Knight Who Refused to Forsake the Virgin', fol. 95v

My primary concern is the series that appears on fols 94r–95v (nos 4–10 above). I will call this the Charter Group, both because it collectively emphasizes Mary's ability to nullify bad contracts and intercede in matters of legality and judgment, and because the only illustration on these folios shows Mary returning a charter to two kneeling devotees (an illustration of no. 8 above, see Plate 5).

The Charter Group illustration immediately communicates to readers, even perusers, that Mary can intercede in matters of law and/or performative text – and this is an important part of the characterization of Marian intercession in this codex – but it has not before been noticed that, in fact, *four* of the stories in the Charter Group are illustrated, because the three other relevant images are distantly separated from the narratives they illustrate. The most remarkable aspect of this group, then, is indeed the interplay of text and image, and the ability of this interplay to suggest a relationship between these miracle narratives (which might otherwise appear an incidental addition at the end of a miscellany) and an entire manuscript schema.

titles for the prose miracles also correspond to *MWME* XXIV), and Whiteford, *Myracles of Oure Lady*, pp. 112–13, 120–1.

57 Oxford is not in fact named in this tale, though the title persists because of analogues. See my discussion below, pp. 133–6, and Appendix 3, where I will refer to it as a 'Marian Miracle of a Clerk' (analogues are also noted in Appendix 3).

58 I call this 'A Scholar at the Scales of Justice'. See Chapter 1, pp. 32–4, and Appendix 4.

Plate 5 The Virgin Mary returns a charter. London, British Library MS
Additional 37049, fol. 95r. © British Library Board

Noticing this connection, and 'reading' the full potential of each medium, means moving between text and image and creating a new grouping of related items through the kind of active reading practice that has already been described by scholars recently working on the book. The Marian illustrations in MS Additional 37049 must be viewed through the lens of narratives they reflect, and this codex teaches its readers not only how to do this, but also, consequently, about Mary's intercessory powers. The Charter Group miracles emphasize Mary's role as an advocate and bearer of text and therefore instruct the reader about this extraordinary aspect of her intercession. The cues that create order in this 'miscellany' (what Brantley might call 'image-text' cues) themselves enact these aspects of Marian intercession,[59] as well as lessons about the uses and dangers of a combined 'visual–textual' devotion to her.

Before I move on to the substance of these arguments, however, I must pause to heed Douglas Gray's caution about perceiving coherency in MS Additional 37049, since, as he rightly says, 'in this area of manuscript study, academic interpreters sometimes feel an excessive urge to find total coherence'.[60] His conclusions about the potential reading practices prescribed by this book's compilation are very much in the spirit of the present investigation:

> As [Fritz] Saxl remarked ... 'in such a collection we cannot expect to find a well-defined order. Image follows image, sometimes connected, often not.' To call MS Add. 37049 a thematically arranged anthology would suggest a careful planning rather than the evidence of a more informal and cumulative compilation would allow, yet to call it a 'miscellany' might overemphasize its 'looseness' of structure. Some thematic groupings are found within the manuscript, but also some sudden shifts. It was probably intended to be read in 'bits,' individual items or sections, and sometimes a grouping might suggest some encouragement to read a series of items together.[61]

This assessment of how the manuscript's texts and images work together allows for various thematic concerns (Gray himself emphasizes the overarching theme of judgment), and allows that these sometimes give way to secondary concerns.[62] I have already called the Marian elements of the codex 'secondary', and I do not intend to treat them in any other way. But to my knowledge, no one has yet paid attention to the elaborate interplay of *Marian* image and legend in this manuscript,[63] and my analysis should complement recent attempts to consider 'the whole book'.

---

59 See *Reading in the Wilderness*, pp. 5–6 n. 29. Brantley borrows 'imagetext' from W. J. T. Mitchell's work on how visuality and textuality work in mixed media. She uses it to denote a certain theatricality in the book's calling up of 'performative modes' (p. 5).

60 'London, British Library, Additional MS 37049', pp. 101–2.

61 Ibid., pp. 102–3.

62 Ibid., pp. 103–6.

63 On the treatment of the Marian material in Brantley, *Reading in the Wilderness*, see n. 48 above. Gray, 'London, British Library, Additional MS 37049', does describe the book's 'prominent'

The Marian material provides a case study of what happens if we read 'in bits' and follow exactly a small grouping that offers 'some encouragement to read a series of items together'. In other words, I am here putting into practice Gray's conjecture about the manuscript's design and intended use, and I am taking it somewhat further by suggesting that the 'bits' and 'series' need not be contiguous. Even Brantley, who argues for an understanding of the manuscript's devotional images and texts in terms of drama and performance (and so might seem to suggest a linear reading) and admits to 'arguing implicitly for a certain unity in the miscellany', is emphatic about how the reading and devotional practices prescribed by this codex are not governed by any theme or 'coherent principle' that can 'explain the sequence of items'. Rather, as the book was apparently primarily the work of one man who was both the main scribe and the artist of the majority of the illustrations, it has a 'unity in its variety' and 'the reading experience establishes crucial relationships among its parts', especially if we imagine readers who knew the book well, who 'worked through the book more than once with the care and intensity appropriate to devotional reading and seeing'.[64] The Charter Group in fact seems to encourage a piecemeal reading practice that expects that kind of knowledge of the book.

I want first to look at the *illustration* of the sixth miracle of the Charter Group (nos 1 and 9 above). Not only has the connection between this illustration and its related narrative not been noticed before, but disconnection has been claimed.[65] In fact, this 'miracle in *tituli*' (on fol. 19r) provides the first image of Mary integrated into the codex (the only one before this is the bust on fol. 1v, a parchment addition to the first quire),[66] and it provides the first illustration of a Marian text also present in the codex, even though it is (in the manuscript's present organization[67]) a full seventy-five pages removed from the Charter Group narrative it clearly reflects. The illustration shows a full-page dialogue between the Soul, God, Christ, Death, Satan, and the Virgin Mary (see Plate 6). It is a 'Debate for the Soul', and it is clearly a judgment scene, wherein Mary advocates for the soul of a sinner after death.[68] These types of visual miracles have been discussed by both Peter Whiteford and Thomas Heffernan as common representations of the Virgin in 'judgement, turning aside the stern justice of God', wherein 'the soul of the appellant calls on the Virgin's intercession, who in turn implores Christ's

Marian content, but he nevertheless overlooks the Charter Group and discusses Marian texts and images as interrelated only when physically adjoined (see pp. 109–10).

64 Brantley, *Reading in the Wilderness*, pp. 10–11.

65 Whiteford, *Myracles of Oure Lady*, pp. 120–1, states that 'no source is known' for the narrative version of the miracle, and the 'miracle in *tituli*' is listed in a separate catalogue entry on p. 112.

66 See Brantley, *Reading in the Wilderness*, pp. 170–1, and n. 53 above.

67 See n. 96 below.

68 Gray, 'London, British Library, Additional MS 37049', p. 104, calls this page a 'spiritual drama' of judgment; and Brantley, *Reading in the Wilderness*, pp. 87–95, discusses it in the context of the *Desert of Religion* and similar medieval illustrations, specifically 'Vado mori' scenes (some of which occur in the same codex).

Plate 6 A dialogue concerning the fate of the soul. London, British Library
MS Additional 37049, fol. 19r. © British Library Board

help, often displaying to him her breasts, and Christ then appeals to the Father, displaying in turn his wounds'.[69]

In the case of the example in MS Additional 37049, Mary asks her son to accept the Soul into heaven. God sits enthroned at the top of the page, holding in one hand an open book, the pages blank, and raising the other hand in blessing. Below and to his left is the crucified Christ, who looks to the enthroned God while one hand cups the wound in his chest and the other (free from the cross) points to Mary. Mary, below God and to his right, stands above a dead body whose infant-like soul rises from him. She looks up to God and forcefully lifts one bare breast toward Christ. On the right side of the corpse stands a skeletal, spear-bearing Death and a club-wielding Satan; on the left stands an angel. Emanating from each participant is a scroll (*titulus*), iconographically used to represent speech. Part of the pedagogy of this image (and others like it) is in the direction of prayer and intercession suggested by the inscribed *tituli*. While Death and Satan, and the angel, simply comment on the state of the Soul and the Body, the Soul ignores them and prays to Mary: 'I hope in nede þu helpe me, gode moder, I pray to þe.' Mary in turn pleads with her son: 'ffor þis þu sowke in þi childhede: son forgyf hym his mysdede.' Christ in turn prays to God the Father: 'I pray þe fader graunt þi son, ffor my sake, my moder bone.' God the Father responds to his son: 'Son ale þu byddes sal al be. No thyng wil I denye þe.'[70] There is a fastidiousness about the theological point here: Mary does not in and of herself have power but rather intercedes on behalf of the sinner by directing her own prayers to her son. Simply put, she is the *mediatrix*.

This visual–textual instruction on the proper role of Mary is not unwarranted: only two folios later (fol. 21r), Marian intercession causes doubt about the relative power of God. In a passage concerning the beauty of the Virgin Mary, which begins alongside a large illustration of her – regal, crowned, and holding the infant Christ – the scribe records the following story about St Ignatius:

> it is sayd of Saynt Ignacius þat of tymes wrote pystyls to þe blyssed virgyn, & sche to hym agayne, þat when he sawe þe blyssed virgyn he felle to þe erthe for þe fayrnes he sawe in hyr face & in hyr body. And whan he rose at hyr byddyng, it is sayd þat he sayd, if he had not bene certyfyed by hyr & by Saynt Ion þe euangelist & verely bene informed in þe faythe, he had trowed þat no oþer god had bene bot sche, for þe wondyrful shynyng of hyr face & excellent fayrnes.[71]

---

[69] I am here quoting Whiteford, *Myracles of Oure Lady*, pp. 16–17, but see also Thomas Heffernan, 'The Virgin as an Aid to Salvation in Some Fifteenth-Century English and Latin Verses', *MÆ* 52 (1983), pp. 229–38.

[70] From my transcriptions.

[71] Appendix 3, 'Blessed Face and Name', lines 7–13.

The choice to focus on this moment of the *vita* of this saint is worth noting because it emphasizes the impact of the visual on devotional reading and writing.[72] Ignatius has a relationship with Mary that involves textual activity – he 'wrote pystyls' and 'sche to hym agayne' – but when that relationship becomes visual ('he sawe'), the nature of his devotion is tested. He must allow that Mary *appears* to be God: there is the potential, because of her image (her face and her body) to believe in 'no oþer god ... bot sche'. He hesitates in his assessment of Mary's divine role exactly at the moment he encounters her visually, and a reader must do the same, since the story is set alongside an illustration of Mary.

All of the problematic elements of this momentary visual confusion are reflected in the 'Debate for the Soul' shown only two pages earlier. While the *text* contained in that image (written in the *tituli*) betrays anxiety to display the correct role of Mary *mediatrix* in the salvation of souls, the mechanism and direction of her speech in the *image* are exceptional. Mary's *titulus*, which in every other case in the illustration is connected to the mouth or head of the speaker,[73] comes streaming from the nipple of the breast that she thrusts toward her son – as if her breast milk pours from her in the form of a scroll.[74] Though the direction of the *tituli* elsewhere reflects the inscribed text within (the Soul's scroll bends toward Mary, the object of its prayer, and Christ's extends upward to God), Mary's *titulus*, which contains a prayer ostensibly directed toward her son, bends back around her and appears to be picked up by the claws of the Holy Spirit (here represented by a dove with the *cruciform nimbus*), who pulls it toward God's open (blank) book. According to Camille, the iconography of the open and unwritten book, especially in England and in the context of a diabolic threat,

> probably originat[es] in Bede's account of the 'records' of sins and good deeds which will confront the soul on the Last Day. The open codex (which is blank) is a visual sign of the process of divine law for a literate audience who was nonetheless attuned to the symbolic rather than the legal power of texts.[75]

Significant here is the power given to Mary to affect this 'open codex'; it is her speech act that is connected to the 'records of sins and good deeds', and it is her act, as opposed to Christ's, that is visually connected to the 'sign

---

[72] The life of St Ignatius of Antioch is a standard in medieval legendaries. His correspondence with Mary is always included, though this encounter is unusual. For a near contemporary English version of the *vita*, see Richard Hamer, ed., *Gilte Legende*, I, EETS, os 327 (London, 2006), pp. 157–61.

[73] In the case of God the Father, the *titulus* comes from the raised hand, but this is typical in depictions of scholars or teachers and not unexpected in an image of God.

[74] Brantley, *Reading in the Wilderness*, p. 89 (fig. 3.5), shows another illustration of Mary holding her breast in a very similar scene in MS BL Cotton Faustina B. VI. In that case, however, Mary stands beside Christ, and her *titulus* extends from behind her head and toward her son.

[75] 'The Devil's Writing', p. 356.

of the process of divine law'. She is the only figure in the illustration whose speech becomes confused with the visual cue of the written scroll: because her *titulus* is not connected to the part of her body that should speak, its significance as a sign of speech becomes strained. Instead, the Holy Spirit carries the scroll toward the blank book of God's judgment, which awaits text, and, in the process, begins to change the questionable speech-act into script. Though an image with *tituli* requires 'a literate audience' to be complete, the text and image here work against each other. What is written within the scrolls makes clear the relationship of each participant to the other, but the image undermines this. To look without reading is to see the 'text' of Mary flowing, with the aid of the Holy Spirit, directly toward the unwritten Book of Judgment. The symbolic power of what emanates from the breast turning into the substance of what is written in the book cannot be overemphasized: Mary's maternal nature is in this case not separate from her legal and literate power, but is rather crucial to what creates that power, and her related ability to inscribe the pages of the blank book establishes in MS Additional 37049 a Marian intercession that is figuratively similar to the position of scribe or compiler.

The Charter Group narrative that works with this illustration (no. 9 above, fol. 95v) places emphasis on Mary's intercession that is subtly different from the visual portrayal:

> þer was a synful man þat felle seke & cald to hym a religious man & mekely prayed hym þat he & alle his breþer suld pray for hym. And he beheste þat he suld amende his lyfe if he myghte lyfe. And when he was recouerd, he was wars þan he was before. *Sone after he fel seke, þe saule passed & come before oure lord Iesu Criste domesman.* And he sawe on his right hande his chosyn, & on his lefte hande reprofed. *When he þoght þat he suld hafe bene sett with þe reprofed þat was dampned, he askyd helpe at Saynt Mary þat sat by þe domesman. Oure lady prayed hyr sone for hym.* Þe domesman sayd hym aghte not to do agayns rightwisnes. Þan þe blissed uirgyn sayd to þe synfull man, '3e wretche, how mykil þe vyce of unkyndnes is & how sorlly þat syn is to ponesche. I am moder of þe kyng & domesman, & I am not hard for þe.' Þan sayd þe synfulman, 'I wate blyssed lady þat mykil is my syn & my wretchydnes. Bot I wate þat þi mercy, þe whilk þat I aske, is mykil more.' *Þan eftyrward oure blyssed lady schewed unto hir son hyr breste & hir pappes, praying hym for þoes þat he sowked to do mercy with þe wretche.* Þan oure lord graunted hym space of lyfe to do penance. And after þat he lyfyd moste holyly & happely endyd [my italics].[76]

The italicized portions of the text above obviously match the 'Debate for the Soul' illustration already discussed. The narrative relationship of the story of a dead man who prays to the Virgin because his soul is in danger of damna-

---

[76] Appendix 3, Charter Group, lines 69–86.

tion is, in any case, similar enough to the illustration to create a connection, especially when Mary's ultimate action in both is to show 'unto hir son hyr breste … praying hym for þoes he sowked to do mercy'.

The differences in the narrative are primarily in the position of Mary, enthroned beside the 'domesman' (the judge), and in the dialogue between the Soul and Mary and between Mary and Christ. Mary's seat beside the judge puts her in a position of authority imaginatively equal to that of God. She does not so much pray to him (as she does in the illustration, looking up from below) as plead with him from her position of equal power. And the fate of the Soul is not as certain here as it is in the compacted version of the dialogue present in the earlier *tituli*. There is some suspense about whether Mary can achieve the judgment desired or even wants to do so. Unlike the illustration, in which her baring of her breast becomes itself the act of judgment, the breast in the narrative is offered as evidence of the validity of Mary's claim – even as a token of the relevant 'law' to be applied, another gesture of 'trothplight'. The emphasis on the (blank) book that was present in the visual representation shifts in the narrative to an emphasis on the function and usefulness of judgment for the sinner through reproof and penance.

This kind of legal debate over the fate of the soul is a consistent feature of Marian miracles in MS Additional 37049. As mentioned above, one reason to designate the Charter Group as such is because it collectively emphasizes Mary's ability to nullify bad contracts and intercede in matters of legal mediation and judgment. In addition to the miracle already discussed, five others in the group are explicit about this mode of intercession (nos 4–6, 8, and 10 above). Three of these narrate the Theophilan fantasy of diabolical legal transaction and Mary's special ability to intercede in such matters, and the illustrator's choice to highlight this in the Charter Group illustration (see Plate 5) is unquestionably a testimony to this. In the miracle to which that illustration is directly connected, for instance (no. 8 above), a young man spends all his money for the love of a woman especially devoted to Mary. When the Devil sees this, he proposes a bargain: if the young man will deny his faith, he will be richer than ever *and* have the woman he desires. The damaged text relates that Satan commands the young man to 'make me a chartyr written', in which he must state, 'I denye þe trowthe … of holy kyrke & þe moder of Iesu Criste.'[77] At some point he regrets his action, and Mary (prompted by the woman's prayers) appears to retrieve the charter and save the man from his legal obligation.

Two other narratives tell of men who very nearly sign similar contracts but ultimately resist, with Mary's help (nos 6 and 10 above).[78] Another (no. 5) tells of a sinful university clerk who is granted a vision of his death and

---

[77] Ibid., lines 62–4.
[78] Ibid., lines 31–42, 86–107. These are clearly analogues of the legend of Theophilus, though see Wright, 'Durham Play of Mary and the Poor Knight' for other texts related to no. 10 ('The Knight Who Refused to Abjure Our Lady').

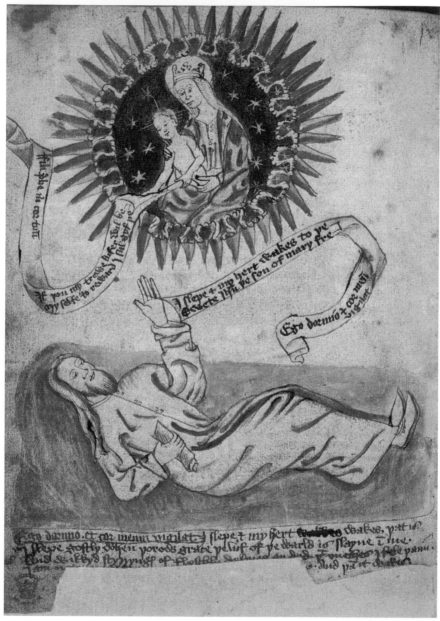

Plate 7 'I slepe & my hert wakes to þe.' London, British Library MS
Additional 37049, fol. 30v. © British Library Board

Mary's mediation at the scales of justice. I have already briefly discussed the 'Scholar at the Scales of Justice' (in Chapter 1), but I will reiterate the crucial point about it, since it is pertinent to the manuscript context here. The clerk sees the Devil place a 'rolle wrytten full of synnes' onto the scales, and, though the case should have gone against him, Mary appears: 'sche toke þe rolle offe þe weyscale & gaf þe clerk it in hys hande & he red it.' I argued above that this is a concise description of Mary's imagined role in English examples of Miracles of the Virgin – this is true – but it is also a concise description of Mary's imagined role in this codex. Mary is able to save the clerk because she can retrieve the 'wrytten rolle'. The clerk's implied ability to handle text is rendered useless at the moment of judgment, while Mary's ability to do so is the emphasis.

In the center of the Charter Group is a single tale seemingly unrelated to the legal-textual theme of the others, but the apparent disconnect is resolved when it is considered with a corresponding illustration, which appears sixty-five pages earlier. This narrative (fol. 95r, no. 7 above) tells of a monk 'ful religios & deuowt to Saynt Mary' who falls into 'dyspayre, þat is wanhope' and prays to Mary until she appears to him in his sleep and comforts him. On fol. 30v, we find an illustration of a reclining, bearded religious man, gazing upward toward an enthroned Virgin, who sits with the infant Jesus on her lap. Macaronic scrolls extend from the hands of the robed man and from Jesus (see Plate 7).

The man's scroll translates Song of Songs 5:2 ('Ego dormio & cor meum vigilat'), 'I slepe & my hert wakes to þe / Swete Iesu þe son of Mary fre.' Jesus's scroll answers, 'Fili praebe mei cor tuum [Son, offer your heart to me]. If þou my trewe lufer wil be / My selfe to reward I sal gyf þe.' Beneath, damaged prose begins: 'Ego dormio et cor meum vigilat. I slepe & my hert wakes. Þat is, I slepe gostly when þorow grace þe luf of þe warld is slayne in me.'[79] Because of the similarity between the appearance of the man in this illustration and two others in the codex (one labeled 'Richard Hampole' in the poem *Desert of Religion*, on fol. 52v), and because of the *Ego dormio* motto (the beginning of one of Rolle's most well-known epistles), this has been regarded as a depiction of Richard Rolle.[80] As both Brantley and Allen have detailed, there are many Rollean elements in this manuscript, and it is evident that 'the [main] scribe of Add. 37049 is devoted to Rolle's catch-words'.[81] Indeed, while the text accompanying the illustration on fol. 30v is not a direct quotation, an excerpt from the *Ego dormio* epistle is on the facing

---

[79] Gray, 'London, British Library, Additional MS 37049', p. 109, also transcribes this text and prints 'I slepe softly' rather than 'I slepe gostly'. I am convinced, however, that the *titulus* reads 'gostly' – a detail that explains why the reclining man's eyes are open.

[80] See Allen, *Writings Ascribed to Richard Rolle*, pp. 307–8; Gray, 'London, British Library, Additional MS 37049', p. 109; and Brantley, *Reading in the Wilderness*, p. 138 (also figs 4.6 and 4.9).

[81] Allen, *Writings Ascribed to Richard Rolle*, pp. 306–11 (here p. 311), and Brantley, *Reading in the Wilderness*, pp. 134–52. Brantley here situates this image in relation to other Rollean elements and the *Desert of Religion* (also associated with Rolle in other codices).

page (fol. 31r),[82] and this illustration is clearly meant to go with that too. But these connections are not mutually exclusive of a connection to the Charter Group narrative on fol. 95r.[83]

Though there are significant differences between the illustration and the narrative to which I connect it, the Rollean aspect adds another layer of visual–textual associations, and the visual representation itself (a reclining man gazing at the Virgin and Child with the biblical motto *Ego dormio* attached) certainly also reflects the narrative of the monk to whom 'on a nyght … oure lady aperyd … & teld hym in his slepe þat his syn was forgyfyn hym'.[84] The most compelling link between these two, however, requires reading the text below the illustration, in which the experience of the spiritual sleeper's enlightenment is associated with the moment when 'luf of þe warld is slayne'. The sleeper is similar to the monk who 'felle in dyspayre' until 'prayinge & lofyng & praysyng' led to sleep that enabled a focused vision of Mary and relief of worldly concerns.[85] The connection between Mary's intercession and written text (though admittedly not legal text in this case) is then enacted in two ways: first, the relationship of text to image forces the reader to contemplate both in order to understand the meaning of the visual representation, and in this instance, because of the nearby Rollean material, to contemplate multiple texts; and second, the 'sleeping' man in the illustration clutches a scroll in his right hand that forces contemplation of text. Though Brantley in her consideration of this image argues that the scroll likely identifies the spiritual sleeper as '*the* author' of the Rollean epistle excerpted on the facing page, she allows that it is 'an unidentifiable scroll that might serve to identify [the sleeper] as *an* author [my italics]'.[86]

What the reclining monk holds out, closest to the viewer, is unknown, but this ultimately permits the viewer/reader to imagine the man as either an author *or* another viewer/reader. The implication is that the man has fallen asleep contemplating text and, at the same moment, has had a spiritual awakening. The didactic lesson about devotional reading is then introduced into a *narrative* because of an additional *visual* detail. On the other hand, even if we imagine that this is Rolle, put here in the unsurprising position of the monk in love with Christ and Mary, the point becomes even stronger, for it is clear that the makers of this codex regard Rolle as the ideal monastic reader and writer.[87] The possibility of a sprawling vacillation between narrative

---

[82] For the full text of Rolle's *Ego Dormio*, see Hope Emily Allen, *English Writings of Richard Rolle Hermit of Hampole* (Oxford, 1931), pp. 60–72.

[83] Gray, 'London, British Library, Additional MS 37049', p. 109, does not knowingly connect the illustration to the miracle on fol. 95r, but he does comment that Mary appears in it 'as if in a vision', thus accurately describing her appearance in the narrative.

[84] Appendix 3, Charter Group, lines 49–51.

[85] Ibid., lines 46–9.

[86] Brantley, *Reading in the Wilderness*, p. 138.

[87] Ibid., figs. 4.6, 4.9. In the labeled illustration of Rolle that accompanies the *Desert of Religion*, and in the similar (unlabeled) depiction of fol. 37r, Rolle is inscribed with the monograph IHC and sits holding a book.

and image thus encouraged by the Charter Group miracles allows a multi-layered meditation on Mary and Marian devotion. With care, the visual and the textual can and should work together when a reader encounters them (compare St Ignatius's moment of doubt!). The connections highlight the role of the reader (the ideal monk, meditating on text and vision), allow that Mary is herself symbolically involved in book production (as one who affects the Book of Judgment), and focus Marian intercession on matters of legal mediation and performative text (the overwhelming content of the narratives).

This is further enriched in the Charter Group, as Marian narrative and images there expand to include the allegorical place of Mary in Judeo-Christian history. In the first narrative of the group (no. 4 above), Mary argues with a group of demons who have claimed the soul of an adulterous canon. The canon, on his way to meet his mistress, falls from a bridge and drowns, but he prays to Mary as this is happening. '[I]n myddes of þe flod', the text tells us, a 'cumpeny' of devils 'raueschyd hys saule to torments', but

> come þe blissed uirgyn gods moder with compeny of saynts to þe place wher fendes tormentyd þe saule, and sayd to þaim, 'Why torment ȝe þe saule of my seruande unrightwisly?' Þai sayd, 'We aske to hafe hym for he was take in oure warke.' Oure lady sayd, 'If he suld be þair whame he seruyd, he suld be oures for he sayd oure matens when ȝe slewe hym, whar fore ȝe ar gylty anence me ffor ȝe hafe done wykkydnes agayns me.' Þan fled þe fendes swyftly away, & þe blissed virgyn bare þe saule to þe body, and raysed þe body up by þe arme fro dowbyl deth, and commaundyd þe watyr to stande on þe ryght hande & on þe left hande lyke a walle & fro þe grownde of þe see broght hym to þe hafen.[88]

With this, the interplay of text and image occurs again on two levels. First, there is an illustration to which this narrative can be connected, sixty-seven pages earlier (fol. 27r, see Plate 8).

It is an unfinished scene with *tituli* that appears to reflect the situation of the adulterous drowned canon. At the bottom right corner of the folio is a naked man immersed in water, his eyes turned upward and his hands together in prayer, a blank *titulus* extending from his mouth. At the top of the page, Mary kneels in prayer before Christ, who sits in judgment, and encircling Mary are eight small angels (a veritable 'compeny'), who likewise raise their hands and eyes in prayer. Blank *tituli* also extend from the mouths of the Virgin and Christ. In the lower left portion of the folio is an English poem rubricated by the first line of the familiar Latin prayer *Ave maris stella*, which begins, 'Hayle se sterne gods modyr holy / Pray þu þi swete son safe us fro foly / Þat walke in þis warld lyke unto þe se / Ebbyng & flowing ful of uanyte.'[89] This figure of the drowning man praying and receiving the intercession of Mary is

---

88 Appendix 3, Charter Group, lines 7–17.
89 From my transcriptions.

Plate 8 A drowning man prays for the Virgin Mary's intercession. London, British Library MS Additional 37049, fol. 27v. © British Library Board

130

certainly a worthy representation of the sinful yet devout drowning canon for whom Mary intercedes with her 'compeny of sayntes'. While the unfinished *tituli* make it impossible to know whether a more explicit connection to the miracle may have been intended, the vernacular prayer that accompanies the image connects the story of the drowning sinner to every reader and turns Mary into a source of salvation to all who are metaphorically drowning.[90]

More significant here, however, is the second visual–textual interplay encouraged by the Charter Group narrative. The argument that Mary puts forth in the miracle concerning the drowned canon is a serious legal one. It points out the flaw in the demons' claim by privileging an overly literal reading of their words. Mary does not dispute that a soul taken in the Devil's work should be damned, only whether this soul was involved in such work at the time of death. Mary claims that at the actual moment of death, since the canon was praying to her, he was in fact doing *her* work. In using the demons' argument against them, Mary pronounces a double judgment: the devils are guilty of stealing from her, and the canon's soul is acquitted of its offense. Important to the related *visual* impact of the story in this codex is that, in recording this swift double act, the scribe clearly connects Mary to the law-bearer Moses: as Mary 'commanndyd þe watyr to stande on þe ryght hande & on þe left hande lyke a wall', she takes action that cannot but signify Moses's parting of the Red Sea. In Exodus 14:21–2, 'when Moses had stretched forth his hand over the sea … the water was divided. And the children of Israel went in through the midst of the sea dried up: for the water was as a wall on their right hand and on their left.'

The connection drawn between Mary and Moses occurs elsewhere in the manuscript too, both visually and textually. In the same text that describes Mary's impact on St Ignatius, her beautiful face is compared to Moses's at the moment he received the law:

> If þe face of moyses so schane for the compeny of þe wordes of god þat þe sonnes of Israel myght not luke in hys face, how mykil more þis blyssed uyrgyn þat was umbyschadowed of þe uertewe of þe aller hyghest & þat þe holy goste lightyd in.[91]

Here the distinction between Mary and Moses – and the usefulness of the comparison – has to do with the differences and similarities between experiencing the written words of God (the inscribing of the Ten Commandments)

---

90 Gray, 'London, British Library, Additional MS 37049', pp. 109–10, also discusses fol. 27r in the context of the codex's Marian content and as a model of its engagement with the reader. He does not connect it to any other text in the codex, but he allows that 'the whole ensemble suggests an intense emotional relationship' between Mary and her devotees (p. 110). Brantley, *Reading in the Wilderness*, p. 154, likewise sees the illustration of the naked drowning man as a representation of the 'general reader' or a type of the 'naked soul', but she therefore seems to suggest (incorrectly, I think) that the *tituli* are intentionally left blank, so that the drowning man 'speaks the main text on the page' (p. 156).

91 Appendix 3, 'Blessed Face and Name', lines 21–4.

Plate 9 Christ and a horned Moses. London, British Library MS Additional 37049, fol. 20v. © British Library Board

and containing the Word of God ('the Word made Flesh'), and this is the same comparison that the single illustration that accompanies the Charter Group makes. That image shows Mary enthroned in heaven and reaching through parted clouds to return to a man and woman a charter, a document spotted with many small lines signifying text (see Plate 5). The same artist twice repeats this image in other parts of the codex, but the examples show *God* enthroned in heaven and reaching through parted clouds to *Moses*.

In the first of these (Plate 9), God extends his hand toward a kneeling, horned Moses (the horns visually mark his Jewishness). The Latin text of the Ten Commandments, interspersed with English verse that translates and describes each command, is written on the rest of page. In the second instance (Plate 10), God reaches through the clouds to the horned Moses and extends to him the tablets of the law, which are dotted with small lines signifying text. The similarity of this latter image to the Charter Group illustration is striking indeed. The narrative and visual connections of Mary to Moses (a connection only clearly accomplished through consideration of the Charter Group) is not only one that implicitly underscores Mary's Jewish identity (and conse-quently her symbolic role as the body that both performs and contains the old and new law), but one that simultaneously emphasizes Mary's role as a law-bearer, as a retriever of text, and as a God-like figure in her granting of text and judgment of souls. In the story of the drowning canon, Mary's action connects her to Moses (the parting of the water), while the nearby Charter Group illustration both connects her to illustrations of God and Moses *and* puts her in the iconographic position of God – not unlike the first illustration discussed above, where visual cues make Mary's body the source of divine text.

While MS Additional 37049 has been called a 'uniformly and completely orthodox' volume,[92] the Charter Group and its related images consistently reflect the same theologically problematic moment of the St Ignatius story also contained in the codex. The image of Mary, narratives of Mary, and devotion to Mary are sometimes at odds and potentially cause moments of doubt that either over- or under-emphasize her position in the economy of salvation and the production of holy text. There is no reason, however, to assume that this amounts to unorthodox content in a manuscript that nowhere else warrants such an evaluation. Rather, the Charter Group encour-ages meditation on exactly this tension, and on the usefulness of Marian devotional images and texts. It is noteworthy that one of this codex's most open discussions of devotional images comes in an illustrated Miracle of the Virgin outside the Charter Group, where we find both encouragement to read the text and images of Marian miracles together and instruction to beware the influence of Marian images. The 'Miracle of a Clerk' (no. 3 above, fol. 27r) tells of a monk who was so devoted to Mary that he traveled to visit

---

[92] Gray, 'London, British Library, Additional MS 37049', p. 99.

Plate 10 Christ gives
the tablets of the law
to a horned Moses.
London, British Library
MS Additional 37049,
fol. 66v. © British
Library Board

an image of her painted by St Luke, but his Marian devotion was negatively impacted by his disappointment in the quality of the image. Eventually he fell sick and was near death, and Mary appeared to him. Beside the narrative, on the left side of the page, is an illustration of a large, barefoot, haloed woman. She has loose blond hair, one hand raised in blessing, and she is clothed in a plain brown dress with an unadorned girdle and headband. Below her is a small tonsured male, tucked into a bed and raising his hands in supplication.

This is a dramatically different image of Mary than offered elsewhere in the manuscript, where she is always regal or connected to her son. But the narrative that accompanies it tells us why:

> It is red in þe myrakils of oure lady þat a clerk luffed wele oure lady, þat in so mykil þat he went unto Rome of deuocion þat he myght se þe ymage of oure lady þe whilk as it is sayd Sayn Luke purtred. Efter when he had sene þat ymage hym þoght it was noȝt so fayre as he trowede. Wherfore his luf & his deuocion was noȝt so mykyl as it was before ... oure blissed lady apperyd unto hym & sayd unto hym, 'Þou went unto Rome þat þu suld se me in myne ymage, and for þe fayrnes of it plesed þe noȝt, þe whilk þu sawe in þe ymage, þi luf & þi deuocyon is lessend to me.' Þe blyssed uirgyn was cled in a blak cote, & abowte hyr a gyrdyll, & a bende in hyr hede, & bare fote. And þan sche sayd ... 'Þus was y anowrned when Gabriel schewed unto me þe incarnacion ... And for þi luf was lessend to me þu sal not be unponesched with þis seknes.'[93]

In a book so clearly designed to inspire simultaneous meditation on images and text, this narrative is both instructive and a caveat. Inasmuch as MS Additional 37049 focuses on Mary, this is a careful reminder of how to approach its Marian content: one must cautiously regard images of Mary, lest they negatively (and therefore wrongly) influence devotion to her. One must 'read' the image with devotion rather than expect the image to inspire devotion. So while an image may be humble, unadorned, or lacking in beauty, it may also, in the right context and read correctly, communicate a fundamental truth.

We can transfer this to the whole book. While MS Additional 37049 is in many ways a humble compilation, it also contains, as Gray has put it, 'extraordinary example[s] of the linking of text and image, exposition and instruction',[94] and the visual–textual instruction offered through its Miracles of the Virgin is one that prescribes the use of the book itself: look at adjacent texts and images, yes, but also travel (to Rome, for instance, or to different parts of a codex) and consider that movement in your experience of devotional reading. We might read this advice as an echo of the postscript of Julian of Norwich's *Revelation of Love*. It advises, 'Beware thu take not on thing after thy affection and liking and leve another, for that is the condi-

---

93 Appendix 3, 'Miracle of a Clerk', lines 1–16.
94 'London, British Library, Additional MS 37049', p. 112.

tion of an heretique. But take every thing with other.'[95] Of course, each of
the illustrations discussed here can stand on its own; none *needs* the Charter
Group miracles to function. Each has its own implicit narrative, and, in the
cases of the Rollean spiritual sleeper and drowning man, the illustrations are
independently connected to different texts, prayers, and biblical citations. But
even the text near these illustrations is not necessarily unrelated to the later
narratives. Each can and does work to complement the image, and moving
between text(s) and image invites a use of this manuscript that is complex. A
full meditation on the Marian images becomes possible only in the reading
of Marian narratives included very late in the codex,[96] for only then comes
the realization that illustrations throughout the manuscript have bearing on
the narratives.

This requires a back-reading of the manuscript, or a rereading of the
manuscript images, but such interactive reading was not unfamiliar to medieval religious. The scribe of the St Albans Psalter copied into his book, which
begins with some forty images of the Life of Christ, the familiar pronouncement of Gregory the Great on the value of images *as* texts: 'Aliud est picturam
adorare, aliud rationem de picturis interroganti, per picture historiam quid sit
adorandum addiscere' (it is one thing to venerate a picture and another to
learn the story which it depicts, which is to be venerated).[97] Though this is
traditionally understood as the beginning of a comment on the usefulness
of images for the illiterate, this line suggests not only that both the image
and the (sometimes written) story are worthy of veneration, but also that
they must be considered together – even if codicologically set apart, as they
are indeed in the St Albans Psalter. In the case of MS Additional 37049,
the delayed position of stories elsewhere depicted is part of a reading practice that invites consideration of the Virgin Mary that is intensely bookish,
intensely textual. Contemplating the Miracles of the Virgin is in this case a
studious act, one that requires reading and rereading, seeing and reseeing –
so that Mary's authority is literally imposed on the reader who chooses to
contemplate it. Camille has noted that, '[a]s opposed to the roll of earlier
times, the codex allowed the reader to recapitulate, skim, check text against
picture and refer forward',[98] and I would add 'backward'. The compiler(s)

---

95 The postscript is found in two manuscripts of Julian's Long Text and is likely scribal, here quoted
    from Jocelyn Wogan-Browne et al., eds, *The Idea of the Vernacular: An Anthology of Middle
    English Literary Theory, 1280–1520* (University Park, PA, 1999), p. 234.
96 While parts of the manuscript may have been unbound or differently organized at some point,
    there is no codicological evidence to suggest that the position of the Charter Group at the *end* of
    the codex ever changed, nor that it was not always at some distance from the relevant illustrations
    discussed above. See James Hogg, 'Unpublished Texts in the Carthusian Northern Middle English
    Religious Miscellany British Library MS Add. 37049', *Essays in Honour of Erwin Stürzl on His
    Sixtieth Birthday*, ed. James Hogg (Salzburg, 1980), pp. 246–8.
97 The Gregory epistle is copied in both Latin and Anglo-Norman on fol. 68v of the St Albans
    Psalter (Hildesheim, St Godehard's Church, MS St Albans Psalter). Digital images and transcrip-
    tions are accessible at http://www.abdn.ac.uk/stalbanspsalter, whence I have taken the Latin. I am
    using the translation of W. Tatarkiewicz, quoted in Michael Camille, 'Seeing and Reading', p. 26.
98 'Seeing and Reading', p. 29.

and the main scribe/artist challenge the reader to do the work of connecting narratives that appear late in the codex to earlier prayers, narratives, *tituli*, and images, and thereby ask for a knowledge of the book and its content that can only come with extended use. And this act of creating a relationship to the codex itself creates a valorization of the written word that enacts the importance of the Book (as a symbol of law and as a text to be read correctly) in Mary's intercessory actions.

We must now ask how this kind of use and characterization of Marian intercession was received. It is always hard, perhaps impossible, to conjure up the reading experiences of the past, of course impossible to know what individual readers thought. Mary was many things by the end of the fifteenth century, and I am only exposing some of her many faces. Miri Rubin has assessed the late medieval understanding of her in this way: 'By the year 1500 Mary had become embedded in private and public worlds of great variety. Mary-language expressed fear and desire, power as well as abjection.'[99] Among 'Mary-languages' that can be situated and examined within the late medieval English landscape, the lawyerly and learned Mary, the capricious and Jewish Mary, constitute one expression of fear and desire within the long English history of Marian devotion, but it is one that functions with a surprising coherence and an observable trajectory.

This book began by questioning why Miracles of the Virgin (and especially English-language examples) look different in England. As should be eminently clear by now, it is partly the fact of their comprising the variable stuff of miscellany and homily that creates the kinds of characterizations of Mary that I have been able to identify. Since continental examples typically 'occupy single manuscripts in their own right, or form major items within *mariales*', the assumption has been that the English situation is 'partially to be attributed to the destruction of [Marian] manuscripts in the sixteenth century' and that both Anglo-Latin and Middle English Marian miracles 'would have been ripe for destruction'.[100] But it seems likely that England's Miracles of the Virgin simply developed independently and differently from continental models, and in different categories. As I outlined in the first chapter, the miscellaneity of English Marian miracles could be advantageous to their exemplarity and in fact expose rather than obscure lines of development; it could establish new groups and patterns of narrative concerns; and it could produce related sets of thematic positions depending on the situations of composition and propagation.[101] The reception history of English Marian miracles – the subject of the final chapter – can tell us something more about this.

---

99 *Mother of God*, p. 349.
100 Whiteford, *Myracles of Oure Lady*, pp. 20, 21.
101 See Chapter 1 above, pp. 16–19.

5

The Fate of English Miracles of the Virgin

> But merci, ladi, at the grete assyse
> Whan we shule come bifore the hye justyse.
>> Geoffrey Chaucer, 'An ABC'[1]

> These wonders (whiche they call miracles) bee wrought dayly in the Churche, not by the power of God, as many thinke, but by the illusion of Sathan rather ... Neither are they to be called miracles of true christen men, but illusions rather, wherby to delude mens mindes, to make them put their faith in our Lady, & in other Saints, and not in God alone.
>> Thomas Bilney c.1531, according to John Foxe[2]

As the Protestant Reformation reached England – bringing with it the rejection of the cult of saints and attacks, rhetorical and real, on shrines, pilgrimage, and associated miraculous events or items – belief in the kinds of Marian intercession described in Miracles of the Virgin could epitomize Catholic 'superstition'. As Ælfric had insisted centuries earlier, the glut of Marian apocrypha that had developed independently of scripture had to be suppressed in favor of biblical accounts (in which Mary features only minimally), since false or unverifiable narratives posed a threat to the honor due to God alone. Marian feasts with apocryphal bases, which had been so central to early English devotion, were to be invalidated. Visual depictions of Mary shifted to meeker and softer representations of Luke's acquiescent maiden.[3] Images and sculptures associated with long-popular shrines and miracles were attacked with words, hammers, and flames.

While I have been advocating for a view of English Marian miracles – particularly the Middle English corpus – that embraces their miscellaneity as representative and thereby reveals visible developments of sets and subsets of miracle narratives like the ones explored in this book, I cannot deny that the complex history of reform attitudes toward Mary and the equally complex history of the English Reformation seem to create a basic evidentiary problem

---

[1]   Benson, *Riverside*, p. 638, lines 36–7.
[2]   Foxe, *A&M*, bk 8, p. 1140 (1570 edition).
[3]   Susan Karant-Nunn and Merry Wiesner-Hanks, eds, *Luther on Women: A Sourcebook* (Cambridge, 2003), p. 34.

for me. Could it be that the English corpus looks the way it does because the sixteenth-century eradication of 'superstitious' texts and images means that the genre is now so badly represented that any traces of development, whether in the whole or in thematically related subsets, are accidental? This question was put to me many times in the course of my research, and even scholars most attuned to the vagaries of the genre will claim that these texts met their 'demise in England' when 'Protestantism ended their popularity', that the reform decades are likely responsible for 'the extent to which the miscellany is responsible for preserving the Middle English miracles', or that we are confronted with losses attributable to 'the deliberate zeal of Protestant reformers'.[4] It is far from obvious, however, that these kinds of Marian texts were systematically seized or sanctioned,[5] and, importantly, there is little evidence that they were ever understood as accessories to dislocated sites or objects of veneration.

Still, there is some indication that reformers were thinking about Marian miracles. When Martin Luther preached his last sermon on the subject of Mary's birth in 1522, he focused on the Gospel of Matthew's account of her lineage and condemned apocryphal accounts as lies, just as Ælfric had condemned near-heretical stories of her Assumption in favor of what could be culled from gospel and archeological evidence.[6] But Luther also included legendary material and *exempla* in his rebuke: Mary had been turned, he said, 'into a judge and a jury or even a god' and would herself cry bloody tears to see 'the way fables have been turned into examples for her people'.[7] Likewise, Hugh Latimer, defending his claim from the pulpit that 'our lady was a sinner' (*c*.1530), echoed Luther with recourse to the Marian devotion of 'not only laye men, but also priestes & beneficed men' who seemed to regard Mary as 'a sauioresse': 'it was neuer said without sinne þat our lady was not saued, but a sauior.'[8] The preacher Thomas Bilney similarly raged (a fuller quotation is at the head of the chapter) that the miracles associated with Mary and others simply served to 'delude mens mindes, to make them put their faith in our Lady, & in other Saints, and not in God alone'.[9]

These are startlingly specific responses to material like that in British Library MS Additional 37049, where Marian images and texts pivot on a

---

4   See Boyd, *Middle English Miracles*, pp. xi, 10; Whiteford, *Myracles of Oure Lady*, p. 20; and Wright, 'Durham Play of Mary and the Poor Knight', p. 254. For a general account of the destruction and dispersal of English texts, see R. M. Wilson, *The Lost Literature of Medieval England* (London, 1952).

5   Restrictions generally focused on service books or texts explicitly associated with Wycliffe, Luther, or Zwingli. See, for instance, the 1530 'Proclamation against erroneous books and heresies' and the 1550 'Act for the abolishing and putting away of divers books and images' in C. H. Williams, ed., *English Historical Documents 1485–1558* (London, 1967), pp. 829–32, 853–4; and 'The names of the bookes that were forbidden at this tyme, together with the new Testament' in Foxe, *A&M*, bk 8, pp. 1157–8 (1570 edition).

6   See Chapter 2, pp. 47–8.

7   Karant-Nunn and Wiesner-Hanks, *Luther on Women*, p. 37.

8   Foxe, *A&M*, bk 11, pp. 1309, 1310 (1563 edition).

9   Ibid., bk 8, p. 1140 (1570 edition).

judgment that sometimes appears to bypass Christ and, at the same time, confront even a learned church father (St Ignatius of Antioch) with the possibility that 'no oþer god had bene bot sche'.[10] Still, MS Additional 37049 was a semi-private devotional production – obviously never attacked or censured despite its clear status as a book of what John Foxe would later call 'monkish miracles & grosse fables'[11] – and the question of how and to what degree *written* stories of miracles might have been targeted in the reform decades is extremely difficult to assess. The destruction of English images, texts, and sites associated with the apparatus of Catholicism, detailed most carefully by Eamon Duffy,[12] implicates the cult of saints, liturgical and polemical texts, public shrines, and the possessions of activists; but how could anyone effectively control or gather preachers' books, miscellanies, private collections, or semi-literary anthologies? Or, in what sense could these 'universal' stories of Marian intercession be counted among the ruins of local shrines or the ashes of associated legendaries and liturgical books? To what degree, indeed, was Mary herself subjected to the same censure as the larger cult of saints? While reformers criticized fine distinctions between *dulia* and *hyperdulia* as incoherent, Mary was very rarely subject to any unqualified attack, in England or elsewhere. Unlike other saints, she was unquestionably worthy of honor and praise; she remained the virgin mother of God and an example of holy behavior. Luther called her a symbol of 'Christianity after the synagogue',[13] and she was, in the sixteenth century, resituated as a model of obedience and faith, even while misguided popular beliefs about her position and power were openly derided.[14]

The process and discoveries of the dissolution of the monasteries, however, made what Miri Rubin has called England's 'disengagement from Mary' one particularly concentrated on the examination of miracles.[15] The many well-known miraculous Marian shrines in England – particularly the shrine of Our Lady of Walsingham – made useful tools for demagoguery, and ambiva-

---

[10] Appendix 3, 'Blessed Face and Name', lines 12–13.

[11] Foxe, *A&M*, bk 1, p. 112 (1570 edition).

[12] *The Stripping of the Altars: Traditional Religion in England, c.1400–c.1580* (New Haven, CT, and London, 1992). On the path of reform in England, see also James Simpson, *Reform and Cultural Revolution*, Oxford English Literary History 2 (Oxford, 2002); Margaret Aston, *England's Iconoclasts, I: Laws against Images* (Oxford, 1988); and Anne Hudson, *The Premature Reformation: Wycliffite Texts and Lollard History* (Oxford, 1988). On restrictions put on the circulation and printing of texts, see Alec Ryrie, *The Gospel and Henry VIII: Evangelicals in the Early English Reformation*, Cambridge Studies in Early Modern History (Cambridge, 2003); and Brian Cummings, 'Reformed Literature and Literature Reformed', *The Cambridge History of Medieval English Literature*, ed. David Wallace (Cambridge, 1999), pp. 821–51.

[13] Karant-Nunn and Wiesner-Hanks, *Luther on Women*, p. 44.

[14] On reform attitudes toward the Virgin Mary, see Christine Peters, *Patterns of Piety: Women, Gender and Religion in Late Medieval and Reformation England*, Cambridge Studies in Early Modern History (Cambridge, 2003), pp. 60–96, 207–45; Karant-Nunn and Wiesner-Hanks, *Luther on Women*, pp. 32–57; and Beth Kreitzer, *Reforming Mary: Changing Images of the Virgin Mary in Lutheran Sermons of the Sixteenth Century*, Oxford Studies in Historical Theology (Oxford, 2004).

[15] *Mother of God*, p. 376.

lence about such places clearly existed even by the late fourteenth century. It has often been repeated that the prologue of *Piers Plowman* satirically describes the 'Eremites on an hep' who 'Wenten to Walsyngham',[16] and that Lollards called the statue of Mary there 'the wyche of Walsingham'.[17] In 1429, Margery Baxter derided the shrine as 'our Lady of Falsingame', and by the 1530s, Bilney had apparently claimed, with some specificity, that 'the miracles done at Walsingham and Canterbury & there in Ipswitch [another Marian shrine] were done by the deuill ... to blind the pore people'.[18] These few examples, however, also show that the focus of contempt was on local abuses, the shrines and associated images or relics, and on the miracle *event* rather than the written account.

Both the association of Marian miracles with shrines and the usefulness of the term 'miracle' in describing a written genre are pertinent here. No English shrine leaves behind narratives of Marian miracles associated with the site, and while I am by no means claiming that available records reflect the situation just as it was, it is notable by comparison that many twelfth- and thirteenth-century collections survive from Marian shrines in northern France, where activity around relics and images had motivated large compilations of Miracles of the Virgin. These survive from Chartres, Laon, Pierre-sur-Dives, Soissons, and Rocamadour. A similar number of English Marian shrines existed throughout the Middle Ages – certainly at Ipswich, Worcester, Doncaster, and Penrice, as well as Walsingham[19] – and it is not impossible that these also inspired written accounts of miracles performed around them. Even if they did, however, we would expect to find miracles of a very different type than those discussed in the previous chapters. Philologists have long separated Miracles of the Virgin into two types – 'general' and 'local', or 'universal' and 'local', sometimes 'popular' or 'local' – and the content of the local narratives is, as Southern put it, 'generally very different from the type of story which formed the foundation of the popular Mary legends' and exerts 'no influence on the early development of these [general] legends'.[20]

16 Derek Pearsall, ed., *Piers Plowman by William Langland: An Edition of the C-Text*, York Medicval Texts (Berkeley and Los Angeles, 1978), Prologue, pp. 51–2.
17 See J. C. Dickinson, *The Shrine of Our Lady of Walsingham* (Cambridge, 1956), p. 27. Hudson, *Premature Reformation*, p. 76 and n. 303, also notes Thomas of Walsingham's emphasis on the Lollards' particular hostility toward the Walsingham shrine.
18 Foxe, *A&M*, bk 3, p. 473 (1563 edition).
19 In June 1538, Latimer suggested that 'Our great Sibyll [the Marian statue at Worcester]' together with 'her older sister of Walsingham, her younger sister of Ipswich, with their two sisters of Doncaster and Penrice' would make 'a jolly muster at Smithfield', the infamous site of the burning of heretics. See Duffy, *Stripping of the Altars*, p. 404.
20 'English Origins', p. 178. A useful summary of the French local collections is given in Ward, *Miracles and the Medieval Mind*, pp. 132–65. The Rocamadour miracles have been translated by Marcus Bull, *The Miracles of Our Lady of Rocamadour: Analysis and Translation* (Woodbridge, 1999). For the others, see Antoine Thomas, ed., 'Les miracles de Notre-Dame de Chartres', *Bibliothèque de l'école des Chartes* 42 (1881), pp. 505–50; Hugo Farsitus, 'Libellus de miraculis B. Mariae Virginis in urbe Suessionensi' *PL* 179, pp. 1777–800; and Herman of Tournai, 'De miraculis S. Mariae Laudunensis, de gestis venerabilis Bartholomaei episcopi et S. Norberti libri tres', *PL* 156, pp. 961–1018.

While some continental collections mix the types,[21] the local miracles are most often codicologically distinct and are concerned to document healings facilitated by a particular image or relic (the Soissons miracles, for instance, recount how Mary's slipper saved many deaf, blind, mute, and lame pilgrims who made their way to the shrine). Such texts were overtly propagandistic and thus may indeed have attracted the attention of commissioners inspecting shrines or pilgrimage sites.

As to whether reformers spoke about 'miracles' as a written genre, both Paul Strohm's examination of genre categories and John Foxe's use of the term are helpful. Strohm argues that the late medieval understanding of 'miraculum' and 'miracle' was 'hardly ever specifically generic' and most frequently evoked an event rather than a narrative.[22] When the English term does describe a genre, it refers to the kinds of narratives that are the topic of this book and survive in droves: the 'large, popular, and somewhat scrappy collections of *exempla*, *gesta*, and *narrationes* which arose for the assistance of sermon writers and the edification of general readers', and sometimes in a sequence of Miracles of the Virgin that call up the notional book of sources discussed in Chapter 1.[23] If we then look to Foxe's *Acts and Monuments*, we see that some ambivalence persists. When William Thorpe was examined before Archbishop Arundel in 1407, according to Foxe, he drew a distinction between the church 'doctors, how they *speke & write* of miracles' and 'þe miracles þat now are *done* [my italics]', and he connected the miracles that people 'here & know' not to text but rather to 'tokens' and 'Images ... shewed or painted'.[24] When Henry VIII wrote to Thomas Cranmer in October 1542 that he had ordered the seizure of 'Images & bones ... & all such *wrytings* & monumentes of fained miracles', he wrote because his orders had *not* been carried out (probably those set out in his 1536 injunction), and his renewal of the request, as entered by Foxe, omitted 'wrytings' and specified rather 'any shrine, couering of shrine, table, *monument of miracles* or other pilgrimages [my italics]'.[25]

The only record of any specific attention to a large collection of Marian miracles (possibly a vernacular one) during the reform era comes in a single letter to Thomas Cromwell from Richard Layton. Reporting on his 1535 visitations of Monk Farleigh, Wiltshire, a cell of Lewes, and Bath Abbey, Dr Layton noted that he was sending to Cromwell, along with other seized items, 'a book of Our Lady's miracles, well able to match the Canterbury Tales;

21 For example, Berkeley, Bancroft Library MS BANC UCB 92 begins with a partial copy of the Soissons miracles that is followed by general miracles (see my 'Anti-Jewish Parody around Miracles of the Virgin?'), and Alfonso X's *Cantigas de Santa Maria* includes many examples derived from local collections (see *CSMD*).
22 Strohm, 'Passioun, Lyf, Miracle, Legende', p. 158 (part 2).
23 Ibid., p. 69 (part 1), p. 159 (part 2). In Chapter 1, see pp. 13–18.
24 Foxe, *A&M*, bk 2, p. 158 (1563 edition).
25 Ibid., bk 3, p. 629.

such a book of dreams as you never saw, which I found in the library'.[26] But much is unclear about the nature and fate of this collection: we do not know from which library it came, nor in what language it was written, nor exactly what Cromwell might have done with it. That Layton connects it to the *Canterbury Tales* may indicate that it is an English-language book, but it may also be a comment on the length of the book, or on its status as fiction ('a book of dreams'). Clearly he associates the book with other suspect items – he sends with it a 'Vincula of S. Petrus' and three combs used by female saints (Mary Magdalene, Dorothy, and Margaret), which he believes to be fakes – but, for all this, we do not know that the book was destroyed. Layton merely submits the items to 'judgment and to the King's pleasure'.[27]

The endless and varied possibilities are part of the scholar's problem, and were also at the time of the dissolution of the monasteries. John Bale and John Leland, who were assigned the work of cataloguing and examining books of monastic libraries, were certainly more anxious to preserve than to remove or destroy them.[28] Leland wrote to Cromwell in 1536 asking for his help in transferring manuscripts to the Royal Library,[29] and Bale famously lamented the loss of English books as a destruction 'without consyderacyon' and 'a most horryble infamy amonge the graue senyours of other nacyons'.[30] In 1560, he made a similar complaint in a private letter to Matthew Parker, Archbishop of Canterbury, and detailed his struggle to retrieve dispersed manuscripts 'in stacyoners and bokebyndeers store howses, some in grosers, sope sellers, taylers, and other occupyers shoppes, some in shyppes ready to be carried over the sea into Flaunders to be solde'.[31] Neither Bale nor Leland were concerned that royal commissioners were seizing books; rather, the problem was the lack of official attention. Books were abandoned and taken by people with no concern for their content. They were sold for parts or relinquished to foreign nations, and the infamy of England was in the passive decision to proceed 'without consyderacyon'.

---

[26] G. H. Cook, ed., *Letters to Cromwell and Others on the Suppression of the Monasteries* (London, 1965), p. 38.

[27] Ibid., pp. 37–8.

[28] For general discussions of the dissolution and the dispersal of the monastic libraries, see C. E. Wright, 'The Dispersal of the Libraries in the Sixteenth Century', *The English Library Before 1700*, eds Francis Wormald and C. E. Wright (London, 1958), pp. 148–75; Joyce Youings, *The Dissolution of the Monasteries*, Historical Problems: Studies and Documents 14 (London, 1971); and R. H. Fritze, '"Truth Hath Lacked Witnesse, Tyme Wanted Light": The Dispersal of the English Monastic Libraries and Protestant Efforts at Preservation, ca. 1535–1625', *Journal of Library History* 18.3 (1983), pp. 274–91. On Leland's life and work, see Simpson, *Reform and Cultural Revolution*, pp. 7–33; J. P. Carley, 'John Leland and the Contents of English Pre-Dissolution Libraries: Glastonbury Abbey', *Scriptorium* 40 (1986), pp. 107–20; 'John Leland at Somerset Libraries', *Somerset Archeology and Natural History* 129 (1985), pp. 141–4; and the bibliography provided by John Chandler, ed., *John Leland's Itinerary: Travels in Tudor England* (Stroud, 1993), pp. xxxiv–vi.

[29] Wright, 'Dispersal of the Libraries', p. 153.

[30] Quoted in ibid., pp. 153–4.

[31] Ibid., pp. 153–4.

A brief (admittedly unsystematic) look at pre- and post-dissolution library catalogues in fact shows that catalogued Miracles of the Virgin do not contradict the surviving evidence. There are two collections of Miracles of the Virgin ('miracula beate marie') in Peterborough's pre-dissolution records, but one is an item in a large religious miscellany, and the other is a self-contained Anglo-Norman ('gallice') collection, which may be, or may be related to, one of the three surviving Anglo-Norman collections.[32] At Worcester Cathedral, whose Marian shrine was among those Latimer wanted burned,[33] Leland catalogued only eleven of the more than 300 codices listed in the pre-dissolution catalogue, but the pre-dissolution list contains no record whatsoever of Miracles of the Virgin.[34] While contemporary witness does, in the Worcester case, provide information about the physical destruction of service books – under the year 1549, an anonymous chronicler wrote, 'This year all bookes of devine service brought to the bisshopp of the sea: videlicet liggers, massebookes, Grailes, pies, portuasses, legendes, and all thees and many others were burnt'[35] – it is not clear that Miracles of the Virgin fit any of these categories. The inclusion in this account of 'legendes' may suggest that some semi-liturgical Marian narratives were destroyed,[36] but the fact that there is no catalogue record of a Marian miracle book at a Marian shrine site before the dissolution is more instructive.

The pre-dissolution catalogue compiled at Syon between 1500 and 1524, on the other hand, contains nearly 1,500 volumes and shows six different listings for Marian miracles – itemized as 'miracula beate marie', or 'mariale de naraccionibus & miraculis gloriose uirginis', or 'diuersa miracula beate marie' – but each of these comprises a text of unknown length *within a miscellany*.[37] Likewise, though the surviving catalogue of gifts made to the library of the Carthusian Abbey of Witham between 1463 and 1474 shows two listings for 'miracula beate marie', one is an item contained in a large anthology of religious and secular material, and the other is a Latin collection that may in fact be extant.[38] It is not obvious, in other words, that Marian

---

32   See Kirsten Friis-Jensen and James M. W. Willoughby, eds, *Peterborough Abbey*, Corpus of British Medieval Library Catalogues (London, 2001), items BP21.255j and BP21.310. For details on the Anglo-Norman manuscripts, see above, p. 5 n. 23.

33   Duffy, *Stripping of the Altars*, p. 404.

34   See R. M. Thomson, *A Descriptive Catalogue of the Medieval Manuscripts in Worcester Cathedral Library* (Cambridge, 2001).

35   Quoted in ibid., p. xxxvii.

36   Strohm, 'Passioun, Lyf, Miracle, Legende', p. 162 (part 2), also notes that, at the end of the Middle Ages at least, 'the term *legende* was simply not generally used to describe Middle English hagiographical collections' and referred more often to the *Legenda aurea* specifically (though there are some ambiguities).

37   See Vincent Gillespie, ed., *Syon Abbey, with the Libraries of the Carthusians*, Corpus of British Medieval Library Catalogues (London, 2001), items SS1.844a, SS1.1104b, SS1.645c, SS1.646b, SS1.646, and SS1.981d.

38   Ibid., items C8.15e and C8.31. The latter is labeled 'Miraculorum regine celi' and may be one of the Latin collections listed in Ward, *Catalogue of Romances*, pp. 586–94 (to which Gillespie refers readers).

miracles ever existed in England in a way radically different from what the surviving corpus shows, that is, as popular items for miscellanies, as Latin and sometimes Anglo-Norman collections, as small groupings within larger compilations, or as *exempla* and *narrationes* in sermons.

Arguments from absence are, of course, difficult at best, but such arguments work on both sides in this case, and it is a truism that absence of proof does not mean proof of absence. Moreover, derision or excision of written Marian miracles – in the only two instances in which I know it occurs – could do more to draw attention to these narratives than erase them from historical knowledge. The twelfth-century miscellany British Library, MS Cotton Cleopatra C. X, for instance, includes among other Latin historical and religious works a collection of forty Latin Miracles of the Virgin, similar to the many Latin collections that circulated in England throughout the Middle Ages that do show a clear relationship to the originary monastic collections that R. W. Southern studied.[39] Several *nota* marks of various dates are in the margins, and on two folios near the end of the collection a sixteenth-century hand has written hostile comments in clear, large print across the top margin: on fol. 133v, 'falsa Miracula falsae dominae' (the false miracles of a false mistress), and on fol. 135v, 'The false Miracula off oure Lady'.[40] The sentiment is clear enough, but the vandal looks more like a reader here, and one who expects future readers at that. The reformer's labels mark the miracles and act as invitations to read them (rather than destroy them) as evidence of Catholic superstition.[41]

This is not unlike Foxe's discussion of the miracle narratives he finds in pre-Conquest saints' lives, which he dismisses as 'lying miracles, falsely forged' or worse, but nevertheless frequently comments that he will simply omit them, or refers his reader to the source texts so that they may judge for themselves.[42] In the case of St Dunstan (Archbishop of Canterbury 960–78), he is so disgusted by 'false & lying miracles' that he cannot 'let passe to speake something of theyr lying' and so proceeds to recount the stories (in summary), including even a very common Marian miracle, 'St Dunstan and the Virgin's Choir', which appears in William of Malmesbury's collection and

---

[39] This collection in fact begins with Dominic of Evesham's 'Elements Series'. It is part of the discussion of Dominic's organization of his miracle collection in Chapter 2 above, pp. 66–7.

[40] The Marian miracles occupy fols 101r–144v. The other *nota* marks on these folios do not appear to be of the same period, and the only other mark in the same script, on the outer margin of fol. 135v, appears to be a pen trial. Neuhaus, *Lateinischen Vorlagen*, lists the contents of the collection (pp. 1–3) and edits some of its miracles as related to the Anglo-Norman examples.

[41] At work here is a thought process similar to the one that creates Augustine's doctrine of Jewish witness, where Jews and Jewish texts must be preserved as evidence of Christian prophecy to facilitate the end of days (see Cohen, *Living Letters of the Law*, pp. 23–65). On the Reformation tendency to compare Catholicism to Judaism, and on Foxe in particular, see Sharon Achinstein, 'John Foxe and the Jews', *Renaissance Quarterly* 54.1 (2001), pp. 86–120.

[42] This is the case, for example, in his discussions of SS Cecilia, Eugenia, Alban, and Oswald. See Foxe, *A&M*, bk 1, pp. 73, 92–3, 112 (1570 edition), and bk 2, p. 163 (1570 edition).

in his *Gesta Pontificam* (to which Foxe more likely had access).[43] What he has in front of him, Foxe says, tells 'how our Lady with her fellowes appeared visibly to hym [Dunstan], singyng this song: Cantemus Domino, sociæ, cantemus honorem. Dulcis amor Christi personet ore pio. Agayne, how the Aungels appeared to him singyng the Hymne called Kyrie Rex splendens. &c.'[44] The hymns of Mary's choir match very closely extant versions of the legend,[45] and Foxe's marginal gloss marks the miracle for further attention: 'the Papistes shame not to ascribe other mens verses also to Mary her selfe.'[46] This paradoxical preservation impulse is likewise evident in British Library MS Stowe 949, a partial *South English Legendary* (one of the four containing the Founding of the Feast of Mary's Conception, along with an apocryphal 'Nativity of Mary and Christ'), which contains a note that it was 'founde apon a donghyll' in the sixteenth century, apparently 'only rescued in order that its contents might demonstrate the worst excesses of medieval religiosity'.[47]

The only non-conjectural example of a 'lost' collection of vernacular Marian miracles is in the large late fourteenth-century Vernon manuscript (Bodleian Library, MS Eng. Poet. a.1), which once included, amidst scores of other Middle English works, a finely illustrated verse collection of forty-one Miracles of the Virgin, of which only eight full narratives and nine illustrations survive (fols 124r–126v).[48] But this too is an example of a 'reformed' codex that paradoxically preserves evidence of what existed and of how it was received. The excision of Marian miracles and images in this case certainly appears to reflect a desire to rid the manuscript of its most ostentatious examples of superstitious worship: 'someone methodically went through the volume from contents-list to end crossing out or erasing the word "pope" and texts relating to St Thomas of Canterbury', and other items were likely removed at this time 'because they contained texts or pictures condemned by Protestant reformers'.[49] Nevertheless, the contemporary contents list details

---

[43] See Carter, 'Historical Content', p. 134. Foxe, *A&M*, explicitly discusses his use of William, whose hagiography he dismisses as 'more legendlike then truthlike' and typical of 'Monkysh story writers' See bk 1, p. 112 (1570 edition), and bk 3, p. 206 (1570 edition).

[44] Foxe, *A&M*, bk 3, p. 206 (1570 edition).

[45] For William of Malmesbury's version of the miracle, see Canal, *El libro de laudibus*, pp. 79–81. On other versions, see index item 'St Dunstan and the Virgin's Choir' in Appendix 4.

[46] Foxe, *A&M*, bk 3, p. 206 (1570 edition).

[47] Thorlac Turville-Petre, review of O. S. Pickering's *The South English Nativity of Mary and Christ*, *Modern Language Review* 73.4 (1978), p. 870. My thanks to Gary Kuchar for suggesting this line of argument by pointing out that it was in fact common for anti-Catholic reformers to preserve or reprint Catholic materials. Professor Kuchar associated it with his work on Richard Crashaw, whose father William printed and translated Jesuit Marian poems to refute them as heretical and disgusting. See *Divine Subjection: The Rhetoric of Sacramental Devotion in Early Modern England* (Pittsburgh, 2005), Chapter 2.

[48] See Carol Meale, 'The Miracles of Our Lady: Context and Interpretation', *Studies in the Vernon Manuscript*, ed. Derek Pearsall (Cambridge, 1990), pp. 115–36. Though the original collection is often described as a compilation of forty-two miracles, Meale correctly notes that one narrative cited in the contents list has been erroneously divided into two (p. 117 n. 10).

[49] Doyle, *The Vernon Manuscript*, p. 11.

the nature of the Marian miracle collection and allows comparison with the style and content of other extant miracles,[50] and the remnant confuses the notion of a careful reform 'vandal' considerably. If the goal was to excise this kind of Marian material, why ignore the three folios that remain?

Anthony Bale has considered that the content of the surviving Vernon miracles may have something to do with their preservation, and his hypothesis is especially interesting in relation to what I have argued are conspicuous and influential themes in English examples of Marian miracles. Three of the surviving complete tales and illustrations are anti-Semitic – this out of four anti-Semitic miracles originally in the collection – and these include a version of 'The Jewish Boy of Bourges', the story of 'The Child Slain by Jews' (an analogue of 'The Prioress's Tale'), and the story of 'The Merchant's Surety' (discussed in Chapter 1).[51] Moreover, the surviving tales are organized so that one of the related illustrations appears on each of the three remaining folios (124v, 125r, and 126r). With this observation, Bale asks provisionally, 'Was antisemitism acceptable for a Reformation audience where Marian "idolatry" was not? Was the image of the Jew the common ground between Catholic and Protestant? … What we can say is that the Reformation reconfiguration of the [Vernon] book left the disesteemed Jewish *topos* intact and largely undiminished.'[52] Indeed, as Bale points out, the codex contains 'a range of fictive Jews' in other contexts, including in the *Northern Homily Cycle* version of the Theophilus legend (fols 203v–205r).[53] It also contains a range of Marian devotional texts that show Mary in her capacity as 'a contemporary force for good in the lives of individual Christians',[54] and these include 'Salutacioun' verses that emphasize Mary's role as a legal intercessor, just as 'Theophilus' and the story of 'The Merchant's Surety' do.

In one Vernon 'Salutacioun to Vre Lady', Mary is the legal document personified. A series of greetings that echo the 'Ave Maria' includes:

> Heil Chartre, þat Ihesus gon a-sele:
> ffor vs, ladi, to þi sone þou pray
> Þat at þe dredful domus-day

---

[50] The remaining narratives show variation in verse form and in tone, and therefore seem to witness multiple authors and sources. See Meale, 'Miracles of Our Lady', pp. 117–20. The titles of the miracles as they appear in the contents list are printed in Horstmann, *Minor Poems*, pp. 138–9.

[51] See Chapter 1, pp. 29–32. The fourth is titled in the contents list 'hou at þe cite of Tholuse þe priuetes were knowe of Iewes' (where it is listed twenty-ninth in the series, see Horstmann, *Minor Poems*, p. 138). This may be related to William of Malmesbury's story of the Jews of Toulouse (see Chapter 2, p. 69), or to the story of the Jews of Toledo (see Chapter 2, pp. 71–2 and Appendix 4).

[52] Bale, *The Jew in the Medieval Book*, p. 77.

[53] The Vernon Theophilus has been edited by Eugen Kölbing, *Englische Studien*, I (Paris and London, 1877), pp. 38–57.

[54] N. F. Blake, 'Vernon Manuscript: Contents and Organisation', *Studies in the Vernon Manuscript*, ed. Derek Pearsall (Cambridge, 1990), p. 50. More specifically, Blake notes that the entire 'second part [of the manuscript] deals essentially with the Virgin Mary, her life and the help she may give to all Christians who seek her protection'.

Vre a-vokes þat ȝe may be,
ffor non oþur þen help us may
Saue þi-self and þi swete sone fre.[55]

Mary alone acts as a defense attorney ('a-vokes') on Judgment Day, and the conflation of this with the appellation that turns her into a charter means that she simultaneously embodies the saving document that she can offer to the judge (her 'swete sone fre') on a sinner's behalf. Or, in a second 'Salutacioun to Vre Lady' that makes explicit the influences that inspire the 'Heil Chartre' lines, Mary accomplishes her legal intercession through sheer physical strength:

Blessed beo, ladi, þi grete strengþe:
…
Þou holdest þe fend vndur foote,
Þou geete from his herte-Rote
    Theophules lettre, þe Clerk.[56]

In this example, the poet has praised each part of Mary's body (her breasts, her thighs, her ears, and on), and her retrieval of Theophilus's charter is as much a fact of her identity and claim on devotion as her virginity, or her womb that bore Christ, or her ears that received the Annunciation and the Holy Spirit – all of which are also celebrated in this poem.

An ability to connect the surviving Vernon miracles to other items in this codex – whether through anti-Semitic content or through the characterization of Mary as a mediator in legal disputes (both meet in 'The Merchant's Surety') – means that the Vernon manuscript examples are not antithetical to my arguments. This reading of 'Reformation reconfiguration' makes the lines of development I have outlined not random but more emphatic; the alteration of this manuscript is a product of choice, and of awareness of generic subsets that can be read and understood as meaningful, as excerptable, and as coherent within their miscellany context, albeit differently depending on shifting historical and cultural situations. If the Vernon manuscript is the quintessential example of the vernacular collections of Miracles of the Virgin that may have been lost to Reformation statutes or reformers' zeal, it is also an example of a book that sets its Marian miracles in relation to other religious texts with similar thematic concerns and Marian characterizations, as it is an object lesson in where a methodical reformer might have stopped short or even revealed late medieval organizations and understandings of the genre. Of course, we cannot know the motivations of any individual reader (and it bears stating that we do not even know with certainty that the thirty-two missing Vernon miracles were excised as part of a reform program), but,

---

[55] Horstmann, *Minor Poems*, p. 136, lines 91–6.
[56] Ibid., p. 130, lines 373–8.

whatever the circumstances of the loss, the legal and anti-Semitic rhetoric of Marian devotion remains also in this example, as do traces of the mechanisms by which Marian miracles might be reconfigured within, and absorb, varying local contexts and ideological agendas.[57]

Chaucer's Miracle of the Virgin

The reform era's most severe limitation on English-language texts came with Henry VIII's 1543 'Act for the Advancement of True Religion and for the Abolishment of the Contrary', a document that betrayed just how potentially all-inclusive its prohibitions were by making allowance for texts that were *not* to fall within its scope.[58] It provided explicitly for the protection of 'the Kings Hieghnes proclamacions iniunctions, translacions of the Pater noster, the Aue Maria and the Crede, the psalters prymers prayer statutes and lawes of the Realme, Cronycles Canterburye tales, Chaucers bokes Gowers bokes and stories of mennes lieues'.[59] This is an interesting group: a list of legal texts, liturgical and perhaps philosophical translations, historiography, and 'literary' (mainly poetic) texts. The *Canterbury Tales* were presumably protectable in part because they were understood as fiction, in part because they were already marked as high English literature, but their position in the list (in fact separated from Chaucer's authorship) affords them an ideologically similar status to the officially mandated prayers and laws of the realm. At the same time, the Act created a situation in which any work ascribed to Chaucer (correctly or incorrectly) could be circulated regardless of its genre or religious content – and one of the things that circulated under Chaucer's name was a fairly typical English iteration of a Marian miracle, known within the *Canterbury Tales* as 'The Prioress's Tale' and otherwise as a version of the 'Child Slain by Jews' story.

As Robert Worth Frank, Jr. pointed out decades ago, amidst a cacophony of critical voices experimenting with the idea that 'The Prioress's Tale' was satiric or ironic, Chaucer was participating in 'the history of [a] genre' when he wrote it.[60] Whether a Marian miracle was 'the illusion of Sathan' (as Bilney

---

57 See also Bale's reading of the 'Miracle of the boy singer' ('Child Slain by Jews') in *The Jew in the Medieval Book*, pp. 76–81, which fits here as a Marian intervention that pivots on a 'legal and material entity' (p. 81).

58 Cummings discusses the long reach of the act in 'Reformed Literature', pp. 842–3. See also Duffy, *Stripping of the Altars*, pp. 432–3.

59 Quoted in C. F. E. Spurgeon, ed., *Five Hundred Years of Chaucer Criticism and Allusion, 1357–1900* (New York, 1960), pp. 84–5.

60 'Miracles of the Virgin, Medieval Anti-Semitism, and the "Prioress's Tale"', p. 178. Frank responds particularly to Florence H. Ridley, *The Prioress and the Critics*, University of California English Studies 30 (Berkeley and Los Angeles, 1965), and her review of criticism on pp. 1–4. More recent surveys and commentaries on the place of 'The Prioress's Tale' within the corpus of Miracles of the Virgin can be found in Boyd, *The Prioress's Tale*, pp. 19–22, 27–50; Stephen Spector, 'Empathy and Enmity in "The Prioress's Tale"', *The Olde Daunce: Love, Friendship, Sex, and Marriage in the Medieval World*, eds Robert R. Edwards and Stephen Spector (Albany,

claimed), or could at least sometimes fall into the categories of 'chronicle' (as it had for William of Malmesbury and Foxe) or 'stories of mennes lieues' (saints' lives? Theophilus?), or indeed *Canterbury Tales*, depended on perceptions of the genre. And by the time Chaucer was working with the form, and then into the sixteenth century, Marian miracles seem to have been uneasily positioned in a middle space between entertainment and devotion. It is evident that they had a literary appeal that was separate from the belief- or truth-claims that shrines, relics, or liturgical texts held, but they could also elicit different responses depending on their contexts.

Both because of 'The Prioress's Tale' and because of the scant piece of Marian devotional poetry he left behind, we can see that Chaucer fully embraced a characterization of the Virgin Mary as a legal advocate with special attachment to gestures of written conveyance. His single surviving devotional poem – 'An ABC', as it is known – is an abecedarian adapted from a prayer in *Le pèlerinage de la vie humaine* of the Cistercian writer Guillaume de Deguileville, and Chaucer's version of it is notable because of its use of legal terminology and emphasis on the image of the court of law.[61] He sets the piece as one in which the penitent's sin has brought an action against him, and he calls on Mary as the only lawyer who can win his acquittal: 'But merci, ladi, at the grete assyse / Whan we shule come bifore the hye justyse.'[62] Chaucer's is a particularly vivid estimation of this mode of intercession. By using the word 'assyse', he links Mary not only to the Last Judgment but to the English judicial system, to the Great (or Grand) Assize created by Henry II to replace trials by battle and provide national institutional structure for the new forms of written law. He sets Mary within the royal court that presided over all inquests, criminal and civil, and which was synonymous with the document (the 'writ of assize') that initiated legal action.[63]

The poem's penitent pleads with Mary to remind Christ that 'with his precious blood he wrot the bille / Upon the crois as general aquitaunce', and to realize that she should therefore be able to 'stinte al his grevaunce'

NY, 1991), pp. 216–18; and Broughton, 'The Prioress's Prologue and Tale', especially pp. 592–8. On satire and anti-Semitism in the tale, see Patterson, '"Living Witnesses of Our Redemption"'; Emmy Stark Zitter, 'Anti-Semitism in Chaucer's *Prioress's Tale*', *The Chaucer Review* 25.4 (1991), pp. 277–84; John Archer, 'The Structure of Anti-Semitism in the *Prioress's Tale*', *The Chaucer Review* 19.1 (1985), pp. 46–54; Denise L. Despres, 'Cultic Anti-Judaism and Chaucer's Litel Clergeon', *Modern Philology* 91 (1994), pp. 413–27; Louise O. Fradenburg, 'Criticism, Anti-Semitism, and the *Prioress's Tale*', *Exemplaria* 1 (1989), pp. 69–115; and Dahood, 'Punishment of the Jews'.

61 See G. R. Crampton, 'Chaucer's Singular Prayer', *MÆ* 59 (1990), pp. 191–213; Helen Phillips, 'Chaucer and Deguileville: The "ABC" in Context', *MÆ* 62 (1993), pp. 1–27; and Alexander Weiss, *Chaucer's Native Heritage* (New York, 1985), pp. 125–70.

62 Benson, *Riverside*, p. 638, lines 36–7.

63 *MED*, *s.v.* 'assise', 1a and 1b. Definition '2' reflects Chaucer's use of the term (as Last Judgment), but all similar uses post-date 'An ABC'. On Henry II and the institution of the Grand Assize, see A. L. Poole, *From Domesday Book to Magna Carta, 1087–1216* (Oxford, 1951), pp. 406–13.

and 'make oure foo to failen'.[64] Christ's good-faith 'bille' appears nowhere in Chaucer's source, but it is a central feature of his extended conceit. The writ of 'general aquitaunce' renders Christ a Theophilan character who can save through legal action, while Mary maintains her (now expected) role as the mediator in legal action that can be validated or invalidated because of a document, or can simply conquer the Devil. Chaucer in fact asserts that this is the role assigned to Mary by God, who promoted her for the express purpose: 'From his ancille he made the maistresse / Of hevene and erthe, oure bille up for to beede.'[65] That is, Mary holds divine power precisely in order that she might offer up the writ of Christ, who 'represseth his justise / After thi [Mary's] wil'.[66] 'An ABC' is a celebration both of her royalty and of the practical reality of what her legal advocacy means for the average (English) sinner. One of Mary's chief virtues as a lawyer, as Chaucer has it, is that she can be had for only a small fee: 'We han ... advocat noon ... for litel hire as yee / That helpen for an Ave-Marie or tweye.'[67] The cost alludes to the common miracle formula of 'The Monk Who Could Learn Only Ave Maria', told in the *South English Legendary* and in many other places in many iterations,[68] and it self-referentially relates also to the poem itself – a Chaucerian bargain with Mary. The broken rhyme and meter in lines 39–40, which include the hope that, lest 'Of verray right my werk wol me confounde', Mary 'correcte' or 'chastyse' something (manuscript witnesses widely disagree, early scribes clearly making the correction themselves), may be a clever gesture that binds Mary to her poet-devotee. It is possible that Chaucer intentionally left something in his work for Mary to correct.[69]

'The Prioress's Tale' is likewise an exploration of Mary's dominion over matters textual and legal, a case study of the implications of these modes of intercession, especially where they intersect with a 'Jewish problem', but this exploration explicitly involves the reception of Miracles of the Virgin, an issue built into the very framework of the *Tales*. The pilgrims' response to a Marian miracle of murder and punishment is ambiguous at best, and generic confusion is embedded in Chaucer's imagination of its immediate reception:

> Whan seyd was al this miracle, every man
> As sobre was that wonder was to se,
> Til that oure Hooste japen tho bigan,
> And thanne at erst he looked upon me,
> And seyd thus: 'What man artow?' quod he.[70]

---

64 Benson, *Riverside*, p. 638, lines 59–60, 63–4.
65 Ibid., p. 639, lines 109–10.
66 Ibid., lines 142–3.
67 Ibid., lines 100–4.
68 See pp. 91–2 above, and 'The Monk Who Could Learn Only Ave Maria' in Appendix 4.
69 I am grateful to Jennifer Miller for sharing this incisive reading with me. On the textual variants, see Benson, *Riverside*, p. 1185 (note for line 39).
70 Benson, *Riverside*, CT VII.691–5.

Critics have offered variable interpretations of the word 'sobre',[71] but these lines reveal almost nothing about the range of possible reactions. It may be that Chaucer intended only an ambiguous gravity. Yet this remains our best window into what force an exceptionally thoughtful medieval writer assigned to a Marian miracle, if not to the genre of which it was a part, and we can say at least that the tale creates an uncomfortable moment, only partially relieved by Harry Bailly's awkward joviality. It is, furthermore, the singular narrative that prompts the Host to look for the first time to the pilgrim Chaucer and demand, 'What man artow?' 'The Prioress's Tale' invites examination of the *author's* character and intentions, albeit displaced by his fictional persona, and this puts a special emphasis on Miracles of the Virgin in the context of the *Canterbury Tales*.

'The Prioress's Tale' is not only part of the 'literature group' (Fragment VII) that includes Chaucer's most explicit discussion of genre and literary valuation;[72] it is the piece that necessitates the discussion. It is here that the tale-telling game breaks down: the pilgrims are frozen in an uncomfortable silence that seems to mark disabled judgment; the Host, at a loss for new participants, suddenly reveals Chaucer; the pilgrim Chaucer responds with a tale so terribly told that it causes another breakdown in the game as he is commanded to stop mid-sentence and try again.[73] The inclusion of a Marian miracle in a contest entered into for the sake of 'pleye', and the ambiguity of the pilgrims' response, questions the utility and status of such tales,[74] which by the late fourteenth century were often overtly connected to Jewish encounters and to English historiography and monastic traditions. The devout Prioress may deny responsibility for the tale when she compares herself to 'a child of twelf month oold, or lesse'[75] – thus identifying herself with the innocent chorister who does not understand his hymn or its violent potential – but Chaucer also has her display the genre's ambivalent alchemy. Her tale begins as an act of devotion, evolves into a brutal and prejudiced wonder tale, and finally brings to mind a violent moment in English history that exposes a problematic engagement with anti-Semitism and law.

This path is most dramatically revealed in the Prioress's framing apostrophes. She complements her initial invocations of God and Mary with a

---

71 See Dahood, 'Punishment of the Jews', p. 489 n. 114.
72 On genre and the construction of fiction in Fragment VII, see Alan Gaylord, '*Sentence* and *Solaas* in Fragment VII of the *Canterbury Tales*: Harry Bailly as Horseback Editor', *PMLA* 82.2 (1967), pp. 226–35; Helen Cooper, *The Structure of the Canterbury Tales* (London, 1983), pp. 165–9; and Lampert, *Gender and Jewish Difference*, pp. 94–7.
73 This of course refers to 'The Tale of Sir Thopas', which I discuss further below, pp. 156–8. On the Thopas/Melibee sequence and its relationship to 'The Prioress's Tale' and to the author's persona, see Lee Patterson, '"What man artow?": Authorial Self-Definition in The Tale of Sir Thopas and The Tale of Melibee', *Studies in the Age of Chaucer* 11 (1989), pp. 117–75, also reprinted in Patterson's collection of essays, *Temporal Circumstances: Form and History in the Canterbury Tales*, The New Middle Ages (New York, 2006), pp. 97–128.
74 Benson, *Riverside*, CT I.772.
75 Ibid., VII.484.

concluding invocation of a boy supposedly murdered by thirteenth-century Lincoln Jews:

> O yonge Hugh of Lyncoln, slayn also
> With cursed Jewes, as it is notable,
> For it was but a litel while ago,
> Preye eek for us, we synful folk unstable,
> That of his mercy God so merciable
> On us his grete mercy multiplie,
> For reverence of his mooder Marie. Amen.[76]

The 1255 murder of Hugh of Lincoln, according to chronicle accounts, involved the Jewish kidnapping of, and reenactment of Christ's crucifixion on, the Christian boy. The Prioress's concluding invocation connects her tale – and this is no new observation – to medieval stories and accusations of Jewish ritual murder, which were unfortunately common in England.[77] Less understood, however, is how the association also creates a connection to matters of English law, for the Prioress's description of the punishment and execution of the accused Jews mirrors the actual punishment imposed after Hugh of Lincoln's murder:

> With torment and with shameful deeth echon,
> This provost dooth thise Jewes for to sterve
> That of this mordre wiste, and that anon.
> He nolde no swich cursednesse observe.
> 'Yvele shal have that yvele wol deserve';
> Therfore with wilde hors he dide hem drawe,
> And after that he heng hem by the lawe.[78]

No known analogue of 'The Prioress's Tale' gives the detail that the presiding legal authority 'with wilde hors ... dide hem drawe, / And after that ... heng hem by the lawe', and it is clear, especially in light of the Prioress's concluding invocation, that this detail is exported from the Lincoln case.[79]

---

[76] Ibid., VII.684–91.

[77] On the Hugh of Lincoln case, see Gavin I. Langmuir, 'The Knight's Tale of Young Hugh of Lincoln', *Speculum* 47 (1972), pp. 459–82; Albert B. Friedman, 'The Prioress's Tale and Chaucer's Anti-Semitism', *Chaucer Review* 9 (1974), p. 118; and Boyd, *The Prioress's Tale*, p. 17. Jewish ritual murder accusations were associated with William of Norwich (*c.1144*), Harold of Gloucester (*c.1168*), Robert of Bury (*c.1181*), Hugh of Lincoln (*c.1255*), and Adam of Bristol (a clearly fictional composition set in the late twelfth century). For an overview of the cases, see Anthony Bale, 'Fictions of Judaism in England before 1290', *The Jews in Medieval Britain: Historical, Literary and Archaeological Perspectives*, ed. Patricia Skinner (Woodbridge, 2003), pp. 129–44, especially pp. 130–5. This work is also importantly reframed in Bale, *The Jew in the Medieval Book*, Chapter 1.

[78] Benson, *Riverside*, *CT* VII.628–34.

[79] I have not seen this observation anywhere except in Dahood, 'Punishment of the Jews', pp. 471–83, where the legal implications of Chaucer's account and its relationship to the Lincoln punishment are discussed in detail. Dahood points out that confusion over the meaning of the verb

Three thirteenth-century chronicle accounts survive – in the Waverly Annals, the Burton Annals, and the *Chronica majora* of Matthew Paris – and the latter two describe the outcome: nineteen Lincoln Jews were, like the Jews in 'The Prioress's Tale', dragged behind horses and then hanged.[80]

Roger Dahood's discussion of whether this punishment, as Chaucer uses it, denotes excessive cruelty or is simply historically accurate reveals pertinent information about the *kind* of law-breaking that the Prioress's execution suggests. In England, Dahood shows, the combined 'punishment of drawing and hanging was reserved for treason', and, indeed, other extant texts reveal that this interpretation of the Lincoln Jews' alleged crime was well known.[81] Chaucer's awareness of the significance is just possible – this particular sentence for treason persisted into the fourteenth century[82] – but even if, after the 1290 expulsion of the Jews from England, collective memory of the reason for such an extraordinary punishment for homicide was lost, it remains likely the Lincoln case was associated with the crown and with the act of expulsion itself.[83] A certain legal interpretation, then, becomes necessary for a full reading of 'The Prioress's Tale'. The specificity that Chaucer assigns to the punishment of the Jews requires a reader to consider their place within English legal categories, even as it invites contemplation of how the Virgin Mary is complicit in the legal justification for the execution.

In Chaucer's version of this story, the miracle is not only that the slain child continues to sing his *Alma redemptoris mater* after his death, but also that the subsequent finding of his body exposes the conspirators and leads to their execution. Chaucer links the miraculous singing to the binding and punishment of the accused Jews:

> This gemme of chastite, this emeraude,
> And eek of martirdom the ruby bright,
> Ther he with throte ykorven lay upright,
> He *Alma redemptoris* gan to synge
> So loude that al the place gan to rynge.

'drawe' has likely restricted thinking about this close connection to earlier chronicle accounts (pp. 466–71). My thanks to Professor Dahood for giving me access to his essay before its publication.

[80] Ibid., pp. 473–4 (the relevant passages are quoted and translated here).

[81] Ibid., pp. 472, 474–6. Dahood cites the Burton Annals' characterization of the Lincoln Jews (and all Jews) as traitors, and a thirteenth-century Anglo-Norman poem that claims Hugh's murderer was executed 'cum traitre', and he notes that Henry II in particular was known for lodging accusations of treason. It is not difficult, in any case, to imagine that the status of Anglo-Jews as wards of the king made such crimes *de facto* treasonous. See Mundill, *England's Jewish Solution*, pp. 45–71.

[82] Dahood, 'Punishment of the Jews', p. 482.

[83] Ibid., p. 477. On the purposeful associations of Hugh of Lincoln and other ritual murder cases with the royal propaganda programs, see also Robin Mundill, 'Edward I and the Final Phase of Anglo-Jewry', *The Jews in Medieval Britain: Historical, Literary and Archaeological Perspectives*, ed. Patricia Skinner (Woodbridge, 2003), pp. 55–70; Mundill, *England's Jewish Solution*, pp. 249–85; and Bale, *The Jew in the Medieval Book*, pp. 137–40.

> The Cristene folk that thurgh the strete wente
> In coomen for to wondre upon this thyng,
> And hastily they for the provost sente;
> He cam anon withouten tariyng,
> And herieth Crist, that is of hevene kyng,
> And eek his moder, honour of mankynde,
> And after that the Jewes leet he bynde.[84]

The miracle of the postmortem singing allows the Christian community to discover the corpse in the Jewry, and the 'provost' praises Christ and Mary for the discovery that so immediately justifies the seizure and execution of the Jews. Mary's intercession is therefore linked not only to the child's ability to sing with a slit throat but quite explicitly to the solving of, and punishment for, the crime that makes the miracle necessary.

It is absolutely crucial to the story's devotional conclusions that we read Mary's involvement in the Jewish 'binding', as the physical effects of her intercession are similarly described elsewhere in the tale. Not only are we to understand that the slain boy is bound in the end, wound up with burial cloth and 'enclosen' in his tomb,[85] but Chaucer also echoes the provost's binding of the Jews in the pious reaction of the abbot who performs the murdered boy's funeral: 'whan this abbot hadde this wonder seyn / ... gruf he fil al plat upon the grounde, / And stille he lay *as he had ben ybounde* [my italics].'[86] Mary's miraculous intercession ultimately has the same effect on the abbot who verifies the miracle as it does on the Jews who necessitated it. Both experience a physical binding as a direct result: Mary binds the Jews 'by the lawe' and the devout Christian audience by 'wonder' – a binding that we might even say extends to the 'sobre' pilgrims who react to the telling of the miracle.

The Tale's connection to Hugh of Lincoln, and the complementary connections of that to a legal punishment for treason and to Mary's direct involvement in the punishment, can only function for an English audience. As Dahood has noted,

> Although the little clergeon's murder is not a ritual murder and occurs in a faraway land, the Prioress's impassioned outburst would have served as a cue to Chaucer's earliest audiences to read Hugh's story as a gloss on the Prioress's Tale. For those of Chaucer's contemporaries familiar with Hugh's story, the invocation and punishment would have brought the little clergeon's murder in distant Asia emphatically home to England.[87]

---

[84] Benson, *Riverside Chaucer*, *CT* VII.607–20.
[85] Ibid., VII.682.
[86] Ibid., VII.673–6.
[87] Dahood, 'Punishment of the Jews', p. 482. On the issue of the dislocation and relocation of Jews in medieval English literature, see also Tomasch, 'Postcolonial Chaucer' (pp. 73–5 on 'The Prioress's Tale').

It would also have brought Marian intercession emphatically home to England, and in a way especially relevant to a significant portion of the Marian miracle genre as it was represented there. If the Tale's ambiguous dislocation to 'Asye' at first seems to make it very much like many other versions of the story, which freely locate and relocate the site of intercession,[88] part of the 'Englishing' of the miracle is in that odd moment of connection to Hugh, and then to English law. This makes an event and a people a century gone return to signify a Marian present, and it makes the English Marian themes I have been discussing uncannily urgent. Chaucer's consciousness of these themes allows him, in a devotional context, to allude to the legend of the monk who can say only 'Ave Maria' and joke that Mary makes a cheap lawyer. In the context of the *Canterbury Tales*, it allows him to experiment with the flexibility of Miracles of the Virgin.

The juxtaposition of 'The Tale of Sir Thopas' is particularly important to this assessment, for Sir Thopas is Chaucer's immediate response to the 'sobre' moment brought on by 'The Prioress's Tale', and it is therefore a crucial component of his imagined reception of a Marian miracle.[89] As Chaucer turns from the story of the child slain by Jews to a romance 'nat worth a toord' (as the Host puts it),[90] he gives a direct response to the Prioress's invocation of Mary, with Sir Thopas's:

> O Seinte Marie, benedicite!
> What eyleth this love at me
> To bynde me so soore?
> Me dremed al this nyght, pardee,
> An elf-queene shal my lemman be
> And slepe under my goore.
>
> An elf-queene wol I love, ywis,
> For in this world no womman is
> Worthy to be my make
>   In towne[91]

There is a double imitation at work here: as Thopas comically parodies the Prioress's longing for Mary's guidance, he also evokes the Marian binding

---

[88] See Bale, *The Jew in the Medieval Book*, pp. 59–66.

[89] Though there are several studies of the Thopas/Melibee link, of Chaucer's authorial persona as sketched in the Thopas/Melibee sequence, and especially of Thopas's parodic relationship to minstrel and romance productions (for which, see the copious notes to Patterson, '"What man artow?"'), little has been made of the relationship of 'Thopas' to 'The Prioress's Tale'. See, however, Lilian Winstanley, ed., *The Prioress's Tale and The Tale of Sir Thopas* (Cambridge, 1922); Lampert's reading of the full sequence in *Gender and Jewish Difference*, pp. 91–100; and Bale's comment in *The Jew in the Medieval Book*, p. 82, that this is 'an interrogation of the limits of genre: it is crucial to remember that "The Prioress's Tale" is placed between a cynical mercantilist take on *fabliau* ("The Shipman's Tale") and an exaggerated low-grade acaudal popular romance ("Sir Thopas")'.

[90] Benson, *Riverside*, *CT* VII.930.

[91] Ibid., VII.784–93.

already twice accomplished in 'The Prioress's Tale' ('What eyeleth this love at me / To *bynde* me so soore? [my italics]'). Both his longing and his binding, however, are ridiculously the stuff of popular romance. Chaucer has Thopas thinking that Mary is as effective an intercessor in his arrogant quest for an 'elf-queene' as she is in the situation of the Prioress's little chorister (who, in some sense, also desires an otherworldly woman), and he is persistent in his biting comparisons of the Prioress and Thopas.

As he introduces Thopas as a stock romance hero – a noble knight, a man with a handsome appearance and expensive clothing, a hunter, a lover, a man on a quest – he recalls his descriptions of the Prioress in the General Prologue, the only other 'story' ascribed to the pilgrim Chaucer. Thopas is someone who has 'a semely nose', where the Prioress sings the Divine Office 'in her nose ful semely'.[92] Sir Thopas has 'lippes rede as rose', just as the Prioress has a mouth 'softe and reed'.[93] Sir Thopas wears a 'robe ... of sykla-toon / That coste many a jane', just as the Prioress has a 'cloke' that is 'Ful fetys' (well made, elegant).[94] His helmet, marked with 'a tour / And ... a lilie flour' – the most familiar symbols of Marian purity – recalls the Prioress's claim in her prologue that she will tell a tale 'in laude ... / Of thee [Mary] and of the white lylye flour / Which that the bar'.[95] The 'Jewes werk' that marks the quality of Thopas's armor inverts the Prioress's account of Marian protection, as it is now Jews who protect the Marian hero, literally providing the material that will keep him from physical harm.[96]

The humorously delicate facial features of both the Prioress and Sir Thopas, and their attention to clothing and appearance, link them both to the here overly marked genre of romance.[97] The series of verbal echoes invites comparison of the Prioress on her quest for the perfect praise of Mary with the unimaginative romance character on a quest for an elf-queen, even as they suggest (tongue-in-cheek) that Thopas's quest is as worthy of Marian inter-cession as the Prioress's, and Thopas as worthy of protection as the Prioress's innocent boy. The Prioress's symbols of Marian purity and hostility reappear together in 'The Tale of Sir Thopas' as literal signs of Marian protection, and this suggests a conscious decision on Chaucer's part to show how the genre and tone of a Miracle of the Virgin might be manipulated in relation to others. Where comparison of the Prioress to Sir Thopas exposes her affectations and

[92] Ibid., VII.729 and I.121–2.
[93] Ibid., VII.726 and I.153.
[94] Ibid., VII.734–5 and I.157.
[95] Ibid., VII.906–7 and VII.461–2.
[96] Ibid., VII.864. On Thopas's 'Jewish' armor, see also Jerome Mandel, '"Jewes Werk" in *Sir Thopas*', *Chaucer and the Jews: Sources, Contexts, Meanings*, ed. Sheila Delany (New York and London, 2002), pp. 59–68.
[97] On Chaucer's use of Sir Thopas as an allusion to popular English tail-rhyme romances, see L. H. Loomis, 'The Tale of Sir Thopas', *Sources and Analogues of Chaucer's Canterbury Tales*, ed. W. F. Bryan and Germaine Dempster (Chicago, 1941), pp. 486–559; and the update by Joanne A. Charbonneau, 'Sir Thopas', *Sources and Analogues of the Canterbury Tales*, II, eds Robert Correale and Mary Hamel, Chaucer Studies 35 (Cambridge, 2005), pp. 649–714.

use of formulaic imagery and vocabulary, comparison of Sir Thopas to the child slain by Jews exposes the fictionality and false gravity of the Prioress's devotional invocations.[98]

I do not suggest that this alleviates the anti-Semitic violence of 'The Prioress's Tale' – Chaucer does not need to be rescued from that – nor do I think that we can conclude certainly that Chaucer intended a satire of a Miracle of the Virgin, or of the Prioress for that matter. Rather, his carefully constructed responses to the story – including the Prioress's tagged-on invocation of Hugh of Lincoln, the pilgrims' 'sobre' silence, the Host's awkward desire for mirth, and 'The Tale of Sir Thopas' itself – render it generically problematic. What is the appropriate response to this now seemingly typical English Miracle of the Virgin? Chaucer, characteristically, does not give a single answer, but he introduces an ambivalence that persists into the Reformation era. We can take his Marian miracle as a very influential model of the genre – at least as one that we can examine in light of its influence on and use by later readers – and it is conspicuous that its generic parameters were wide and long. Whether Marian miracles were to be understood as devotional, historiographical, or fictional was clearly a working question for Chaucer, as it was for those in the fifteenth and sixteenth centuries who responded to 'The Prioress's Tale' in particular and to the *Canterbury Tales* in general.

When Latimer preached a sermon before Henry VIII in 1549, he invoked the *Canterbury Tales* as a negative model: 'if good lyfe do not insue and folow upon our readynge ... we myghte as well spende that tyme in reading prophane hystories, of canterbury tales, or a fit of Roben Hode'.[99] For Latimer, the *Tales* were emphatically separated from spiritually beneficial texts, as they were for Cranmer, who echoed the sentiment around the same time:

> If we receiue and repute the gospel as a thing most true and godly, why do we not live according to the same? If we count it as fables and trifles why do we take upon us to give such credit and authority to it? ... If we take it for a Canterbury tale, why do we not refuse it? Why do we not laugh it out of place, and whistle at it?[100]

How might Chaucer's Marian miracle fit into this? If it could be easily recognized as a fable to 'laugh ... out of place, and whistle at' – and I have argued that Chaucer himself may imply the same – then in what sense could such a text be threatening or maintain any devotional utility? This is a reformer's tactic too, one that removes religious authority from the voices of 'literary' writers or tellers by emptying them of spiritual depth or importance, but of

---

[98] The name 'Thopas' may also be an allusion to, or inversion of, the Prioress's label for the slain child, the 'gemme of chastite, this emeraude' (at VII.609). See Charbonneau, 'Sir Thopas', pp. 655–7.

[99] Quoted in Spurgeon, *Five Hundred Years of Chaucer*, p. 89.

[100] Ibid., pp. 88–9.

course responses to certain of the Canterbury tales were much more variable than Latimer and Cranmer suggest.

Reframing Chaucer's Miracle of the Virgin

'The Prioress's Tale' could be made appropriate to a legendary or *mariale*, and it could be linked or unlinked to Chaucer, remade and reframed, depending on a compiler's predilections. Five fifteenth-century manuscripts contain the excerpted 'Prioress's Tale': MSS Chetham's Library 6709, British Library Harley 1704, British Library Harley 2251, British Library Harley 2382, and Bodleian Library Rawlinson C. 86. Anthony Bale's work on the tale in these contexts is thorough, and there is no need to repeat it here (though it might be inserted almost whole).[101] But where Bale sees rare evidence of the reception of medieval anti-Semitic *exempla* and 'quasi-historical texts' in England,[102] I see also the history of Marian miracles. To be sure, the overlap is critical to my arguments, as is the notion that the English Marian miracles are by their very nature miscellaneous (that is, they are exemplary and meant to function in the 'radical … openness, fluidity, and abundance of meanings' that Bale assigns more generally to anti-Semitic tales),[103] but the evidence, and indeed Bale's conclusions, must be inflected differently if we are looking for Mary as well as the Jew in the fifteenth-century iterations.

In MS Harley 1704, for instance, 'The Prioress's Tale' is set in an anthology of devotional material,[104] and its prologue is significantly rewritten and truncated to remove the suggestion of any specific speaking voice. As Bale puts it, 'Narrative self-examination is deleted in preference for the invocation of the Virgin.'[105] The whole work is disconnected from Chaucer, titled only 'Alma Redemptoris Mater' – even though an expunged line from the Wife of Bath's Prologue suggests that the scribe probably had access to a copy that included other Canterbury tales[106] – and this reworking of the child slain by Jews story therefore 'foreground[s] the very song absent from the Tale' (the words are never given, and the young boy does not understand its meaning).[107] This reframing announces the tale itself as a kind of Marian hymn, and it is the hymn that is striking on the page. It is the visual focus for any reader or

---

101 *The Jew in the Medieval Book*, pp. 88–103.
102 Ibid., p. 50, where he uses 'quasi-historical' to describe *exempla* in their monastic historio-graphical contexts.
103 Ibid., p. 91.
104 For a list of contents and a brief description, see John M. Manly and Edith Rickert, eds, *The Text of the Canterbury Tales, Studied on the Basis of All Known Manuscripts*, I (London, 1940), pp. 238–40.
105 Bale, *The Jew in the Medieval Book*, pp. 92–3 (here p. 92).
106 Ibid., p. 210 n. 160. The line 'alas that euer loue was synne' (*CT* III.614) is copied immediately after 'The Prioress's Tale' on fol. 31r. Manly and Rickert, *Text of the CT*, p. 240, also note this, but do not connect it to the Wife of Bath.
107 Ibid., p. 93.

peruser of the book, because the scribe has boxed each instance of the phrase 'Alma redemptoris' or 'Alma redemptoris mater' (there are five, six including the title) in red ink.

This personal devotional emphasis is likewise present in the Chetham's manuscript, a vernacular legendary compiled by the Augustinian canon William Cotson in 1490.[108] In this codex, 'The Prioress's Tale' and 'The Second Nun's Tale' are together situated between Lydgate's *Lyf of Our Lady* and four saints' lives also ascribed to Lydgate. The two Canterbury tales occupy a single quire, which suggests that they were sought out and copied for inclusion, and Cotson, who recorded his name and vocation on three separate folios, claimed that the entire compilation was 'to the honour lawde and worshippe of almighty Godde and of owre Blessid lady his moder and all the saynts whos lyvis shall folowe'.[109]

In MS Harley 2251, 'The Prioress's Tale' (beginning on fol. 72v) is organized generically, along with John Lydgate's only Miracle of the Virgin (fols 70v–72v), a work known as the 'Legend of Dan Joos', which has Mary once again repaying simple devotion by leaving a written record in the form of an inscribed flower.[110] These two keep company with several other Marian items, including Chaucer's 'An ABC' (fols 49r–51v). Though the book is really a vernacular literary anthology, heavily Lydgatian and including secular poetry on many subjects (beasts, tragedy, instructions to kings, a letter to Alexander the Great, etc.),[111] it is again clear that, as Bale puts it, the '"Prioress's Tale" is taken seriously, and devoutly, and offered as a reflection of religious and familial relations'.[112] This is accomplished in part by the omission of the final stanza on Hugh of Lincoln in this instance – an omission of the associations with England's 'real' anti-Semitic history – and the addition instead of Lydgate's 'Praise of St Anne'. This reframing 'consolidates the foreignness' of the Tale's 'Asian' setting and of Jews themselves, focuses on the lineage and tutelage of the Virgin Mary, and makes '[t]he story of the Jews' murder of the Christian boy ... connected with and displaced by instructional family concerns and the register of everyday hagiography'.[113]

In the fourth example (MS Harley 2382), the Marian devotional motivations and hagiographical modes imposed on the compilation are in many ways the most interesting in the context of the present study. Manly and Rickert called Harley 2382's script 'a loose, careless, ugly cursive' and dismissed the whole anthology as 'a book which a country parson might have written for

---

[108] See Manly and Rickert, *Text of the CT*, pp. 82–4; and Bale, *The Jew in the Medieval Book*, pp. 97–8.

[109] Quoted in Manly and Rickert, *Text of the CT*, p. 84.

[110] Cf. the similar story in the *SEL* sequence, pp. 91–2 above. Lydgate's miracle is printed in Boyd, *Middle English Miracles*, pp. 56–60, and its origins and relationships to other Marian miracles discussed in Boyd, 'The Literary Background of Lydgate's "The Legend of Dan Joos"'.

[111] On the manuscript, see Manly and Rickert, *Text of the CT*, pp. 241–4, and Bale, *The Jew in the Medieval Book*, pp. 93–6.

[112] Bale, *The Jew in the Medieval Book*, p. 95.

[113] Ibid.

himself', but this manuscript nonetheless engages 'The Prioress's Tale' as a work central to its organizational scheme.[114] The Marian miracle is again set in a Lydgatian devotional context here, and the scribe seems to have purposefully grouped it with other devotional material and started a 'Prioress's Tale group' in the midst of Lydgate's *Testamentum*. Bale argues that this strange embedding of text within text acts as one of several 'witnesses to the spiritual conversion of "Lydgate" the poet-narrator' and therefore proves that 'The Prioress's Tale' was 'integral to the compilation's moral concerns',[115] but it seems to me that the codex's hagiographical and Marian foci are, in this case, also markers of the perceived devotional utility of 'The Prioress's Tale'. While contemporary notes on the interruption of the *Testamentum* – 'Quare plus xii folio post' on fol. 96v, and 'Quare plus xx folios post' at 108r – allow easy (if cumbersome) navigation to its continuation, the intervening folios create an interesting group in and of themselves: they include 'The Prioress's Tale', labeled only 'ffabula monialis de sancta maria' (the nun's story of St Mary, fols 97r–100r); 'The Second Nun's Tale', likewise disconnected from its Chaucerian context and labeled 'Vita Sancte Cecilie' (fols 100v–108r); a life of St Erasmus ('De sancto Erasmo martire', fols 109r–111r); a long *Charter of Christ* ('Testamentum Christi', fols 111v–118r); and the 'Childe of Bristowe' (fols 118v–127r).

This section of the codex situates Chaucer's Miracle of the Virgin as a devotional piece on several registers. The collation with saints' lives means that Chaucer's version of the story of the slain boy reads as a *vita* or *passio* itself, and its position in a sequence that includes a long *Charter of Christ* connects the Marian miracle genre to its documentary and anti-Semitic motifs. The long *Charter* figures Mary as the blood and flesh that enables the 'sealing' of the document (Christ's body), and in it Christ describes his mother pained and swooning at the Jewish violence against him.[116] The particulars of the version of the *Charter of Christ* found in this manuscript (a copy of what is known as the 'B-text') also encourage the reader to identify with the devout child of 'The Prioress's Tale', by placing the reader in the position of the innocent schoolboy who does not know his Latin but insists on his devotion nonetheless. It begins on fol. 111v: 'Whoso will euer rede this boke / And wiþ gostly eyen ther on loke / To other scole dar he not wende / To saue his soule fro þe fende.'[117] The suggestion is that the reader need not go

---

[114] See Manly and Rickert, *Text of the CT*, pp. 245–8 (here p. 247). Bale, *The Jew in the Medieval Book*, gives this codex the least attention of the five (see pp. 96–7).

[115] Bale, *The Jew in the Medieval Book*, p. 97. Though Manly and Rickert suggest that the compilation was piecemeal and haphazard, Bale notes that '[s]ignatures on the booklets show that the copying was continuous' (p. 211 n. 171) and makes clear that the texts that seem to 'interrupt' continuous copying are in fact positioned intentionally.

[116] For the text of various versions of the long *Charter*, see Spalding, *Middle English Charters of Christ*, pp. 18–81.

[117] From my transcription, but cf. Spalding, *Middle English Charters of Christ*, pp. 46–7 (the start of a parallel edition of four manuscripts). Green, *Crisis of Truth*, pp. 262–4, uses these lines as

'day by day to scole',[118] as the child of 'The Prioress's Tale' does, to achieve the same spiritual ('gostly') literacy for which he is rewarded by Mary. This expects not only that 'The Prioress's Tale' may be understood as one in which learning and interpretation matter distinctly (see my reading in Chapter 1),[119] but also that the *Charter of Christ* (a textual and legal embodiment of the flesh born of Mary) is a gloss on the Miracle of the Virgin.

The 'Childe of Bristowe', which follows the *Charter of Christ* (fols 118v–127r), is likewise concerned with a boy, his schooling, and his devotion, and it might even be called a Marian miracle in this sequence. It tells of a child whose father 'put hym vnto lore, / To lerne to be a clerke'.[120] When the father wants his son to learn law, however, the boy refuses and takes on an apprenticeship with a merchant instead. He is nonetheless eventually called upon to act as a makeshift lawyer for his father, since, as he explains, 'ther was no-man but y / That wolde be his attourny / At his endynge day.'[121] He is thereafter so concerned with his father's salvation that he prays and begs and bankrupts himself, working tirelessly and selflessly until he earns his father's heavenly bliss. His employer is so impressed with his devotion that, after the father's death, he makes him his heir and requests in exchange only that he be *his* attorney as well.[122] Ultimately, in the context of 'The Prioress's Tale' and of the influential Marian characterizations I have outlined, the good son of the 'Child of Bristowe' can be read not only as analogous to the little chorister of 'The Prioress's Tale', but more obviously as analogous to the Virgin Mary.

This apparently carelessly written 'country parson' book, then, is a compilation that announces itself as specifically Marian, and 'The Prioress's Tale' constitutes a pivotal moment in its arrangement. The whole codex begins with pieces 'De nativitate beate marie' and 'De purificacione beate marie' (both parts of Lydgate's *Life of Our Lady*, but not marked so, fols 1r–74v), and the two pieces that precede Lydgate's *Testamentum* are 'De assumcione Sancte marie' (fols 75r–86r), and an 'Oratio Sanctam Mariam' (fols 86v–77r). All of these are marked with running headers in brown ink, underscored with red, and each part ends with an indication of careful organization (e.g., 'Explicit liber secundus' on fol. 28r to mark the end of the nativity narrative in the *Life of Our Lady*). The explicits sometimes further emphasize the Marian scheme (e.g., 'Explicit quintus liber de sancte marie' on fol. 74v, or 'Explicit sextus liber de sancte marie' on fol. 86r), so that the first two-thirds of the codex seems to have been self-consciously structured as a *mariale* that begins with the birth of Mary, proceeds through the birth and life of her son (other

an example of 'an advertisement for ... talismanic properties' in 'a culture where books and charters were regularly fetishized as objects of awe and mystery'.
118 Benson, *Riverside*, *CT* VII.504.
119 See pp. 26–9.
120 The text has been edited in Horstmann, *Altenglische Legenden*, pp. 315–21 (here p. 315, lines 38–9).
121 Ibid., p. 321, lines 511–13.
122 Ibid., lines 541–6.

sections of the *Life of Our Lady* are marked as the Nativity, Circumcision, and Epiphany of Christ), and leads eventually to miracle texts.[123] Annotations within this 'revision' of 'The Prioress's Tale', moreover, include notes that connect Mary to Moses (Mary's identification as the 'bushe unbrent' is annotated with 'Rubum quem uiderat moyses'), and highlight the child's Marian song ('Infans canebat alma redemptoris mater' annotates the first mention of the child's singing in the Jewry).

In addition to the evident private-devotional use of 'The Prioress's Tale' throughout the fifteenth century, however, it is important to note that the miracle tale might also maintain its more ambiguously 'literary' position in secular compilations. The final example of its repositioning is in MS Rawlinson C. 86, which is a very different kind of anthology from those discussed above, and especially from MS Harley 2382. The perceived utility of the tale is not clear in this case. The book seems to be a London merchant's anthology that provides a 'courtly reading' of the tale in 'a civic, indeed secular, textual context' (it includes romances, secular poetry, verses on the death of Edward IV, verses ascribed to 'Quene Elyzabeth', recipes, and other Chaucerian texts).[124] What is most remarkable in its copy of 'The Prioress's Tale' is that it ends mid-stanza at the moment when the Jews are arrested and sentenced to death – with the line 'Euill shall þey haue þat evill deserve' – and therefore omits the chorister's death and burial, much of what makes the story a miracle tale at all, and ominously sets the full force of the narrative pathos on Jewish guilt and insult of Mary. Despite its general 'courtly' aspect, however, this manuscript begins with *The Northern Passion* ('Passio Domini', fols 2r–30v) and includes a 'Lament of Mary', both of which might be read as necessitating the ambiguous moment of Jewish punishment with which this compiler ends 'The Prioress's Tale'.[125] Bale's assertion that the copyist's stopping place indicates that there is 'no Marian gloss on this harsh portrait of child murder and retribution' is perhaps contradicted by the presence elsewhere in the manuscript of portraits of Jewish conspiracy and violence, and of Mary's grief and outrage.

The combined evidence of these excerptions and appropriations of Chaucer's version of the 'Child Slain by Jews' miracle offers powerful examples of the variable use and reception of a Marian miracle. As Bale puts it, these compilers 'do not defer to Chaucerian authority but rather to Marian and

---

123 Mary Beth Long, 'Corpora and Manuscripts, Authors and Audiences', *A Companion to Middle English Hagiography*, ed. Sarah Salih (Cambridge, 2006), p. 63 n. 59, suggests that the position of 'The Prioress's Tale' here and in the Chetham's manuscipt may indicate that the compilers 'considered the *Prioress's Tale* a saint's life', but more likely it fit the category 'hagiography' generally. In MS Harley 2382, however, it might be conceived of as *part* of Mary's life.

124 For a full list of contents, see Manly and Rickert, *Text of the CT*, pp. 472–5. See also Bale's discussion in *The Jew in the Medieval Book*, pp. 98–102 (here p. 101).

125 See F. A. Foster, ed., *The Northern Passion*, EETS, os 145 (London, 1913); and Rose Cords, 'Fünf me. Gedichte aus den Hss. Rawlinson Poetry 36 und Rawlinson C. 86', *Archiv für das Studien der neueren Sprachen und Literaturen* 135 (1916), pp. 300–2 (where the *Lament of Mary* is printed).

Christian authority', and they show how such a tale could be 'open, fluid and inherently transgressive, malleable to changing concerns and contextual specificities'.[126] 'The Prioress's Tale' was copied and resituated by regular canons and humble parsons, by London courtly readers, and by a compiler working 'to the honoure and lawde and worshippe … of owre Blessid lady'. It could be set among secular poetry, among the 'fables and trifles' of Latimer and Cranmer (indeed of Chaucer), and among the devotions of religious who appreciated Lydgatian poetic manners. In its fifteenth-century reframings, Chaucer's Miracle of the Virgin allows us to see an English example of the genre – English in its appropriation of the themes I have been discussing and especially in its status as a 'miscellany' piece – as it was written, rewritten, and received within the changing religious and literary tastes of the late medieval and early modern periods.

Coda: The Fate of a Marian Shrine

The miracle of the foundation of the Shrine of Our Lady at Walsingham is told in the anonymous 'Walsingham Ballad' (also called the 'Pynson Ballad', printed *c.*1496).[127] It is described there as one of many associated with the shrine: 'here Our Lady hath shewyd many myracle / Innumberable … / Four hundreth yere and more, the cronacle to witnes.'[128] While we do not know what 'cronacle' lists them, the poet describes Marian miracles in which pilgrims were healed of various afflictions, the dead resurrected, shipwrecks averted, demons banished, temptations relieved, and comfort obtained,[129] and all began with the construction of the Lady Chapel in the year 1061. Mary appeared then to a noble English widow of Walsingham and instructed her to build a replica of her home at Nazareth (the house in which the Annunciation happened). In the Ballad, the transplanting of the Nazarene setting stands as both a demonstration of Mary's special affection for England and a recognition of Marian Jewishness. The poet compares England 'to the londe of promysson', and he concludes that Mary is the 'glory of Jerusalem / Cyprus of Syon and Ioye of Israel',[130] so that Norfolk becomes a new Israel, remade in the image of a Christianized Holy Land.[131] All of this is well known, the

---

126 *The Jew in the Medieval Book*, pp. 102, 103.
127 Richard Pynson was the printer (book no. 1254 of Pepys Library, Magdalene College, Cambridge). The unique copy is edited in Dickinson, *Shrine of Our Lady*, pp. 124–30, divided into twenty-one stanzas. As the edition contains no line numbers, I will cite it according to page and stanza numbers.
128 Ibid., p. 128, stanza 14.
129 Ibid., p. 128, stanzas 15–16.
130 Ibid., p. 129, stanza 19; p. 130, stanza 21.
131 The Roman Catholic National Shrine of Our Lady, Walsingham, still repeats this foundation story and welcomes those who visit its website to 'England's Nazareth' (www.walsingham.org. uk/romancatholic/). The shrine is a place of renewed activity today, for both the Roman Catholic and Anglican Churches.

poet says, for 'bokes make remembraunce', and this and other Walsingham miracles are told frequently by 'olde cronyclers'.[132]

There was clearly some tradition of miracle narratives around the shrine, but there is little evidence to substantiate this late medieval poet's claims for the antiquity and iterability of the Walsingham stories. The Augustinian priory there was dismantled at the end of the 1530s,[133] and the ruins of the texts of Walsingham are not so easy to see as the ruins in the Norfolk countryside. No library catalogues survive, and the only real suggestions of lost texts are in the 'Walsingham Ballad' and in John Capgrave's early fifteenth-century mention of the existence of Walsingham annals. Some local miracles are recorded by Thomas of Walsingham (1377–1422), and some others by the Dutch humanist Desiderius Erasmus in his account of the shrine,[134] but these do not reflect the copious 'chronicle' content to which the Ballad poet adverts. If the content of the Marian texts that might have been at Walsingham are ultimately unknowable, however, what can be gleaned about the shrine's final decades provides a glimpse of the influence of Miracles of the Virgin nonetheless.

Erasmus, who spent the better part of twenty years visiting, living, and teaching in England,[135] made two pilgrimages to Walsingham, one in the summer of 1512 and another probably in 1514. In 1526, he published his colloquy *Peregrinatio religionis ergo* (Pilgrimage for Religion's Sake) – a satirical dialogue between his alter ego 'Ogygius' ('simple-minded') and his old friend 'Menedemus' ('stay-at-home') – and he began it with an account of his second visit to Walsingham.[136] The colloquy's characterization of the Virgin Mary, and its clever criticisms of the shrine and its custodians, are valuable evidence of the life of a medieval Marian shrine in its final years, even more so because they constitute the commentary of an outsider observing the English situation (even if parodically). While we might not look at Erasmus's descriptions as factual or unbiased, the humor in his account reveals some

---

132 Dickinson, *Shrine of Our Lady*, p. 127, stanza 12; p. 129, stanza 18.

133 The first Act for the Dissolution of the Monasteries was issued in 1536, but addressed only those houses with annual incomes under £200 (Walsingham made considerably more than this). The second Act was issued in 1539, and the chantries were finally dissolved in 1547. For full texts of the acts, see Williams, *English Historical Documents*, pp. 770–7.

134 These are discussed in Dickinson, *Shrine of Our Lady*, pp. 19–20, 53–8. Dickinson also prints (as Appendices 2 and 3) cartulary lists of priors and canons that are among the only records of the priory's activity.

135 Erasmus was frequently in England between 1498 and 1517. He was at Oxford for a time and, between 1514 and 1517, was Lady Margaret Professor of Divinity and Professor of Greek at Cambridge. On his time and influence in England, see John Joseph Mangan, *The Life, Character, and Influence of Desiderius Erasmus of Rotterdam* (New York, 1927), especially Chapters 9–10 and 21–25; and John C. Olin, *Christian Humanism and the Reformation: Selected Writings of Erasmus*, 3rd ed. (New York, 1987), pp. 1–37. On his influence on the religious thought and historical sensibilities of the period, see Istvan Pieter Bejczy, *Erasmus and the Middle Ages: The Historical Consciousness of a Christian Humanist* (Leiden and Boston, 2001).

136 See Craig R. Thompson, trans., *The Colloquies of Erasmus* (Chicago and London, 1965), pp. 285–7. Thompson also notes that an anonymous English translation was printed in 1536 or 1537 (p. 285).

of the aspects of Marian devotion that were, by the end of the Middle Ages, conspicuous enough to be lampooned.

The colloquy's discussion of Walsingham begins with a letter of complaint from Mary, addressed to 'Glaucoplutus' (a Greek version of 'Ulrich', Zwingli's first name). In it, Mary first praises Luther's disciples for unburdening her of the incessant pleadings of devotees from all walks of life, but she also laments the dispossession of the cult of saints and warns that she will not be put out, 'nisi simul eiecto filio ... aut hunc una mecum extrudes, aut utrumque relinques, nisi mavis habere templum sine Christo' (unless at the same time you eject my Son ... Either you expel him along with me, or you leave us both here, unless you prefer to have a church without Christ).[137] Though the letter goes to Zwingli and plays on Reformation convictions about Marian mediation generally, this characterization of Mary is emphatically English. Ogygius claims that he can validate the letter because he has the autograph copy, in 'manum angeli, qui est virgini ab epistolis' (written in the hand of the angel who is the Virgin's secretary), and the hand is easily identifiable because it is the same one that inscribed 'epitaphium Bedae' (Bede's epitaph) in Durham Abbey: 'elementorum figurae per omnia congruunt' (the shape of the letters agree entirely).[138] Erasmus's fantasy of the Marian document calls up images of the law-bearing Mary so frequently associated with her miracles in the examples I have studied, and it insists on a Marian link between the writing of English history and the history of English writing.

This estimation also influences Erasmus's caricature of English fastidiousness and learning. He had written Greek verses in honor of Mary on the occasion of his first visit to Walsingham, and the community there had been heroically struggling to understand them ever since. He is approached, consequently, as the man 'qui ante biennum affixisset votivam tabellam literis Hebraicis' (who two years earlier had put up a votive tablet in Hebrew), for the English canons, he says, 'quidquid non intelligunt, Hebraicum vocant' (call Hebrew anything they don't understand)![139] He describes their labors:

> quantopere sudatum sit a multis, ut versus eos legerent, quot frustra extersa perspicilla. Quoties advenisset aliquis vetustus Theologiae aut Iuris Doctor, adductus est ad tabellam, alius dicebat esse literas Arabicas, alius ficticias. Tandem repertus est qui legeret titulum. Is descriptus erat verbis ac literis Romanis, sed maiusculis; Graeci versus descripti Graecis maiusculis, quae prima specie videntur referre maiusculas Latinas. Rogatus descripsi senten-

---

[137] All Latin citations of the *Peregrinatio religionis ergo* follow Desiderius Erasmus, *Colloquia familiaria*, Perseus Digital Library [online] (Stoa Consortium, 1997). Full hyperlinked text available from: http://www.stoa.org/hopper/text.jsp?doc=Stoa:text:2003.02.0006:colloquium=39. English translations follow Thompson, *Colloquies*, pp. 287–312 (here p. 291), as does the note on the meaning of the name 'Glaucoplutus' (p. 286).

[138] Thompson, *Colloquies*, p. 289.

[139] Ibid., pp. 299–300. Erasmus did not know Hebrew himself (or at least not very well). On his linguistic training and skills, see Erika Rummel, *Erasmus as a Translator of the Classics*, Erasmus Studies (Toronto, 1985).

tiam carminum Latine, verbum verbo reddens. Huius opellae quum praemi-
olum oblatum constanter recusarem, affirmans nihil esse tam arduum quod
in Virginis sanctissimae gratiam non essem cupidissime facturus, etiam si
literas iuberet illinc perferre Hierosolymam.

How hard many persons toil to read those lines and how often they wipe
their spectacles in vain. Whenever some aged D.D. or J.D. came along
he was marched off to the tablet. One would say the letters were Arabic;
another, that they were fictitious characters. Finally one was found who
could read the title. It was written in Roman words and letters, but in capitals. The Greek lines were written in Greek capitals, which at first glance
look like Roman capitals. Upon request, I gave the meaning of the verses
in Latin, translating word for word. I refused the small tip proffered for this
bit of work, declaring there was nothing, however difficult, that I would not
be very eager to do for the sake of the Most Holy Virgin, even if she bade
me carry a letter from there to Jerusalem.[140]

The notion that Mary might require devoted couriers to run her letters all
over the world again evokes the image of Mary *legislatrix*, but the fictional-
ized account of toil over Marian text is also a commentary on certain preoc-
cupations of Marian devotion in England. The confusion of languages and
alphabets – Hebrew, Arabic, Roman, Greek, or altogether fictitious – is an
exaggerated criticism of the state of English monastic life and learning at the
end of the Middle Ages, but behind it is a parody of the English willingness
to believe in the importance of Marian text. If the verses are unreadable,
they are potentially miraculous – like those in the 'Blood on the Penitent
Woman's Hand' story[141] – and they hold a Marian lesson for those who gaze
at the Walsingham image. If they are in Hebrew – and the false recognition
reveals also a willingness to accept the Jewish language as appropriate to
Mary – they reflect the pseudo-Nazarene location. Erasmus's comment that
'they call Hebrew anything they don't understand', then, satirizes both the
English construction of 'otherness' and the English construction of Marian
devotion as an encounter with Jewishness.

But not long after the *Peregrinatio religionis ergo* was published, Walsingham was dissolved, and the shrine that had become the quintessential
example of the superstitious pilgrimage site and the excesses of Mariolatry
was a target of royal investigations that explicitly queried the validity of its
miracles. When the Walsingham canons accepted Henry VIII as head of the
English Church in 1534, they also subjected their priory to the visitations
and valuations of his royal commissioners.[142] One sixteenth-century miscellany (British Library MS Harley 791) preserves a list of nineteen questions
labeled 'Walsingham' (fol. 27r–v). These were clearly written after Erasmus's
colloquy – two of the questions relate directly to the information reported

---

[140]   Thompson, *Colloquies*, p. 300.
[141]   See Chapter 1, pp. 23–6, and Appendix 2.
[142]   Dickinson, *Shrine of Our Lady*, p. 59.

there – and it has long been assumed that they were generally influenced by Erasmus's account.[143] The majority, nevertheless, are non-specific. They interrogate the value of offerings made at the shrine, the value of movable goods related to the shrine, and the nature and validity of the relics there, and there is a striking focus on Marian miracles. Items 10–18 (almost all of those on fol. 27v) expressly query miracles, whether performed, written, or told. One asks 'what is the gretest miracle and most undoubted which is said to have ben doon by oure lady hire' and 'what prouffe [do] they have of the facte or the narracion therof'? Another queries the truth of the foundation miracle related in the 'Walsingham Ballad': 'what is the saying of the buylding of oure lady chappell?' Another addresses the use of Marian miracles as sermon *exempla*, 'whether the miracles were wonte to be declared in pulpite hertofor. And for what cause they were so?' Yet another implies that there had recently been a suspicious upsurge in miracles: it asks 'wheter our lady false doon so many miraclis nowe of late', when offerings had increased at the shrine. Three others question belief in Marian intercession more broadly: even if there is proof of a miracle, instructs the document, the commissioner should ask 'whether the same might not procede of the immediate helpe of god', and why a miracle 'shuld be imputed to oure lady' or 'to the image of our Lady in this house more than another?' Do 'they know not that men shulde not be light of credite to miracles?' And 'what pruffe were they wont to take of the miraclis that the pilgrims did reporte shulde be made by our Lady?'

Collectively, these give the impression of a near-compulsive interest in the miracle problem. The visitation questions cover all modes of circulation – miracles done, narrated, preached, and perhaps even written (at least there is clear allusion to the foundation story and to Erasmus's accounts) – and there seems to be consideration of both the local and general miracle types (those associated with this site, but also those that arriving pilgrims might tell). But this does not confirm that royal commissioners were gathering and destroying miracles collections and preachers' anthologies (the concern was more likely for the staging of fake miracle events that attempted to defraud believers of money). Rather, the Walsingham inquiry record makes clear that Marian miracles had hit both theological and social chords. They were a locus of conflict, of community, of class distinction (the royal commissioners versus the canons versus the mass of pilgrims), and they could prompt meditation on the nature of Marian intercession specifically and English religiosity generally.

By 1536, perhaps as a consequence of the type of inquiry preserved in MS Harley 791, most of the ornaments and valuables around the shrine had been sequestered, and visitations had produced reports that the entire house

---

[143] Dickinson, *Shrine of Our Lady*, discusses the Harley MS 'Articles of Inquiry' on pp. 61–2, and does assume that they are based on Erasmus. What follows, however, is based primarily on my own examinations and transcription of the text.

was the seat of 'much superstition in feigned relics and miracles'.[144] A year later, when several letters between royal officials suggested that there was a conspiracy at Walsingham to resist dissolution, Cromwell ordered the execution of all those involved, and the subprior and one layman were drawn, hanged, beheaded, and quartered on 30 May 1537.[145] In January 1538, a Walsingham woman was 'set in stocks for spreading rumours that the image from the despoiled shrine had begun to work miracles' again, and a magistrate wrote to Cromwell that he could not 'perceyve butt the seyd Image is not yett out of sum of ther heddes'.[146] The famous statue was seized and reached London on 18 July 1538, along with the statue of Our Lady of Ipswich, and it is likely that both were destroyed before the month was out. In August 1538, the Walsingham canons officially relinquished the priory and all its possessions to the king.[147]

The fear that monasteries might be reestablished, or that pilgrimage sites might endure and the rumors of miracles persist despite official injunctions, meant that religious houses, including Walsingham, were physically destroyed. As Margaret Aston puts it, 'Many of those who witnessed it must have found it a mournfully memorable sight. For the ending of monastic life in England was accomplished in quite as spectacular a way as that of revolutionary France.'[148] The buildings were razed, dismantled, carted away, sold for parts, and the ruins of centuries were created within a few years. By the end of the sixteenth century, one poet could lament the utter ruin of Walsingham:

> Levell levell with the ground the towres doe lye,
> Which with their golden, glitteringe tops pearsed once to the skye.
> …
> Weepe, weepe O Walsingham, whose dayes are nightes,
> Blessinge turned to blasphemies, holy deeds to despites.
> Sinne is wher our Ladie sate, heaven turned is to hell,
> Sathan sittes wher our Lord did swaye, Walsingham oh farwell.[149]

The nebulous role of Marian miracles in the lives of pilgrims and reformers can be seen in the remnant of Walsingham documents. These serve as contemporary witnesses to the power that Marian stories could have in the most fraught historical moments.

---

144 Ibid., p. 62.
145 Ibid., p. 64. The suspected Walsingham 'traditionalist plot' is also discussed in Duffy, *Stripping of the Altars*, pp. 397–403.
146 Duffy, *Stripping of the Altars*, p. 403.
147 Dickinson, *Shrine of Our Lady*, p. 65.
148 *Lollards and Reformers: Images and Literacy in Late Medieval Religion*, History Series 22 (London, 1984), p. 320.
149 'In the wrackes of Walsingham', in MS Bodl. Rawlinson Poetry 219, fol. 16r–v. The text dates to the last quarter of the sixteenth century and has been tentatively ascribed to Phillip, Earl of Arundel. See Dickinson, *Shrine of Our Lady*, pp. 67–8.

Yet the shrine's fate is not the fate of the English Miracles of the Virgin. The little, scattered narratives that are the subject of this book were surely caught up in the fits of devotion and merriment and conflict that resulted in the razing of Walsingham and other Marian shrines, but they resisted localization. They were aggressively exemplary. To return to R. W. Southern's words, 'they appealed to too many people to be confined', and they did not implicate 'the reputation of any church or corporate body'.[150] The evidence of Miracles of the Virgin in the medieval English landscape shows that they were most dynamic in their miscellaneity – that difference that this project started with – and that their cultural and social importance lay exactly in those interactions that have, in part, contributed to the feeling that they show no development. Marian intercession appealed to a rapidly changing, rapidly literate world, and this is modeled in the miracles' variable discursive modes, and most interestingly revealed when their content intersects the most difficult upheavals of the age: the rapid codification of law in the thirteenth century, the expulsion of the Jews, and the Protestant Reformation.

[150]   *Making of the Middle Ages*, pp. 246, 248.

Afterword

There are many *desiderata* at the conclusion of this study. From some angles it seems as if all paths of inquiry lead to these texts. But any reader attuned to a single miracle or group of miracles, or to a particular century or language or genre, will be struck by what has not been said. There is important work to be done on the possibility of Marian miracles in English drama, on gender issues within and around these tales, on associated reading habits and patronage of royalty, on further source work and continental comparisons, on the relationships between local and general miracles, on the many English illustrations of Marian miracles,[1] and especially on the Anglo-Norman collections. I have focused on what struck me many years ago as some conspicuous organizing features of the supposedly disorganized English examples, and on one through-line of development traceable from the earliest iterations of the Theophilus legend in England and down to the end of the Middle Ages. But there is much more that might be said, and I hope that it will be said.

The presence in the medieval consciousness, however, of a Marian figure of ferocity and learnedness and usefully ambiguous Jewish-Christian religious identity is an important corrective to the often too-easily accepted notion that the object of Marian devotion was either consistently gentle and maternal or somehow (simply) all-meaningful. I do not think that Mary could be all things to all people. Rather, surviving Miracles of the Virgin show that she could fulfill very specific functions in the English imagination, and that those functions could shift with regional and temporal conditions. The sign 'Mary' had a range of possible meanings, yes, but these are the kinds of texts that hold up mirrors. Mary's legal and Jewish embodiments in these miracles are a performance of English and Christian law, made flexible and accessible. Her unstable and potentially infinite performances mark her as a flashpoint, a creative and paradoxical sign, in some of the most familiar medieval English literary and theological negotiations. The figure that stands out at the end of this study – the figure of Mary *legislatrix* – is also a figure of English desire and identity.

---

[1] Queen Mary's Psalter (MS BL Royal 2 B. VII) immediately comes to mind. It includes a full collection of Miracles of the Virgin (over forty of them) in the margins of fols 204v–232r, but these exist only in the form of illustrations (the associated texts are psalms and canticles). My thanks to Maidie Hilmo for drawing my attention to these.

Appendix 1

'The Founding of the Feast of the Conception' in the *South English Legendary*

A Note on the Manuscripts

There are more than fifty extant manuscripts of the *South English Legendary*. Its earliest form dates *c*.1270–1285, and the earliest example (in Bodleian, MS Laud Misc. 108) is not much later. The number of items in a full *Legendary* varies considerably, but the majority (excluding fragments) includes a series of six Miracles of the Virgin, which are appended to the 'Life of Theophilus' (see Chapter 3).[1] The story of the founding of the Conception is separate from these, extant in only four late examples, all of which date between the late fourteenth and mid-fifteenth century. These are: Bodleian Library MS Bodley 779, fols 244v–245v (hereafter 'B'); Lambeth Palace Library MS 223, fols 31v–33r (hereafter 'L'); British Library MS Stowe 949, fols 100v–102r (hereafter 'S'); and Bodleian Library MS Eng. Poet. a. 1, fols 6v–7r (the Vernon Manuscript, hereafter 'V'). I have had the opportunity to examine B and S *in situ*, and L and V in facsimile. The Conception legend comprises a prologue to apocryphal narratives of the Virgin Mary's birth and life in all but S, where it concludes the apocryphal story.[2] I print S here, however, since the most significant variants tend to be different from each other or take the form of additions to S, which appears to be the earliest of the four. I amend in S only obvious errors, and I note only additions or variants that may change meaning or emphasis; I have not noted orthographic variants, minor changes in word order or (added or omitted but not grammatically influential) pronouns, nor have I noted substitutions of very common synonyms. Abbreviations are silently expanded and punctuation and capitalization altered for ease of reading.

---

[1] On the manuscripts and complex dissemination history, see Manfred Görlach, *Textual Tradition of the SEL*; and Charlotte D'Evelyn, *The South English Legendary: Introduction and Glossary*, EETS, os 244 (London, 1959).

[2] O. S. Pickering has edited the 'Nativity of Mary and Christ' from this manuscript (S) in *The South English Nativity of Mary and Christ*, Middle English Texts 1 (Heidelberg, 1975). On this edition and the manuscript's quality, see also Thorlac Turville-Petre's review of Pickering's edition in *Modern Language Review* 73.4 (1978), p. 870.

Text

Welle we witen whanne & whou þe feste schal ben yholde
Þe Concepcioun of ur lady, as þe bok us tolde.
Nas þe feste noþing ykud wiþouten eny fayle
Atfore þat Wyliam conquerour wan Englond in batayle
5 & slowh Harald in batayle, þat oure kyng was þo.
Þan was Wiliam conquerour kyng & duk also.
Kyng he was of Englonde & duk of Normanndie.
Of boþe þe londes he held þe seignorie.
Wel swiþe sone þerafter wel wyde sprong þe sauwe
10 Þat Harald þe king of Engelond wiþ treison was aslawe.
Þo þe king of Denemark þat forsoþe wuste,
Þat ilke tyme to king Harald hadde mest truste,
He let of Dauenische men ȝarken gret nauye
& þouhte þe king Wiliam ofsechen & destruye,
15 And is oste gan gaderen wiþ þe Normanns to fihte,
Uorsoþe it was þat king Willam nas nout kyng wiþ rihte.
So sone so it wuste þe unkynde kyng William
Þat þe kyng of Denemarke wiþ is pouwer cam,
Swiþe riche ȝiftes ouer see he him sende
20 To uoreward þat he hamward aȝen wiþ his poer wende.
He sende him by is messagers boþe gold & fe
& of riche cloþes swiþe gret plente
Wiþ þe wyseste man ychosen of þe contreye,
Þat was Elsy þulke tyme abbot of Rameseye.
25 Him he het þoru alle þing þarewiþ for to go,
For he was þe wiseste man þat men wusten þo.
Þe abbot say þat he nede moste & sone forþ he wende
To Denemarch wiþ is presaunt, as þe king him sende.

1 **Welle we witen**] B Alle ȝe wetyn, L Wole ȝe now wete, V Wolle ȝe wite
2 **þe bok us**] V a maister me   **tolde**] L *expunges* telles
4 **conquerour**] BLV bastard
5 **ure kyng was**] L was þe kyng
6 **conquerour**] BLV bastard
8 **seignorie**] V maystrie
10 **wiþ treison**] L þen
11 **Þo**] SL *omit word* (þo *or* whan)   **king**] L duke   **þat forsoþe**] V þe soþe þerof
12 BSV *insert* he *after* **Harald**   **mest truste**] V much triste
13 **ȝarken**] B gadre, L ordeyne   **nauye**] V rayne
14 **destruye**] V distrayne
16 **soþe it was**] L hem þoȝt, V soþe he wuste
20 **poer**] V ost
24 **Elsy**] B elsine, V *omits name*
25 **het þoru**] L bede ouer
26 **wusten**] B foundin, VL fond(e)
27 **þat**] V *omits word*

He hadde þe wynd & wederinge boþe softe & stille
30 & þerto spedy passage at is oune wille.
Sone so he ariued was, is presaunt so faire he dude
Þat þe king wel corteysliche aueng it in þe stude.
His erles & is baronnes eke he delede it al aboute
& bihet hom faire ynou heom þat were wiþoute.
35 So hendeliche wiþ hem he spak by on & by on
& made of hem is gode frendes þat eror weren is fon.
Þo he hadde þat iȝiuen aboute of iewis what he wolde,
& of stones preciouse, of suluer & of golde,
At þe kyng curteysliche þere is leue he nom
40 So þat to is schip aȝen wiþ gret honour he com.
He nadde yseyled in þe see bote one wel schorte þrouwe
Þat þe wynd him aȝen sone bygan to blouwe
& þe stormes of þe see so grete gonne aryse
Þat þe schipmen euerichon sore hem gan agrise.
45 Ar it were of þe day our ney any tyde,
Þe schip was ydriue up & doun in þe see wel wilde.
Þo nusten hii what to done or what þing hem was best,
Uor uurste her ropes bursten alle & seþþen hor mast.
Here steresman þat was ne couþe heom noþing rede
50 Bote to ur leuedy ȝerne þat hii bede.
Among alle þat þerinne weren sorwe þer was ynou
Þat monye for wo þat þerinne were by þe toppe hem drou.
Hii nusten to whiche londe þe wynd hor schip ladde,
Neren hii neuir half bifore syker sore adradde.
55 Iesu Crist godes sone & is moder Marie
Hii bytoken al & some here schip for to gye.
A wel briht aungel in þe see þo cam gon þere
As druȝe auote upon þe watre as he alonde were
Wiþ clene cloþes, & white ycloþed he him hadde.

29 **softe**] B loud
30 **spedy**] BV redy
31 **ariued**] V at ned **presaunt so faire**] L message soone
32 **it**] V him
33 **delede it**] V biheold
38 V *reads* in none maner þere dwellen lengore he nolde   BL *insert* & oþer nobley(ne)s *after*
suluer
41 **one wel schorte**] B a litil, L a short
43 **stormes of**] B wawis in
44 **everychon**] V on and on wel
45 **our ney any**] B mydmorn, V ouerneih atte
46 **wel wilde**] BL ful wide (*or* wyde), V wel wyde
50 **to ur**] B alle to oure, L rad hem to oure, V bad hem to ur
52 **Þat money for wo þat þerinne were**] V euerich mon him self for wo
57 **þo**] V to hem   **þere**] L nere
58 **auote**] V *omits word*

60   To þis abbot Elsy wel myldeliche he gradde.
       Him he het þat he scholde wiþoute fayle fonde
       & wiþ him baldeliche speke & bad him up stonde.
       Þis godeman þat er of þe weder agros
       Of þe tiþinge he was glad & þe raþer he aros.
65   Þe aungel him seide, '3if þat þou þenkest, godeman, alyue
       Euirmore in Englonde hol & sound aryue,
       Auouwe þat þou schalt & þat þou wolt euir after þis day,
       Of oure leuedy Marie, wiþouten eny delay,
       To holden þe Concepcion, þe derworþe feste,
70   & halewi here in eueri toun schal ben þin biheste.
       Byhote þou most wiþ gode wille & taken it an honde
       To teche men forþere ouer al in Engelonde
       Þat hii after þis day hey3liche holde
       Þe feste of þe Concepcioun, as ich eror tolde,
75   Þo þat heo yconceyued was & þo heo was bi3ute,
       For me herde neuir telle ne fond it ywrite.'
       To þis holy aungel spak þis godeman,
       'Þe feste of þe Concepcioun halewe I ne can,
       What day ne what tyme ur lady was bi3ete,
80   For I ne herde neuir telle ne fond it ywrite,
       Ne nouþer of þe seruise þat falleþ to þe feste
       Siker I not no betere þan a wylde beste.
       Þerefore þou most me teche neodfulliche nou
       Which tyme ich her schal holden & hou.'
85   'Bote tel þe eyteþe day in þe byginnynge
       Of Decembre as he ualleþ wiþoute lesinge,
       & þulke sulue day, ich do þe to wyte,
       Of Anna heo conceyued was, of Ioachim by3ete.'

---

60 **þis]** S is   **Elsy]** B elsine, V elsyn   S *in right margin in a sixteenth-century hand* howe & wherefore the feste of the Concep*cion* of our lady was kept and fyrste ordynyd
63 **weder]** BV water (*or* wadur)
67 **þat þou schalt & þat þou wolt]** B þu wat þat þu chalt (*with illegible scribal error before* þat), V þow most þat þou wolt
68 **leuedy]** B ladyes day
72 **men forþere]** B ilk man fer & ner, L men þis þinge ferþer   V *inserts* to al *after* in
73 **Þat hy]** B & euir   **hey3liche]** V evere þe feste
75 **Þo ... þo]** BL how ... how
76 V *reads* Loke þou do as ich þe teche þat hit ne beo for lete   **me]** B i
77 V *reads* þo þat aungel þis hedde iseid onswerde þis holy mon
78 L *inserts* he saide *after* **Concepcioun**
80 B *reads* for neuer 3it in no stede ne coulde i finde it wrete, L *reads* for neuer 3ett in no stid I ne couþe hit under 3eten, V *reverses the order of lines* 79 *and* 80 *and reads* ne herde ich neuere telle ne fond ich neuere iwrite
82 V *reads* Nam ich no wysore but as hit was a beeste
84 V *reads* which tyme þe feste schal beo iholde and which maner and hou *and then inserts two lines:* þo þe aungel sauh þis þat hit was to done / he bi gon to teche stilleliche and sone
85 BV *omit* **Bote**   B *inserts* he sayde *after* **tel**(le)

     'Þei þou me habbe þis ytauht, more þou most me wyse:

90 Whiche schal þulke feste day ben oure seruyse?'

     'Bote þe seruyse þou schalt nyme of hire burþetime,

     & riht so heyȝe ordre nyme forþ, matynes & prime,

     Bote whare þat þou fyndest Natiuitas ywrite

     Þere schal Concepcio forþ ben ysmyte.'

95 Þis abbot auouwede auou þat he wolde euirest more

     Holden þe Concepcion & don after is lore.

     He byhet hym ouer al halyday to bede

     Fer & ner in ech contre where þat he ȝede

     & to done also þe seruise, þat was his auou,

100 Clanliche of þe Burþtime as we yseþ nou.

     So sone he hadde þe uou ymad, þe tempest him wiþdrou.

     Þis abbot þonkede God & oure leuedy & was glad ynou.

     Þe cloude bygan to abreyde & þe sonne schon.

     Þe see was as stille as it were a ston.

105 Þe aungel after þulke tyme ne schewid him namore.

     Hii schipede forþ in þe see & þonkede godes ore

     And ariuede in a lutel while up in Engelonde.

     Of grace þat hii hadde yfounde hii þonked godes sonde,

     & þis þat hem bytidde hii tolden wel wide,

110 By este by weste & by souþe & by þe norþ side.

     Hii haleweden þe feste so as hii byhete

     & beden ouer al wher hii come þat hii nout ne lete.

     Alle þat habbeþ yherde of our leuedyis Concepcioun

     Of here synnes god hem ȝiue, þoru is grace, remissioun.

89 V *inserts* þe abbot seide *at start of line*

90 **oure]** V of hire swete

91–2 V *substitutes four lines:* þou ne schalt nouþur sigge þe more ne þe lasse / nouþur at euensong at matins ne at masse / at underne and eke at non at midday and at prime / þou schalt bi ordre take as in hire burþtyme

92 **& riht so heyȝe ordre nyme forþ]** B Al of þe selue ordre   L *reads* þe *for* heyȝe

94 **Concepcio]** V þe Concepcion   **ysmyte]** L ysete

95 **auou]** V *omits word*   **euirest more]** V hire fest euermore

97 **halyday to bede]** S to bede to bede

98 S *omits line (line from B inserted above)*, L *reads* fer & ner by þe contreyes whereso euer he ȝede, V *reads* fer and neer bi þe cuntreye wher þat he eode

101 **him]** L *omits word*

102 **ynou]** V and louh

103 B *inserts* bryȝt *after* **sonne**

104 **see]** V weder

105 **schewid]** V seȝen

107 **And ariuede in a lutel while]** V heo a loondeden in a luytel toun   **while]** BL sto(u)nde

108 **þonked]** V herieden

109 V *inserts* al *after* **&**

111 BV *insert* holy *after* **þe**

112 **ouer al]** BL all oþer

113 **þat habbeþ yherde]** B þo þat now haue herd

113–14 V *omits lines*

114 **ȝiue þoru is grace]** B grante plener, L graunte full

Appendix 2

'Blood on the Penitent Woman's Hand'

A Note on the Manuscript and Related Texts

The text printed below comes from Bodleian Library MS e Museo 180, a late fifteenth-century manuscript that contains a full *de tempore* sermon cycle, including some material from John Mirk's *Festial*. It can be found on fols 62v–64r, where it concludes a sermon on penitence designated for the third Sunday after Pentecost (*sancte trinitatis*). The codex is closely related to three others, all of which record very nearly the same sequence of homilies, two of which are written entirely in the same hand.[1] The sermon that precedes this *exemplum* also appears in Gloucester Cathedral Library MS 22 (in the second binding), and Lincoln Cathedral Library MS 50.[2] I have been unable to examine these, however, and so cannot verify whether the *exemplum* (or the same version of it) is appended in these cases.

The e Museo 180 version appears really to be a combination of two common Marian miracle stories, catalogued in the *MWME* XXIV as 'Blood on the Penitent Woman's Hand' and 'Woman who Committed Incest'.[3] The first type features Christ as the direct intercessor (the blood comes from the wound in his side rather than a murdered infant) and not the Virgin Mary. Analogues of this type can be found twice in both British Library MS Royal 18 B. XXIII and John Mirk's *Festial*, and in the *Gesta Romanorum*.[4] One of the versions in Royal 18 B. XXIII is the only analogue I have seen that has the blood on the woman's hand turning into Latin text (or text at all), though the Latin is significantly different and no vernacular translation is provided.[5] The second type, in which the Virgin Mary intercedes to save an incestuous woman from a devil, can be found in British Library MS Additional 39996,

---

[1] See Fletcher, 'Unnoticed Sermons'. One of these (Gloucester Cathedral Library MS 22) has sections that are written by a different scribe. Of the related codices, Fletcher suggests that e Museo 180 is 'textually the best of the four' (p. 516).

[2] For more information, see Whiteford, *Myracles of Oure Lady*, pp. 127–8.

[3] See Appendix 4 for more detail.

[4] See Willy L. Braekman and Peter S. Macaulay, 'Two Unpublished Middle English Exempla from MS. Royal 18 B. XXIII', *Neuphilologische Mitteilungen* 72 (1971), pp. 97–104; Ross, *Middle English Sermons*, pp. 216–17 (notes on pp. 262–3); Erbe, *Mirk's Festial*, pp. 90, 95–6; and Sydney J. H. Herrtage, ed., *The Early English Versions of the Gesta Romanorum*, EETS, es 33 (London, 1879), p. 393.

[5] Braekman and Macaulay, 'Two Unpublished Middle English Exempla', p. 99: 'on hire thomme þise wordes Casus cecidisti. carne cocata. In secundo digitu. Demoni dedisti deo dicata In tercio digitu Resurgens a reatu. regina rogata In quarto digitu. puerum perdidisti. pena palliata. In quinto digitu Monstrat manifeste manus maculata.'

178

the *Alphabet of Tales*, and *Jacob's Well*. Only in the latter two has the woman slain a newborn – though Latin, French, Spanish, and Italian analogues of this type do include the slaying of the child – and none of this type mentions blood on the hand or miraculous text.[6]

In the e Museo 180 text that follows, abbreviations are silently expanded and punctuation and capitalization minimally modernized. I note the very few scribal corrections, in case they should prove helpful in any comparison to the related codices.

Text

Narracio. Accordyng to this we fynde among the myrakils of oure lady that there was some tyme a gentil woman. And sche was full of deuocion and used many deuowte prayers to owre lady. And sche used grete penaunce, as fastyng and almes dedys doyng with many other good dedis of devocion,
5 þe whiche perteyned to good lyvyng. So þe deuil had grete enuy to hyr and tempted hyr to fowle lyuyng, and so ouercame hyr þat hyr owne sonne had to do withe hyr in þe synne of lechery, thorow hyr owne desyre be þe deuils temptacion. And be hym sche had a childe, þe **[63r]** whiche was kept priuy frome all pepill. And at the burthe of this child was no creature but
10 god and sche hyr self hyr sonne & the deuill, the whiche child when it was borne sche brake the neke there of & so slew it. And in the brekyng of the neke of þis childe ther fell iiii droppis of bloode upon hyr ryȝte hond, the whiche blood grew in to iiii uersis of herd latyn. Sche kowde rede hem but sche kowde not understonde þem. And sche had assayed with dyuers licors
15 many tymes and ofte to whassche hem a wey and it wold not be. Also sche had beried hir child prively and so fro þat tyme sche contenewid still in synne withe hyr sonne, and had left all hyr good dedys and good lyuyng and liuyd so in þe deuyls seruyce. But at þe last þe quene of comforthe and moder of merci owre lady Seynt Mary the moder of Iesu, sche had
20 pite and compassion up on hyr be cawse of hyr firste lyuyng. And so this glorius uirgyn in an euyntyde as þe curat of the chyrche, a gracius disposed preste, was walkyng in the chirche in his deuyne seruice seyng and other

1 **Narracio]** in margin
9 ch *(presumably the beginning of 'child') expunged before* **burthe**
22 man *expunged before* **preste**

6   See Tryon, 'Miracles of Our Lady in Middle English Verse', pp. 360–1; Banks, *Alphabet of Tales*, pp. 220–2; and Brandeis, *Jacob's Well*, pp. 66–7. The latter two, set in Rome, include court proceedings in which the Virgin Mary appears to defend the incestuous woman; and the *Jacob's Well* version is notable for its possible connection to 'The Prioress's Tale', as the woman throws her slain child 'in a gonge'. The 'Roman' version was part of the original Vernon manuscript collection of Marian miracles too: the contemporary contents list notes (the twenty-seventh miracle in the list) a tale 'Of a wommon off Rome þat conceyuede bi heore owne sone, & slou heore child' (Horstmann, *Minor Poems*, p. 138 n. 2). Other analogues are catalogued under 'Incest Between Mother and Son' (*CSM* Number 17) in the *CSMD*.

holy prayers. Sche a-**[63v]**perid to hym bodily and bad hym aske this gentil
woman, þis synner, whi sche was not so uertuesly disposed as sche was
25   wont to be long a fore þat tyme. 'And when þu hast asked hyr þis question
þen forthe with sche wyll desyre to be confessyd, but sche wil not in hyr
confescion tell hyr greues synnes, the whiche bythe so abhomynabill, but if
sche wyll schryue hyr of þem els þei wil be þe cawse of hyr dampnacion.
And þerfore take hyr ry3te honde and rede to hyr her synnes, the whiche is
30   and schall be couerde withe a clothe abowte hyr honde.' & on the morow
this synfull woman cam to þe chirche, more for babans of the worlde þen
for deuocion. And this curat dyd as he was comawndyd of owre lady. And
for grete schame sche went to schrifte to hym but sche wold not schryue
hyr of tho synnes, þe whiche scholde be the cawse of hyr dampnacion, and
35   there he toke hyr be the hande and toke awey the clothe. And red the versis
þat grew of the bloode. Casu cecidisti carne cecata / Demoni dedisti dona
dicata // Monstrat maliciam manus immaculata Recedit rubigo regina **[64r]**
Rogata // Thu blynde in flesche hast fall in a case / Þu hast geuen to þe fende
þings þat riche was / That berthe witnes þe rede honde þat thu has / The
40   rednes is a go pray to þe quene of grace. When sche herd all þis then sche
wept sore and withe þe teeris þat fel downe sche wassched the blody uersis
clene a wey, wherbi they understode that hyr synnes were clene for 3euen
of god. So euery synner be sory for his offens, make confescion of mowthe.
And in like wise fulfill þi penaunce withe duw satisfaccion. Þen ioye schall
45   be in heuen of thi conuersion. To þe whiche ioye &cetera.

29 hede *expunged after* **take**

180

Appendix 3

The Charter Group Miracles and Other Short Texts from British Library MS Additional 37049

A Note on the Manuscript

British Library MS Additional 37049 is a mid- to late fifteenth-century religious miscellany of Carthusian English (probably northern) provenance. All of its texts are in English, with occasional macaronic verses and prayers, and it is heavily illustrated with colorful and amateurish (though not unbeautiful) drawings in a style indicative 'of informal rather than liturgical devotion'.[1] Both its texts and illustrations, which must be read together, are primarily concerned with the suffering of Christ, the fate of the body and soul after death, and the role of the Virgin Mary in Christian salvation. Douglas Gray has called it 'an English vernacular example of a "spiritual encyclopedia of the later Middle Ages"',[2] and Jessica Brantley has published a very learned book on the entire codex, though discussion of the Marian miracles printed here are not a part of it (for which see my analysis in Chapter 4).[3] Plates of its illustrations are now widely accessible, both in Brantley's book and in James Hogg's work,[4] but many of its shorter texts remain unedited.[5]

The texts printed here are: a group of three brief notices on the face and name of the Virgin Mary (fol. 21r–v), including a 'Note on the Beauty of the Virgin' (fol. 21r), a 'Rhapsody on the Name of Mary' (fol. 21v), and the 'Tale of the Lazy Servant of St Anselm' (fol. 21v); a 'Marian Miracle of a Clerk' (fol. 27r); and seven Miracles of the Virgin that appear together near the end of the manuscript (fols 94r–95v). The 'Marian Miracle of a Clerk', which concerns a clerk who questions the quality of an icon painted by St Luke,

1   Brantley, *Reading in the Wilderness*, p. 4.
2   'London, British Library, Additional MS 37049', p. 100. Gray makes the same comment in his *Themes and Images*, p. 52.
3   Brantley does, however, consider the texts on fol. 21r–v (printed below) within her discussion of meditation on 'holy names'. See *Reading in the Wilderness*, pp. 184–7. See also p. 115 n. 49 above.
4   Hogg's work includes a manuscript description and partial edition, as well as reproductions of all illustrations. See, respectively, 'Unpublished Texts in the Carthusian Northern Middle English Religious Miscellany' and *An Illustrated Yorkshire Carthusian Religious Miscellany*. A description is also in George F. Warner, ed., *Catalogue of Additions to the Manuscripts in the British Museum in the Years 1900–1905* (London, 1907), pp. 324–32. Illustrations most relevant to my discussion are reproduced above, in Plates 5–10.
5   Brantley, *Reading in the Wilderness*, pp. 307–25, provides a detailed list of the manuscript's contents with notation of which texts have yet to be edited, along with current bibliographical references keyed to individual items.

appears also in Wynkyn de Worde's late fifteenth-century collection *Myracles of Oure Lady* and has been edited by Peter Whiteford in that context, but there are notable differences between that version and the one here.[6]

The final seven consecutive prose Marian miracles form a unit that I call the Charter Group. The label refers both to their organization around a single illustration of Mary returning a charter to devotees and to their general content, which by and large focuses on Mary's legal and textual intercessions. The Charter Group is severely damaged: the lower outside corners of the folios are lost due to tearing, so that about one-fifth of the pages is missing. In what follows, I have represented damaged text with bracketed ellipses ([…]), though, because of the nature of the damage, this does not always represent an equal amount of missing text. Throughout, I have completed damaged words without comment only when I am certain of my reading; otherwise, provided letters will appear within the brackets. Abbreviations are expanded and scribal corrections inserted silently, punctuation and capitalization minimally modernized. Editorial titles are inserted in square brackets ([ ]) and follow those used in Brantley's contents list and the *MWME* XXIV.[7]

Texts

[On the Blessed Face and Name of Mary, fol. 21r–v]

[21r, Note on the Beauty of the Virgin] Of þe fayrnes of Saynt Mary gods moder oure lady. Oof þe fayrhed of Saynt Mary, Alexander says þat thre fayrnesses is. One is natural, ane oþer is spryrttual, þe thyrd is essencyal. Ffayrhed natural worschipt hyr body. Ffayrhed spyrtual anowrnyd hir mynde. Þe endles fayrnes þat is essencial inhabyt bodely in þe chawmer of þe uyrgyn wome. Mary had swylk natural fayrnes þat I hope neuer woman in þis lyfe had swylk fayrnes. Fforþi it is sayd of Saynt Ignacius þat of tymes wrote pystyls to þe blyssed virgyn, & sche to hym agayne, þat when he sawe þe blyssed virgyn he felle to þe erthe for þe fayrnes he sawe in hyr face & in hyr body. And whan he rose at hyr byddyng, it is sayd þat he sayd, if he had not bene certyfyed by hyr & by Saynt Ion þe euangelist & verely bene informed in þe faythe, he had trowed þat no oþer god had bene bot sche, for þe wondyrful shynyng of hyr face & excellent fayrnes. And be certayn argument we may prefe þat sche was fayrest of body. ffor

5

10

1–2 **Of þe fayrnes of Saynt Mary gods moder oure lady. O]** *in red*
1–10 **Of þe fayrnes of … in hyr body. And whan he rose]** *at left, within the text block (sharing 24 lines of the page), an illustration of a crowned Virgin Mary and infant Christ with dove. Reproduced in Brantley,* Reading in the Wilderness, *p. 188 (Figure 5.12).*

6   See *Myracles of Oure Lady*, pp. 71–2 (item 46), and p. 94, where analogues are briefly discussed. Whiteford also catalogues the Miracles of the Virgin in this manuscript on pp. 120–1.
7   The 'Marian Miracle of a Clerk' (fol. 27r) is an exception. Brantley and *MWME* XXIV call this 'Marian Miracle of the Clerk at Oxford' or 'The Clerk of Oxford', but I have adjusted the title, as Oxford is not named in this version.

15   it is written of hyr son Iesu þat he was fayrest before þe sonnes of men.
And certayne so þe moder was fayrest before þe doghtyrs of men. Ffor þi
ilk deuowte seruant to hyr says, 'Quia pulcra es amica, &c.' Þat is, 'How
fayr art þu my frende, how fayr & how semely.' It is sayd þat fro þat tyme
þat sche had conceyfed þe son of rightwysnes þat a brightnes of þe son

20   schane in hyr face, þat Ioseph myght not se in hyr face before sche was
delyuered. If þe face of moyses so schane for the compeny of þe wordes of
god þat þe sonnes of Israel myght not luke in hys face, how mykil more þis
blyssed uyrgyn þat was umbyschadowed of þe uertewe of þe aller hyghest
& þat þe holy goste lightyd in. **[21v, Rhapsody on the Name of Mary]**

25   Ffrebertus says, 'A Mary, a þu gret, a þu mylde. A þu onely lufabyll. Mary
þu may neuer be neuynde bot þu kyndels, nor þoght bot þu comforths &
fedes þe affections of þi lufer.' Also a conuers sayd, 'A, þu glorios lady
Saynt Mary blyssed uirgyn moder of god, doghtyr of Iesu, hande mayden
of Iesu, moder of Iesu, nures of Iesu, systyr of Iesu, ffrend & lufer of Iesu,

30   luf of Iesu, swetnes of Iesu. A, Mary of Iesu, ffor þu dwels in Iesu, & Iesu
in þe, fforþi he þat lufes Iesu, he lufes þe, and he þat lufes þe lufes Iesu.
Ffor by inseperabyl luf ȝe ar ioyned togedyr, fforþi by grace I couet to hafe
in my mynde þe name of Mary closed within þe name of Iesu, and þe name
of Iesu closed with in þe name of Mary. And so by þe name of Ihesu & þe

35   name of Mary, I sal hafe þe moder & þe son, þe fadyr & þe holy goste, ffor
none may say 'lord Iesu' bot in þe holy gost. And wher þe holy gost is þer
is þe holy trynyte indyuysibill incomprehensybyll, o god almyghty.' **[Tale
of the Lazy Servant of St Anselm]** Þer was a seruand of Saynt Ancelme
þat when his feloo bad hym ryse of his bed opon a Sonday & go to þe kyrk

40   with þaim, ha lay styll & wald not ryse for þaim & bard þe chawmer dore
after þaim, þat þai suld not let hym to hafe his ese. And þan come þer a
fende to a hole & cald opon hym & sayd þat he had broght hym a gyft. &
þan he rase naked & come to þe hole, þer as a child myght not pas forthe
at. & þo he sawe when he put forthe his hande ane ugly roghe deuyll with

45   byrnand eene, sprenkylland mowthe & nosethryls lowande lyke to a bere,
þat toke hym by þe arme. And he wald hafe crost hym bot he myght not,
for he was flayd oute of wytte. & þan þe fende puld hym oute at þat lytel
wyndow withouten any horte & keste hym opon hys bake & flow forthe
with hym sum tyme in þe ayer & by þe erthe & þorow woddes. And when

50   he felde it was a fende þat barc hym he gret & made gret sorow, blamyng
his slewthe, tellyng his synnes, & beheste to amende hym if he myght
stape þat perell. & þan he askyd help of sayntes to pray for hym before þe
maieste of god, be whome he coniured þe fende to tell hym whyter he wald
bere hym. & þe fende sayd, 'To hell.' Þan þe fende bare hym þorow clewes

55   & cragges depe & strayte, & þan he cryde & sayd, 'Lord Iesu Criste by
þe uirtew of þi passion & þe prayer of þi blissed moder, haf mercy on me

34–5 **þe name of Ihesu & þe name of Mary]** þe name of Mary & þe name of Mary
before correction

wretche. And glorios uirgyn Mary hafe mercy on me in þis gret nede lyke
to perresche.' & sone þe enmy stode stil & sayd, 'Þu syngs to me a bytter
sange þat rehersis þe name of Mary.' And þan with a gret ugly crye he kest
60 hym downe opon a hepe of stones & vanysched away. Þan wyst he not wher
he was & made gret sorow & prayed, and son come in a mans lyknes ane
angel & askyd whyne he was & why he was nakyd. & þan he teld hym al
how he was delyuerd by þe help of Saynt Mary. & þan seyd þe angel, '&
þow had not cald þe name of oure lady þu had entyrd into helle […] fro
65 now forthe be deuowte to þi delyuerer & forgyt not þat þu suffers. Þu […]
so fer fro home þat be mans helpe þu cummes neuer agayne.' And þ[…]
he was made slepyng with þe angel help brought to þe same in war he […]
was, layd in a hows opon a hyghe balke. & when he felt hym selfe þer he
[…] of þe name of Saynt Mary besyly. And when his felows soght [hym]
70 þai hard hym cryyng of þe name of Saynt Mary & with mykil lab[our] gat
hym downe & warmed hym at a fyre, for he was ner hard lost. […] And þan
þe remelande of his lyfe he led in þe drede [of …].

[Marian Miracle of a Clerk, fol. 27r]

It is red in þe myrakils of oure lady þat a clerk luffed wele oure lady, þat in
so mykil þat he went unto Rome of deuocion þat he myght se þe ymage of
oure lady þe whilk as it is sayd Sayn Luke purtred. Efter when he had sene
þat ymage hym þoght it was noȝt so fayre as he trowede. Wherfore his luf
5 & his deuocion was noȝt so mykyl as it was before, or he sawe þat ymage.
Nerþeles he luffed hyr, bot not so intentyfly as he dyd before. At þe last he
fell seke & as he lay be hys one in his chawmer opon a day, oure blissed
lady apperyd unto hym & sayd unto hym, 'Þou went unto Rome þat þu suld
se me in myne ymage, and for þe fayrnes of it plesed þe noȝt, þe whilk þu
10 sawe in þe ymage, þi luf & þi deuocyon is lessend to me.' Þe blyssed uirgyn
was cled in a blak cote, & abowte hyr a gyrdyll, & a bende in hyr hede,
& bare fote. And þan sche sayd to þe seke clerke, 'Þus was y anowrned
when Gabriel schewed unto me þe incarnacion of þe son of god, and wer
not bot at þi luf & þi deuocion had bene to me, þu suld noȝt hafe bene in
15 heuen with me before my son. And for þi luf was lessend to me þu sal not
be unponesched with þis seknes, unto þe thyrd day. And þan sal I mete þe.
And for þan forth þu sal be in ioye.' & so sche went fro hym.

[The Charter Group Miracles, fols 94r–95v]

[94r, Prologue] Also it is gode for to hafe a special luf […] moder &
euermore calle on hyr in al […] prayers unto hir as Aue maria & […] socord
many a synful wretche & s[…] hir myrakels. [The Drowned Sacristan]

Miracle of a Clerk] *On the left, running alongside the entire miracle, an illustration
of the humbly clad Virgin Mary standing over a small clerk praying from his bed. On
the same page, above the miracle, the end of the 'Indulgences of St Clement', with an
illustration of a tree/cross on the right.*
Drowned Sacristan] *cf. Plate 8 above, from fol. 27v of the same manuscript.*

How þer was a chanon [...] of our lady Saynt Mary devoutely [...] avowtre.
5 & cumyng homeward [...] to passe þe watyr. And he [...] Mary. And when
he began [...] in myddes of þe flod a cumpeny [...] **[94v]** schyp bothe, &
raueschyd hys saule to torments. On þe thyrd day come þe blissed uirgyn
gods moder with compeny of saynts to þe place wher fendes tormentyd
þe saule, and sayd to þaim, 'Why torment 3e þe saule of my seruande
10 unrightwisly?' Þai sayd, 'We aske to hafe hym for he was take in oure
warke.' Oure lady sayd, 'If he suld be þair whame he seruyd, he suld be
oures for he sayd oure matens when 3e slewe hym, whar fore 3e ar gylty
anence me ffor 3e hafe done wykkydnes agayns me.' Þan fled þe fendes
swyftly away, & þe blissed virgyn bare þe saule to þe body, and raysed þe
15 body up by þe arme fro dowbyl deth, and commaundyd þe watyr to stande
on þe ryght hande & on þe left hande lyke a walle & fro þe grownde of
þe see broght hym to þe hafen. Þan þe chanon gretly gladdyd fel downe
before hyr & sayd, 'My dere swete lady what sal I gyf þe for þis benefyce
þat þu has done to me?' Gods moder sayd, 'I preye þe þat þu falle no more
20 in avowtry. & þu sal halow þe feste of my concepcion & preche it to oþer.'
And fro þens forth he lyfed hermet lyfe, and to alle þat couet it he teld
what befelle hym. Þerfore blissed be oure lady Saynt Mary. **[A Scholar at
the Scales of Justice]** Also in þe same boke, it tells how þer was a clerke
in ane unyversite synfully lyfyng. He was raueschyd to þe dome. And he
25 sawe fewe gode deds of his belayd in þe to weyscale. Þe fende held a rolle
wrytten full of synnes & layd it in þe toþer party of þe weyscale þat bowed
downe. Wherfore sentence suld hafe gone agayn þe synful man. He was
ferd & beheld to Saynt Mary þat stode nerhande & sche toke þe rolle offe
þe weyscale & gaf þe clerk it in hys hande & he red it. & sone he went
30 to confession to schryfe hym, & chawnged his abet & mendyd his lyfe. &
fro [þen for]th seruyd Saynt Mary deuoutely. **[A Compact with the Devil
Rescinded]** Also it is teld [...] clerke þat oure lady Saynt Mary toke hym
oute of [...] cause he put his body & his saule in [...]is gode to euere
creature to put to þat blyssed [...]es in welthe & in woo þair body & þayr
35 [...]ion & tribulacion commytt þaim holy to hir [...]ne þat verely trests
in hyr [...]rd ritches with gret treuell [...] wastyd & gone he was sory. Þe
[...] sayd þat he suld make hym rytcher [...k]e Criste & his Cristyndom &
[...] for to forsake Criste he dyd me [...] with gret trauell he has taken [...]
sacraments of holy kyrke. Loo [...]se. Þan sayd oþer fendes. 'Hym [...]gyn
40 Mary be whome þay [...]t many forsake Criste **[95r]** & noght his glorios
moder. Sche helped þaim. And þan when þis man wald not forsake Saynt
Mary sche purchest & gat hym forgifnes. **[A Monk of Cluny Rescued**

35–6 **trests in hyr]** *followed by a space of about four words (line not filled)*
Monk of Cluny Rescued] *cf. Plate 7 above, from fol. 30v of the same manuscript.*

from Despair] Also in ane abbay of cluny was a monke ful religios &
deuowt to Saynt Mary so þat his life schane in uertews as a lantyrne in þe
45 sight of god. Bot ofte tymes a god tylman tylles lande yll. So þis monke
synned. And for þat syn he felle in dyspayre, þat is wanhope. At þe laste
by þe grace of criste he soght socour at gods moder a ȝere contynewly,
dwellying in wakyng, in sorowynge, in prayinge & lofyng & praysyng of
þe blissed virgyn moder of god. & on a nyght þe sterne of þe see þat is
50 oure lady aperyd to hym & teld hym in his slepe þat his syn was forgyfyn
hym þorow hir prayer. Þan he thanked god & his glorios moder Mary with
al þe myght of his body & his saule. **[The Devil and a Young Man Make
a Charter]** Also it is red þat a ȝong man luffed a ȝonge woman þat was
ful deuowte to Saynt Mary. And þe ȝonge woman prayed oure blyssed lady
55 to kepe hyr fro þat ȝonge man. And he dyspendyd all his godes for to gytt
hyr. Þe deuyl seynge þat come to hym & sayd, if he wald denye & forsake
before his lord þe prince of deuyls þos thynges, þat þe prince of deuyls suld
neuyn unto hym. He suld make hym dowbyll rycher þan he was, and he suld
hafe þe woman to his wyll þat he d[esyred …] amonesched hym þat he suld
60 not make þe tok[…] hym. Þan he ȝode with þe fende in to preuy pl[ace …]
fendes war. Þan þe kynge of deuyls sayd, […] welcum. Aske what þu wyll
& I sal gyf þe[…] sal make me a chartyr written with þi[…] thyngs þat I
byd þe. When þe chartyr wa[s …] say þus, 'I denye þe trowthe of þe […]
of holy kyrke, & þe moder of Iesu Criste […]deryng of þat, þat he sayd
65 made þ[…] selfe. And þan al þe fendes uaneschyd […] sorow þat he made
þe chartyr. And […] wher he fande þe ȝonge woman […] aperyed & sayd to
hym, 'I delyuer […] here prayd for þe þat I suld refre[…] þe whilk þu made
to þe de[uyl …] breke gods byddynge. And […] weddyd þe same mayden
[…] **[95v, The Virgin Bares Her Breasts for a Sinner]** Also þer was a
70 synful man þat felle seke & cald to hym a religious man & mekely prayed
hym þat he & alle his breþer suld pray for hym. And he beheste þat he suld
amende his lyfe if he myghte lyfe. And when he was recouerd, he was wars
þan he was before. Sone after he fel seke, þe saule passed & come before
oure lord Iesu Criste domesman. And he sawe on his right hande his chosyn,
75 & on his lefte hande reprofed. When he þoght þat he suld hafe bene sett
with þe reprofed þat was dampned, he askyd helpe at Saynt Mary þat sat by
þe domesman. Oure lady prayed hyr sone for hym. Þe domesman sayd hym
aghte not to do agayns rightwisnes. Þan þe blissed uirgyn sayd to þe synfull
man, 'Ȝe wretche, how mykil þe vyce of unkyndnes is & how sorlly þat
80 syn is to ponesche. I am moder of þe kyng & domesman, & I am not hard
for þe.' Þan sayd þe synfulman, 'I wate blyssed lady þat mykil is my syn

---

43–52 **Also in ane abbay … myght of his body]** *on the left, an illustration of the Virgin*
Mary reaching through clouds to return an inscribed charter to a kneeling man and
woman (sharing sixteen lines of the page). The male figure exceeds the boundary of the
text block, so that his back and feet extend well into the inner margin. See Plate 5 above.
Virgin Bares Her Breasts] *cf. Plate 6 above, from fol. 19r of the same manuscript.*
79 **sorlly]** *first letter of word blotted out*

& my wretchydnes. Bot I wate þat þi mercy, þe whilk þat I aske, is mykil
more.' Þan eftyrward oure blyssed lady schewed unto hir son hyr breste
& hir pappes, praying hym for þoes þat he sowked to do mercy with þe
85 wretche. Þan oure lord grauntyd hym space of lyfe to do penance. And after
þat he lyfyd moste holyly & happely endyd. **[The Knight Who Refused
to Abjure Our Lady]** In diocesi leodiensi be syde floraunce was a ȝonge
knyght þat in tornyaments & in vanytes had wastyd al his godes. And þerfor
began for to dyspayre. Þan þerfore on of hys men led hys mayster on a nyght
90 in to a wodde & cald a fende as he was wont to doo oþer tymes. Þan þe
knyght askyd hym with whome he spake. He awnswerd, 'Make ȝe no force.
Wil ȝe not be rytche as ȝe war?' Þe knyght sayd, 'Ȝis, if it may be done at
gods will.' Þan his seruand sayd to þe fende, 'Lo, I hafe broght ȝow a nobil
man my lord þat ȝe restore hym to his ritches.' Þe fende sayd, 'He sal fyrst
95 forsake [...] & make me homage.' Þe knyght as if it wer dredynge & [...]e
intysynge of his man, & for hoope to be ritche, he [...] þe fende aftyr þat
sayd, 'Þe behofes to forsake [...] knyght sayd, 'Þat sal I neuer doo' & went
away [...] þe blissed uirgyn Mary & felle downe be [...]ng & sorowynge. In
þat same tyme a [...]ht of hym alle his godes come in to þe [...] þe ȝonge
100 knyght þus praye & gretyng [...] a pyler for to se þe endynge. Bothe þe
[... bliss]ed uirgyn Mary spake þorow þe [...]n þus, 'My suettest son hafe
mercy [... an]swerd noght & turned hys [...] prayd eftsones þe child turned
[...] þis man forsoke me. What [...] ymage of þe uirgyn rase up & [...] &
fel downe to his feete & [...] forgyf hym þis syn. And þan þe [...] moder
105 I myght neuer denye [...]e I forgyf al. Þe ȝonge [... or]y for his syn, bot
glad he [...] & ȝode to þe ȝonge knight [...]edde hir. I s[...]eȝode al [...]
ew ay[...]s. & [...] syn [...]ed.

Knight Who Refused to Abjure] *A complete prose summary of this miracle survives
as a dramatic prologue in Durham Dean and Chapter MS I.2 Archdiac. Dunelm 60. See
Wright, 'Durham Play of Mary and the Poor Knight', p. 255.*
89 **þerfore]** *in margin*

Appendix 4

An Index of Miracles of the Virgin
Collated with Existing Lists

A Note on Titles and Catalogues

The breadth of international scholarship on Miracles of the Virgin over the last century or so (beginning with Adolfo Mussafia's work in 1886–98) has put into use a frustrating variety of editorial titles for individual miracles. As is often the case with exemplary literature, the number of analogues or related narratives associated with a given tale increases the confusion. Many scholars writing on Marian miracles will use titles eclectically, and some knowledge of existing catalogues is necessary for comparative work and source studies. For the most part, I have titled miracles in accordance with either the *MWME* XXIV or Peter Whiteford's catalogue of Middle English miracles (in *The Myracles of Oure Lady*). Whenever generally accepted titles misrepresent the content of an English version of a common tale or gloss over important distinctions between versions, however, I have made small adjustments or omitted titles altogether, and some collation with available lists is therefore of interest.

To facilitate further research, I index here all Miracles of the Virgin discussed in this book, collated wherever possible with three important reference works that will, in turn, provide further bibliographical information. Albert Poncelet compiled almost 1,800 Latin incipits in his 'Index miraculorum B. V. Mariae quae saec. VI–XV latine conscripta sunt', *Analecta Bollandiana* 21 (1902), pp. 242–360, and these are now available online as the *Electronic Poncelet*, maintained through Oxford's *CSMD*. The Oxford database, which was launched in 2005 and continues to evolve, is an important new resource for scholars interested in Marian legends. Though its focus is the large thirteenth-century Galician-Portuguese verse collection of the Castilian King Alfonso X, it incorporates user-friendly cross-references, bibliographies, summaries, keyword links, and manuscript and analogue information that are wide-ranging and searchable. *MWME* XXIV catalogues information specific to extant Middle English miracles and includes content summaries and bibliographies keyed to individual miracles (as endnotes).

In what follows, miracles are ordered alphabetically, according to the titles I habitually use or (when I have not used a title) according to a *CSMD* or *MWME* XXIV heading. Each entry includes first a list of related titles, then information on versions discussed in this book (listed as *MVME*, with page numbers), and finally references to the relevant catalogues. Catalogue numbers may refer to analogues and/or to the tale(s) discussed in the present volume, but the data will frequently pertain to tales not directly connected to my discussions (e.g., I examine 'Blood on the Penitent Woman's Hand' in a unique version that is likely a combination of one or more related tales, for which see Appendix 2). Finally, it should be noted that the Poncelet numbers do not always denote separate versions of a miracle, since an incipit may vary even when the narrative it introduces is nearly identical to another; conversely, one number may refer to an incipit (and version) in use in many manuscripts. Poncelet's list, however, is extremely useful for identifying miracles and investigating possible sources.

'Blood on the Penitent Woman's Hand'

Variant/related titles: 'Blood on a Woman's Hand', 'The Devil as a Clerk', 'Incest', 'Incest Between Mother and Son', 'Mary Saves an Incestuous Woman', 'The Virgin Befriends a Woman Accused of Incest', 'Woman who Committed Incest'

MVME	MS Bodl. e Museo 180	23–6, 178–80
Cf.	*CSM* No. 17	
	MWME XXIV [37] [171] [192]	
	Poncelet Nos 47, 360, 424–5, 450, 483, 625, 662, 950, 1001, 1010, 1090, 1267, 1300, 1406, 1559, 1588, 1590	

'Childbirth in the Sea'

MVME	Dominic of Evesham (in 'Elements Series')	63 n. 63
Cf.	*CSM* No. 86	
	Poncelet Nos 25, 499, 810, 811, 968	

'A Compact with the Devil Rescinded'

Variant/related titles: 'The Clerk who Refused to Forsake the Virgin', 'The Devil and a Young Man Make a Charter'

MVME	MS BL Additional 37049 (Charter Group)	117, 125, 185
Cf.	*MWME* XXIV [55] [63]	

'The Devil and a Young Man Make a Charter'

Variant/related titles: 'The Clerk who Refused to Forsake the Virgin', 'A Compact with the Devil Rescinded'

MVME	MS BL Additional 37049 (Charter Group)	117–18, 125, 186
Cf.	*MWME* XXIV [55] [63]	

'The Devil in Service'

MVME SEL   90
Cf.   *CSM* No. 67
          MWME XXIV [67]
          Poncelet Nos 346, 380, 511, 666, 700–2, 989, 1339, 1393, 1435,
          1439–40, 1444, 1628

'The Drowned Sacristan'

Variant/related titles: 'Ave on the Tongue', 'The Drowned Clerk', 'The Incontinent Monk'
MVME MS BL Additional 37049 (Charter Group)   117, 129–31, 133,
                                                                                          184–5
Cf.   *CSM* No. 11
          MWME XXIV [73]
          Poncelet Nos 13, 36, 187, 201, 398, 422, 434, 444, 466, 468, 470,
          475, 552, 564, 594, 600, 641, 650, 791, 821, 832, 850, 852, 1006,
          1011, 1017, 1045, 1105, 1110, 1353, 1355, 1451, 1503, 1687

'Eulalia'

MVME John Mirk's *Festial* (MSS BL Harley 2403, Cotton Claudius
A. II)   106–7
Cf.   *CSM* No. 71
          MWME XXIV [77]
          Poncelet Nos 73, 521–3, 597, 1043, 1305, 1571

'The Founding of the Feast of the Conception'

Variant/related titles: 'Abbot Elsinus', 'Conceptio (Elsinus)', 'How the Feast
of Our Lady's Conception was Established', 'The Origin of the Festival of
the Conception of Our Lady'
MVME SEL (MSS BL Stowe 949, Bodl. Bodley 779, Bodl. Eng. poet. a. 1,
Lambeth Palace Library 223)   3, 19–23, 146, 173–7
Cf.   *MWME* XXIV [84]
          Poncelet Nos 260, 292, 316, 404–5, 714, 745, 1676, 1698, 1700,
          1702, 1781

'Hildefonsus of Toledo'

Variant/related titles: 'Hildefonsus', 'Toledo'
MVME William of Malmesbury   71
Cf.   *CSM* No. 2
          Poncelet Nos 117, 568, 590, 660, 873, 884, 973, 1002, 1153, 1227,
          1626, 1720, 1730

'How a Scribe Painted a Miraculous Image'

Variant/related title: 'A Scribe Paints a Miraculous Image'
MVME MS BL Harley 2403 (John Mirk's *Festial*)   39, 107, 110
Cf.   *MWME* XXIV [152]

'How Our Lady Came to the Devil Instead of the Victim'

Variant/related titles: 'The Knight and His Wife', 'Our Lady Comes to the Devil instead of the Victim', 'A Pauper Knight's Pact with the Devil', 'Virgin Comes to the Devil Instead of His Victim'
MVME SEL   90–1
Cf.   *CSM* No. 216
          MWME XXIV [128]
          Poncelet Nos 1005, 1069, 1082–3

'How Our Lady Restored a Scribe's Arm'

Variant/related titles: 'How Our Lady Restored a Scribe's Hand', 'John of Damascus', 'A Scribe's Hand Restored'
MVME MS BL Harley 2403 (John Mirk's *Festial*)   105, 107–11
Cf.   *CSM* No. 265
          MWME XXIV [153]
          Poncelet Nos 15, 905–6, 1009

'The Jewish Boy'

Variant/related titles: 'Jew of Bourges', 'Jewish Boy Covered with Her Cloak', 'Jewish Boy of Bourges'
MVME Dominic of Evesham (in 'Elements Series')   63–8
          SEL   87–8, 90
          William of Malmesbury ('Jewish Boy of Pisa')   69–70
Cf.   *CSM* No. 4
          MWME XXIV [98]
          Poncelet Nos 95, 131, 228, 234–5, 274, 403, 532, 534, 759, 826,
          833, 835, 904, 910–13, 915, 917, 1000, 1139, 1159, 1222, 1254,
          1407, 1483–5, 1492, 1647, 1745

'The Jews of Toledo'

Variant/related titles: 'Christ Image Pierced by Jews', 'Toledo'
MVME SEL   87–8, 90
          William of Malmesbury   71–2
Cf.   *CSM* No. 12
          MWME XXIV [167]
          Poncelet Nos 16, 283, 291, 883, 914

'The Jews of Toulouse'

Variant/related titles: 'Jew Struck by a Knight', 'One-Eyed Knight and Jew'
MVME William of Malmesbury   69, 147 n. 51
Cf.   Poncelet Nos 1077, 1780

'Julian the Apostate'

Variant/related title: 'Death of Julian'
MVME Ælfric, *Catholic Homilies* I, *Lives of Saints*   48, 50–1, 53–4
           Dominic of Evesham (in 'Elements Series')   63, 65
           MS BL Royal 18 B. XXIII   94
           William of Malmesbury   71
Cf.   *CSM* No. 15
           MWME XXIV [101]
           Poncelet Nos 318, 506, 563, 803, 889, 918–19, 921–2, 1012, 1140,
           1205

'The Knight Who Refused to Abjure Our Lady'

Variant/related titles: 'Christ Denied but not the Virgin', 'Unwilling to Deny
Mary'
MVME MS BL Additional 37049 (Charter Group)   117, 125, 187
Cf.   *MWME* XXIV [105]
           Poncelet Nos 169, 707(?), 776, 849, 894, 938, 983, 1251, 1547

'The Legend of Dan Joos'

Variant/related titles: 'The Five Psalms', 'Five Psalms with the Initials MARIA'
MVME John Lydgate   14 n. 11, 15, 160
Cf.   *CSM* No. 56
           MWME XXIV [80]
           Poncelet Nos 578–80, 598, 994, 1102, 1508

'The Lily in the Wine Pot'

Variant/related title: 'The Jew and the Wine Pot'
MVME John Mirk's *Festial*   39–40
Cf.   *MWME* XXIV [96]

'Marian Miracle of a Clerk'

Variant/related titles: 'The Clerk of Oxford', 'Marian Miracle of the Clerk at
Oxford', 'St Luke's Portrait of Mary' (very loosely related)
MVME MS BL Additional 37049   117, 133–6, 184
Cf.   *MWME* XXIV [49]
           Poncelet Nos 270, 272, 373, 857, 1567, 1608

'Mary of Egypt'

Variant/related titles: 'The Conversion of Mary of Egypt', 'The Life of Mary of Egypt', 'St Mary of Egypt'

MVME	Paul the Deacon of Naples	44, 45 n. 14, 51–2
	SEL	85 n. 33
Cf.	*MWME* XXIV [58]	
	Poncelet Nos 679, 1039	

'The Merchant's Surety'

Variant/related titles: 'Jew Lends to Christian', 'Jew Lends to Christian: Sails to Alexandria'

MVME	MS Bodl. Eng. poet. a. 1 (Vernon MS)	29–32, 147, 148
	William of Malmesbury	69
Cf.	*CSM* No. 25	
	MWME XXIV [112]	
	Poncelet Nos 41–2, 165, 171, 174, 213, 232–3, 237, 555, 559, 709, 771, 797, 875–6, 981, 1241, 1331, 1410, 1748, 1759	

'The Monk and Our Lady's Sleeves'

Variant/related titles: 'How Our Lady's Psalter was Made', 'Our Lady's Psalter'

MVME	MS Bodl. Digby 86	5
	MS National Library of Scotland, Advocates 19.2.1 (Auchinleck MS)	5
	Thomas Hoccleve	14 n. 11, 15–16
Cf.	*MWME* XXIV [130]	

'A Monk of Cluny Rescued from Despair'

Variant/related title: 'The Monk Who Despaired'

MVME	MS BL Additional 37049 (Charter Group)	117, 126 9, 185–6
Cf.	*MWME* XXIV [113]	

'The Monk Who Could Learn Only Ave Maria'

Variant/related titles: 'Clerk of Chartres', 'A Monk Learns Only Ave Maria', 'Saved by Learning Two Words', 'Saved by Two Words', 'The Unshriven Clerk'

MVME	*SEL*	90, 91–2, 151
Cf.	*CSM* No. 24	
	MWME XXIV [120] [168]	
	Poncelet Nos 201, 297–8, 336, 339, 459, 478, 629, 639, 668, 836–8, 941, 988, 996, 1021, 1068, 1078, 1084, 1338, 1341, 1343, 1352, 1357–8, 1360, 1370, 1429–30, 1637	

'The Oxford Scholars'

Variant/related titles: 'The Oxford Scholar', 'Oxford Scholar Led to Heaven'
MVME *SEL*   90, 92
Cf.   *MWME* XXIV [131]
         Poncelet No. 1249(?)

'The Prioress's Tale'

Variant/related titles: 'The Child Slain by Jews', 'Chorister Killed by Jews',
'The Chorister Slain', 'The Miracle of the Boy Singer'
MVME Chaucer   14 n. 11, 15, 26–9, 149–59
         MSS BL Harley 1704, BL Harley 2251, BL Harley 2382,
         Bodl. Rawlinson C. 86, Chetham's Library 6709   159–64
         MS Cambridge, Trinity College 0.9.38   28–9
Cf.   *CSM* No. 6
         MWME XXIV [45] [140]
         Poncelet Nos 382, 487, 645, 809, 1250, 1507, 1631, 1755

'St Dunstan and the Virgin's Choir'

Variant/related title: 'St Dunstan'
MVME Foxe, *A&M*   145–6
Cf.   *CSM* No. 288
         Poncelet Nos 45, 150, 412, 1048, 1193, 1625

'A Scholar at the Scales of Justice'

Variant/related titles: 'Divine Judgment', 'A Drop of Blood on the Scales of
Justice', 'A Hand on the Scales of Justice', 'Our Lady's Hand and the Scales
of Justice', 'Sins Outweighed by a Drop of Christ's Blood', 'Virgin Tips
Scales', 'The Virgin's Weight Added to a Good Scale', 'The Wicked Clerk's
Vision of Judgment'
MVME MS BL Additional 37049 (Charter Group)   32–3, 117, 125–7, 185
Cf.   *MWME* XXIV [72] [90]
         Poncelet Nos 22, 193, 654, 1470

'Tale of the Lazy Servant of St Anselm'

Variant/related titles: 'The Lazy Servant of St Anselm', 'A Monk Stays in
Bed', 'The Servant of St Anselm Carried Off by a Devil', 'The Sleeping
Monk Awakened'
MVME MS BL Additional 37049   117, 183–4
Cf.   *MWME* XXIV [109] [117] [159]

'Theophilus'

Variant/related titles: 'The Legend of Theophilus', 'The Life of Theophilus', 'Theophilus the Penitent'

MVME	Ælfric, *Catholic Homilies* I	47–54, 62
	Dominic of Evesham (in 'Elements Series')	62–6, 68, 73–4
	MS BL Additional 49999 (William de Brailes, illustrations)	75–80
	MS BL Royal 18 B. XXIII	93–6
	MS Bodl. Rawlinson Poetry 225	97–102
	MS Lambeth Palace Library 209 (Lambeth Apocalypse, illustrations)	79–81
	Paul the Deacon of Naples	42–7, 51–2, 54–62
	SEL	82–90, 92–3
	William of Malmesbury	62, 69–74
Cf.	*CSM* No. 3	
	MWME XXIV [163]	
	Poncelet Nos 74–5, 79, 113, 401, 416, 486, 567, 574, 640, 664, 692, 729, 758, 946, 1044, 1171, 1376, 1577, 1634, 1663, 1716–18	

'The Virgin Bares Her Breasts for a Sinner'

Variant/related titles: 'A Goliard Saved by the Virgin', 'Virgin Bares her Breast', 'The Virgin Pleads for a Sinner's Soul'

MVME	MS BL Additional 37049 (Charter Group, miracle in *tituli*)	117, 120–5, 186–7
Cf.	*MWME* XXIV [86] [170] [175]	
	Poncelet Nos 183, 191	

'The Walsingham Ballad'

Variant/related titles: 'The Foundation of the Chapel at Walsingham', 'The Pynson Ballad'

MVME	Cambridge, Magdalene College, Pepys 1254	164–5, 168
Cf.	*MWME* XXIV [83]	

Bibliography

Achinstein, Sharon, 'John Foxe and the Jews', *Renaissance Quarterly* 54.1 (2001), pp. 86–120

Allen, Hope Emily, *English Writings of Richard Rolle Hermit of Hampole* (Oxford, 1931)

——, *Writings Ascribed to Richard Rolle Hermit of Hampole and Materials for His Biography* (New York and London, 1927)

Archer, John, 'The Structure of Anti-Semitism in the *Prioress's Tale*', *The Chaucer Review* 19.1 (1985), pp. 46–54

Ashe, Laura, 'The "Short Charter of Christ": An Unpublished Longer Version, from Cambridge University Library, MS ADD. 6686', *MÆ* 72 (2003), pp. 32–48

Ashford, William Ray, ed., *The Conception Nostre Dame of Wace* (Chicago, 1933)

Aston, Margaret, *England's Iconoclasts, I: Laws against Images* (Oxford, 1988)

——, *Lollards and Reformers: Images and Literacy in Late Medieval Religion*, History Series 22 (London, 1984)

Atkinson, Nancy E. 'John Mirk's Holy Women', *Papers on Language & Literature* 43 (2007), pp. 339–62

Bale, Anthony, 'Fictions of Judaism in England before 1290', *The Jews in Medieval Britain: Historical, Literary and Archaeological Perspectives*, ed. Patricia Skinner (Woodbridge, 2003), pp. 129–44

——, *The Jew in the Medieval Book: English Antisemitisms, 1350–1500* (Cambridge, 2006)

Banks, Mary Macleod, ed., *An Alphabet of Tales*, EETS, os 127 (London, 1904)

Bär, Franz, *Die Marienlegenden der Strassburger Handschrift Germ. 863* (Strasbourg, 1913)

Barr, Beth Allison, *Pastoral Care of Women in Late Medieval England*, Gender in the Middle Ages (Woodbridge, 2008)

Bartlet, Suzanne, 'Three Jewish Businesswomen in Thirteenth-Century Winchester', *Jewish Culture and History* 3.2 (2000), pp. 31–54

Baswell, Christopher, 'Latinitas', *The Cambridge History of Medieval English Literature*, ed. David Wallace (Cambridge, 1999), pp. 122–51

Bejczy, Istvan Pieter, *Erasmus and the Middle Ages: The Historical Consciousness of a Christian Humanist* (Leiden and Boston, 2001)

Benson, Larry D., ed., *The Riverside Chaucer*, 3rd edn (Boston, 1987)

Binski, Paul, *Medieval Death: Ritual and Representation* (Ithaca, NY, 1996)

Bishop, Edmund, *Liturgica historia* (Oxford, 1918)

Blake, N. F., 'Vernon Manuscript: Contents and Organisation', *Studies in the Vernon Manuscript*, ed. Derek Pearsall (Cambridge, 1990), pp. 45–60

Bloomfield, Morton, *Piers Plowman as a Fourteenth Century Apocalypse* (New Brunswick, NJ, 1961)

Boyarin, Daniel, *A Radical Jew: Paul and the Politics of Identity* (Berkeley and Los Angeles, 1994)

Boyd, Beverly, 'Hoccleve's Miracle of the Virgin', *Texas Studies in English* 35 (1956), pp. 116–22

——, 'The Literary Background of Lydgate's "The Legend of Dan Joos"', *MLN* 72 (1957), pp. 81–7

——, 'The Rawlinson Version of Theophilus', *MLN* 71 (1956), pp. 556–9

——, ed., *The Middle English Miracles of the Virgin* (San Marino, 1964)

——, ed., *The Prioress's Tale*, A Variorum Edition of the Works of Geoffrey Chaucer (Norman, OK, 1987)

Braekman, Willy L. and Peter S. Macaulay, 'Two Unpublished Middle English Exempla from MS. Royal 18 B. XXIII', *Neuphilologische Mitteilungen* 72 (1971), pp. 97–104

Brandeis, Arthur, ed., *Jacob's Well*, Part I, EETS, os 115 (London, 1900)

Brantley, Jessica, *Reading in the Wilderness: Private Devotion and Public Performance in Late Medieval England* (Chicago and London, 2007)

Bridgett, Thomas Edward, *Our Lady's Dowry, or, How England Won and Lost that Title* (London, 1890)

Brooke, Christopher and Rosalind Brooke, *Popular Religion in the Middle Ages: Western Europe 1000–1300* (London, 1984)

Broughton, Laurel, 'The Prioress's Prologue and Tale', *Sources and Analogues of the Canterbury Tales*, II, ed. Robert M. Correale and Mary Hamel, Chaucer Studies 35 (Cambridge, 2005), pp. 583–647

Brown, Carleton, 'The Prioress's Tale', *Sources and Analogues of Chaucer's Canterbury Tales*, ed. W. F. Bryan and Germaine Dempster (New York, 1958), pp. 477–85

Budge, E. A. W., ed. and trans., *The Miracles of the Blessed Virgin Mary and the Life of Hannâ*, Lady Meux Manuscripts (London, 1900)

——, ed., *Maríu Saga*, Norske Oldskriftselskabs Samlinger (Christiana, 1871)

Bull, Marcus, *The Miracles of Our Lady of Rocamadour: Analysis and Translation* (Woodbridge, 1999)

Camille, Michael, 'The Devil's Writing: Diabolic Literacy in Medieval Art', *World Art: Themes of Unity in Diversity: Acts of the XXVIth Congress of the History of Art*, II, ed. Irving Lavin (University Park, PA, 1989), pp. 355–60

——, 'Seeing and Reading: Some Visual Implications of Medieval Literacy and Illiteracy', *Art History* 8.1 (1985), pp. 26–49

Canal, José, 'El libro "De Miraculis Sanctae Mariae" de Domingo de Evesham (m.c.1140)', *Studium Legionense* 39 (1998), pp. 247–83

——, ed., *El libro de laudibus et miraculis Sanctae Mariae de Guillermo de Malmesbury, OSB*, 2nd edn (Rome, 1968)

Carley, J. P., 'John Leland and the Contents of English Pre-Dissolution Libraries: Glastonbury Abbey', *Scriptorium* 40 (1986), pp. 107–20

——, 'John Leland at Somerset Libraries', *Somerset Archeology and Natural History* 129 (1985), pp. 141–54

Carter, Peter, 'The Historical Content of William of Malmesbury's Miracles of the Virgin Mary', *The Writing of History in the Middle Ages: Essays Presented to Richard William Southern*, ed. R. H. C. Davis and J. M. Wallace-Hadrill (Oxford, 1981), pp. 127–65

Chandler, John, ed., *John Leland's Itinerary: Travels in Tudor England* (Stroud, 1993)

Charbonneau, Joanna A., 'Sir Thopas', *Sources and Analogues of the Canter-*

bury Tales, II, ed. Robert Correale and Mary Hamel, Chaucer Studies 35 (Cambridge, 2005), pp. 649–714

Chiesa, Paolo, 'Le tradizioni del Greco: l'evoluzione della scuola Napoletana ne X secolo', *Mittellateinisches Jarbuch* 24/25 (1989/90), pp. 67–86

Clanchy, M. T., *From Memory to Written Record* (Cambridge, 1993)

Clayton, Mary, *The Cult of the Virgin Mary in Anglo-Saxon England*, Cambridge Studies in Anglo-Saxon England 2 (Cambridge, 1990)

——, 'Feasts of the Virgin in the Liturgy of the Anglo-Saxon Church', *Anglo-Saxon England* 13 (1984), pp. 209–33

Clemoes, Peter, ed., *Ælfric's Catholic Homilies, The First Series*, EETS, ss 17 (London and New York, 1997)

Cohen, Jeremy, *The Friars and the Jews: The Evolution of Medieval Anti-Judaism* (Ithaca, NY, and London, 1982)

——, *Living Letters of the Law: Ideas of the Jew in Medieval Christianity* (Berkeley and Los Angeles, 1999)

Cook, G. H., ed., *Letters to Cromwell and Others on the Suppression of the Monasteries* (London, 1965)

Cooke, Thomas D. (with Peter Whiteford and Nancy Mohr McKinley), 'XXIV. Tales: 3. Pious Tales: I. Miracles of the Virgin', *A Manual of Writings in Middle English, 1050–1500*, IX, ed. Albert E. Hartung (New Haven, CT, 1993), pp. 3177–258, 3501–51

Cooper, Helen, *The Structure of the Canterbury Tales* (London, 1983)

Copeland, Rita, *Rhetoric, Hermeneutics, and Translation in the Middle Ages: Academic Traditions and Vernacular Texts* (Cambridge, 1991)

Cords, Rose, 'Fünf me. Gedichte aus den Hss. Rawlinson Poetry 36 und Rawlinson C. 86', *Archiv für das Studien der neueren Sprachen und Literaturen* 135 (1916), pp. 292–302

Cothren, Michael W., 'The Iconography of Theophilus Windows in the First Half of the Thirteenth Century', *Speculum* 59.2 (1984), pp. 308–41

Crampton, G. R., 'Chaucer's Singular Prayer', *MÆ* 59 (1990), pp. 191–213

Crane, T. F., ed., *Liber de Miraculis Sanctae Dei Genitricis Mariae* (Ithaca and London, 1925)

Cummings, Brian, 'Reformed Literature and Literature Reformed', *The Cambridge History of Medieval English Literature*, ed. David Wallace (Cambridge, 1999), pp. 821–51

Dahood, Roger, 'The Punishment of the Jews, Hugh of Lincoln, and the Question of Satire in Chaucer's Prioress's Tale', *Viator* 36 (2005), pp. 465–91

Dasent, George Webbe, *Theophilus in Icelandic, Low German, and Other Tongues* (London, 1845)

Despres, Denise L., 'Cultic Anti-Judaism and Chaucer's Litel Clergeon', *Modern Philology* 91 (1994), pp. 413–27

D'Evelyn, Charlotte, *The South English Legendary: Introduction and Glossary*, EETS, os 244 (London, 1959)

D'Evelyn, Charlotte, and Anna J. Mill, eds, *The South English Legendary*, I–II, EETS, os 235–6 (London, 1956)

Dewick, E. S., ed., *Facsimiles of Horae de Beata Maria Virgine from English Manuscripts of the Eleventh Century*, Henry Bradshaw Society 21 (London, 1902)

Dexter, Elise F., ed., 'Miracula Sanctae Virginis Mariae', *University of Wisconsin Studies in the Social Sciences and History* 12 (1927), pp. 1–60

Dickinson, J. C., *The Shrine of Our Lady of Walsingham* (Cambridge, 1956)

Donovan, Claire, *The de Brailes Hours: Shaping the Book of Hours in Thirteenth-Century Oxford* (London, 1991)

Doyle, A. I., *The Vernon Manuscript: A Facsimile of Bodleian Library, Oxford, MS Eng. poet. a.1.* (Cambridge and Wolfeboro, NH, 1987)

Duffy, Eamon, *The Stripping of the Altars: Traditional Religion in England, c.1400–c.1580* (New Haven, CT, and London, 1992)

Ellis, F. S., ed., *Lives of the Saints, as Englished by William Caxton* (London, 1900)

Elvins, Mark Turnham, *Catholic Trivia: Our Forgotten Heritage* (London, 1992)

Erasmus, Desiderius, *Peregrinatio religionis ergo, Colloquia familiaria*, Perseus Digital Library [online] (Stoa Constorium, 1997). Available from: http://www. stoa.org/hopper/text.jsp?doc=Stoa:text:2003.02.0006:colloquium=39

Erbe, Theodor, ed., *Mirk's Festial: A Collection of Homilies by Johannes Mirkus*, EETS, es 96 (London, 1905)

Farsitus, Hugo, 'Libellus de miraculis B. Mariae Virginis in urbe Suessionensi', *PL* 179, pp. 1777–1800

Fletcher, Alan J., 'John Mirk and the Lollards', *MÆ* 56 (1987), pp. 217–24

——, 'Unnoticed Sermons from John Mirk's *Festial*', *Speculum* 55.3 (1980), pp. 514–22

Foster, F. A., ed., *The Northern Passion*, EETS, os 145 (London, 1913)

Foxe, John, *Acts and Monuments [...], The Variorum Edition* [online], (hriOnline, Sheffield, 2004). Available from: http://www.hrionline.shef.ac.uk/johnfoxe/

Fradenburg, Louise O., 'Criticism, Anti-Semitism, and the *Prioress's Tale*', *Exemplaria* 1 (1989), pp. 69–115

Frank, Robert Worth, Jr., 'Miracles of the Virgin, Medieval Anti-Semitism, and the "Prioress's Tale"', *The Wisdom of Poetry: Essays in Early English Literature in Honor of Morton W. Bloomfield*, ed. Larry D. Benson and Siegfried Wenzel (Kalamazoo, MI, 1982), pp. 177–88

Friedman, Albert B., 'The Prioress's Tale and Chaucer's Anti-Semitism', *Chaucer Review* 9 (1974), pp. 118–29

Friis-Jensen, Kirsten and James M. W. Willoughby, eds, *Peterborough Abbey*, Corpus of British Medieval Library Catalogues (London, 2001)

Fritze, R. H., '"Truth Hath Lacked Witnesse, Tyme Wanted Light": The Dispersal of the English Monastic Libraries and Protestant Efforts at Preservation, *ca.* 1535–1625', *Journal of Library History* 18.3 (1983), pp. 274–91

Fuiano, Michele, *La cultura a Napoli nell'alto medioevo*, Storia e pensiero (Naples, 1961)

Gautier de Coinci, *Les miracles de Nostre Dame*, ed. V. F. Koenig, 2nd edn, Textes littéraires français (Geneva, 1966–70)

Gaylord, Alan T., '*Sentence* and *Solaas* in Fragment VII of the *Canterbury Tales*: Harry Bailly as Horseback Editor', *PMLA* 82.2 (1967), pp. 226–35

Gelley, Alexander, 'Introduction', *Unruly Examples: On the Rhetoric of Exemplarity*, ed. Alexander Gelley (Stanford, CA, 1995), pp. 1–24

Gillespie, Vincent, 'Medieval Hypertext: Image and Text from York Minster', *Of the Making of Books: Medieval Manuscripts, Their Scribes and Readers.*

Essays Presented to M. B. Parkes, ed. P. R. Robinson and Rivkah Zim (Brook-field, VT, and Aldershot, 1997), pp. 206–29

——, ed., *Syon Abbey, with the Libraries of the Carthusians*, Corpus of British Medieval Library Catalogues (London, 2001)

Godden, Malcolm, *Ælfric's Catholic Homilies, Series I and II: Commentary*, EETS, ss 18 (Oxford and New York, 2000)

——, 'Experiments in Genre: The Saints' Lives in Ælfric's Catholic Homilies', *Holy Men and Holy Women: Old English Prose Saints' Lives and Their Contexts*, ed. Paul Szarmach (Albany, NY, 1996), pp. 261–87

Gonzalo de Berceo, *Milagros de Nuestra Señora* (Barcelona, 2002)

Görlach, Manfred, *The Textual Tradition of the South English Legendary*, Leeds Texts and Monographs (Leeds, 1974)

Graef, Hilda, *Mary: A History of Doctrine and Devotion* (New York, 1963)

Gray, Douglas, 'London, British Library, Additional MS 37049 – A Spiritual Encyclopedia', *Text and Controversy from Wyclif to Bale: Essays in Honour of Anne Hudson*, ed. Helen Barr and Ann M. Hutchison (Turnhout, 2005), pp. 99–118

——, *Themes and Images in the Medieval English Religious Lyric* (London and Boston, 1972)

Green, Richard Firth, *A Crisis of Truth: Literature and Law in Ricardian England*, The Middle Ages Series (Philadelphia, PA, 1999)

Gregg, Joan Young, *Devils, Women, and Jews: Reflections of the Other in Medieval Sermon Stories*, SUNY Series in Medieval Studies (Albany, NY, 1997)

Hamer, Richard, ed., *Gilte Legende*, I, EETS, os 327 (London, 2006)

Hamilton, Hans Claude, ed., *Historia rerum Anglicarum Willelmi Parvi*, Publications of the English Historical Society, II, rpt (Vaduz, 1964)

Harvey, P. D. A. and Andrew McGuinness, *A Guide to British Medieval Seals* (London, 1996)

Heffernan, Thomas, 'The Virgin as an Aid to Salvation in Some Fifteenth-Century English and Latin Verses', *MÆ* 52 (1983), pp. 229–38

Herrtage, Sydney J. H., ed., *The Early English Versions of the Gesta Romanorum*, EETS, es 33 (London, 1879)

Hogg, James, 'Unpublished Texts in the Carthusian Northern Middle English Religious Miscellany British Library MS Add. 37049', *Essays in Honour of Erwin Stürzl on His Sixtieth Birthday*, ed. James Hogg (Salzburg, 1980), pp. 241–84

——, ed., *An Illustrated Yorkshire Carthusian Religious Miscellany, British Library London Additional MS. 37049*, III, Analecta Cartusiana 95 (Salzburg, 1981)

Horstmann, Carl, *Altenglische Legenden, neue Folge* (Heilbronn, 1881)

——, ed., *The Early South English Legendary*, EETS, os 87 (London, 1887)

——, ed., *The Minor Poems of the Vernon MS*, EETS, os 98 (London, 1892)

Hoyle, Victoria, 'The Bonds that Bind: Money Lending between Anglo-Jewish and Christian Women in the Plea Rolls of the Exchequer of the Jews, 1218–1280', *Journal of Medieval History* 34 (2008), pp. 119–29

Hudson, Anne, *The Premature Reformation: Wycliffite Texts and Lollard History* (Oxford, 1988)

Jackson, Peter and Michael Lapidge, 'The Contents of the Cotton-Corpus Legendary', *Holy Men and Holy Women: Old English Prose Saints' Lives and Their Contexts*, ed. Paul Szarmach (Albany, NY, 1996), pp. 131–46

Jenkinson, Hilary, ed., *Calendar of the Plea Rolls of the Exchequer of the Jews Preserved in the Public Record Office, Edward I 1275–1277*, III (London, 1929)

Jennings, J. C., 'The Origins of the Elements Series of the Miracles of the Virgin', *Mediaeval and Renaissance Studies* 6 (1968), pp. 84–93

——, 'The Writings of Prior Dominic of Evesham', *The English Historical Review* 77 (1962), pp. 298–304

Jessop, Augustus and M. R. James, ed. and trans., *The Life and Miracles of St William of Norwich* (Cambridge, 1896)

Justice, Steven, *Writing and Rebellion: England in 1381*, The New Historicism: Studies in Cultural Poetics 27 (Berkeley and Los Angeles, 1994)

Karant-Nunn, Susan, and Merry Wiesner-Hanks, eds, *Luther on Women: A Sourcebook* (Cambridge, 2003)

Kjellman, H., ed., *La deuxième collection anglo-normande des Miracles de la Sainte Vièrge et son original latin*, Bibliotheca Ekmaniana Universitatis Upsaliensis (Paris and Uppsala, 1922)

Knowles, David, ed. and trans., *The Monastic Constitutions of Lanfranc* (London, 1951)

Kölbing, Eugen, ed., *Englische Studien*, I (Paris and London, 1877)

Kreitzer, Beth, *Reforming Mary: Changing Images of the Virgin Mary in Lutheran Sermons of the Sixteenth Century*, Oxford Studies in Historical Theology (Oxford, 2004)

Kuchar, Gary, *Divine Subjection: The Rhetoric of Sacramental Devotion in Early Modern England* (Pittsburgh, PA, 2005)

Kulp-Hill, Kathleen, ed. and trans., *The Songs of Holy Mary of Alfonso X, The Wise*, Medieval and Renaissance Studies (Tempe, AZ, 2000)

Kunstmann, Pierre, *Le Gracial*, Publications médiévales de l'Université d'Ottawa 8 (Ottawa, 1982)

Lampert, Lisa, *Gender and Jewish Difference from Paul to Shakespeare*, The Middle Ages Series (Philadelphia, PA, 2004)

Langmuir, Gavin I., 'The Knight's Tale of Young Hugh of Lincoln', *Speculum* 47 (1972), pp. 459–82

——, *Toward a Definition of Antisemitism* (Berkeley and Los Angeles, 1990)

Lazar, Moshe, 'Theophilus: Servant of Two Masters. The Pre-Faustian Theme of Despair and Revolt', *MLN* 87.6 (1972), pp. 31–50

Levi, Ezio, ed., *Il libro dei cinquanta Miracoli della Vergine*, Collezione di opere inedite o rare dei primi tre secoli della lingua (Bologna, 1917)

Lewis, C. S., *The Discarded Image: An Introduction to Medieval and Renaissance Literature* (Cambridge, 1964)

Lochrie, Karma, *Margery Kempe and Translations of the Flesh*, New Cultural Studies Series (Philadelphia, PA, 1991)

Long, Mary Beth, 'Corpora and Manuscripts, Authors and Audiences', *A Companion to Middle English Hagiography*, ed. Sarah Salih (Cambridge, 2006), pp. 47–69

Loomis, L. H., 'The Tale of Sir Thopas', *Sources and Analogues of Chaucer's Canterbury Tales*, ed. W. F. Bryan and Germaine Dempster (Chicago, 1941), pp. 486–559

Madicott, J. R., *Simon de Montfort* (Cambridge, 1996)

Mâle, Emile, *Religious Art from the Twelfth to Eighteenth Century* (New York, 1958)

Mandel, Jerome, '"Jewes Werk" in *Sir Thopas*', *Chaucer and the Jews: Sources, Contexts, Meanings*, ed. Sheila Delany (New York and London, 2002), pp. 59–68

Mangan, John Joseph, *The Life, Character, and Influence of Desiderius Erasmus of Rotterdam* (New York, 1927)

Manly, John M. and Edith Rickert, eds, *The Text of the Canterbury Tales, Studied on the Basis of All Known Manuscripts*, I (London, 1940)

Marcus, Jacob Rader, ed. and comp., *The Jew in the Medieval World: A Source Book, 315–1791*, rev. Marc Saperstein (Cincinnati, 1999)

Meale, Carol M., 'The Miracles of Our Lady: Context and Interpretation', *Studies in the Vernon Manuscript*, ed. Derek Pearsall (Cambridge, 1990), pp. 115–36

Meersseman, G. G., *Kritische glossen op de Griekse Theophilus-legende (7e eeuw) en haar Latijnse vertaling (9e eeuw)* (Brussels, 1963)

Mettmann, Walter, ed., *Cantigas de Santa Maria*, I–III (Coimbra, 1959–72)

Meyer, Paul, 'Notice du MS Rawlinson Poetry 241', *Romania* 29 (1900), pp. 27–47

Miélot, Jean, *Les Miracles de Nostre Dame* (Paris, 1928)

Morgan, Nigel J., 'Texts and Images of Marian Devotion in Thirteenth-Century England', *England in the Thirteenth Century: Proceedings of the 1989 Harlaxton Symposium*, ed. W. M. Ormrod (Stamford, 1991), pp. 69–103

——, ed., *The Lambeth Apocalypse: Manuscript 209 in the Lambeth Palace Library* (London, 1990)

Mundill, Robin, 'Edward I and the Final Phase of Anglo-Jewry', *The Jews in Medieval Britain: Historical, Literary and Archaeological Perspectives*, ed. Patricia Skinner (Woodbridge, 2003), pp. 55–70

——, *England's Jewish Solution: Experiment and Expulsion, 1262–1290*, Cambridge Studies in Medieval Life and Thought (Cambridge, 1998)

Mussafia, Adolfo, *Studien zu den mittelalterlichen Marienlegenden*, Sitzungsberichte der kaiserlichen Akademie der Wissenschaften zu Wien, Phil.-hist Klasse (Vienna, 1886–98)

Neuhaus, Carl, ed., *Die lateinischen Vorlagen zu den alt-franzosischen Adgar'schen Marien-Legenden*, Part I (Aschersleben, 1886)

——, *Adgar's Marienlegenden nach der Londoner Handschrift Egerton 612* (Heilbronn, 1886)

Newman, Barbara, *God and the Goddesses: Vision, Poetry, and Belief in the Middle Ages*, The Middle Ages Series (Philadelphia, PA, 2003)

Nirenberg, David, *Communities of Violence: Persecutions of Minorities in the Middle Ages* (Princeton, NJ, 1996)

Olin, John C., *Christian Humanism and the Reformation: Selected Writings of Erasmus*, 3rd edn (New York, 1987)

Palmer, Philip and Robert More, *The Sources of the Faust Tradition from Simon Magus to Lessing* (New York, 1965)

Patterson, Lee, '"Living Witnesses of Our Redemption": Martyrdom and Imitation in Chaucer's Prioress's Tale', *JMEMS* 31 (2001), pp. 507–60——, *Temporal Circumstances: Form and History in the Canterbury Tales*, The New Middle Ages (New York, 2006)

——, '"What man artow?" Authorial Self-Definition in The Tale of Sir Thopas and The Tale of Melibee', *Studies in the Age of Chaucer* 11 (1989), pp. 117–75

Paul the Deacon of Naples, 'Miraculum S. Mariæ de Theophilo Poenitente', *Acta Sanctorum*, IV February (Feb., I, *BHL* 8121), pp. 483–7

Pearsall, Derek, ed., *Piers Plowman by William Langland: An Edition of the C-Text*, York Medieval Texts (Berkeley and Los Angeles, 1978)

——, ed., *Studies in the Vernon Manuscript* (Cambridge, 1990)

Pedrick, Gale, *Monastic Seals of the XIIIth Century* (London, 1902)

Pelikan, Jaroslav, *Mary Through the Centuries: Her Place in the History of Culture* (New Haven, CT, and London, 1996)

Peters, Christine, *Patterns of Piety: Women, Gender and Religion in Late Medieval and Reformation England*, Cambridge Studies in Early Modern History (Cambridge, 2003)

Phillips, Helen, 'Chaucer and Deguileville: The "ABC" in Context', *MÆ* 62 (1993), pp. 1–27

Pickering, O. S., 'A Middle English Prose Miracle of the Virgin, with Hidden Verses', *MÆ* 57.2 (1988), pp. 219–39

——, *The South English Nativity of Mary and Christ*, Middle English Texts 1 (Heidelberg, 1975)

Plenzat, Karl, *Die Theophiluslegende in den Dichtungen des Mittelalters* (Berlin, 1926)

Poole, A. L., *From Domesday Book to Magna Carta, 1087–1216* (Oxford, 1951)

Powell, Susan, 'John Mirk's *Festial* and the Pastoral Programme', *Leeds Studies in English* 22 (1991), pp. 85–102

Radermacher, Ludwig, *Griechische Quellen zur Faustsage*, Akademie der Wissenschaften zu Wien, Phil.-hist Klasse (Vienna and Leipzig, 1927)

Ridley, Florence H., *The Prioress and the Critics*, University of California English Studies 30 (Berkeley and Los Angeles, 1965)

Rigg, J. M., ed., *Calendar of the Plea Rolls of the Exchequer of the Jews Preserved in the Public Record Office, Henry III 1218–1272*, I (London, 1905)

Ross, Woodburn, ed., *Middle English Sermons*, EETS, os 209 (London, 1940)

Rubin, Miri, *Corpus Christi: The Eucharist in Late Medieval Culture* (Cambridge, 1991)

——, *Gentile Tales: The Narrative Assault on Late Medieval Jews* (New Haven, CT, 1999)

——, *The Mother of God: A History of the Virgin Mary* (New Haven, CT, and London, 2009)

Rummel, Erika, *Erasmus as a Translator of the Classics*, Erasmus Studies (Toronto, 1985)

Ryrie, Alec, *The Gospel and Henry VIII: Evangelicals in the Early English Reformation*, Cambridge Studies in Early Modern History (Cambridge, 2003)

Savage, Henry L., ed., *St Erkenwald: A Middle English Poem*, rpt (Hamden, CT, 1972)

Schmidt, A. V. C., ed., *The Vision of Piers Plowman: A Complete Edition of the B-Text* (London, 1987)

Schmitt, F. S., ed., *S. Anselmi Cantuariensis Archiepiscopi opera omnia*, III (Edinburgh, 1946)

Schreckenberg, Heinz, *The Jews in Christian Art* (New York, 1996)

Shea, Jennifer, 'Adgar's *Gracial* and Christian Images of Jews in Twelfth-Century Vernacular Literature', *Journal of Medieval History* 33.2 (2007), pp. 181–96

Siegmund, Albert, *Die Überlieferung der griechischen Christlichen Literatur*, Abhandlungen der bayerischen Benediktiner-Akademie (Munich, 1949)

Simpson, James, *Reform and Cultural Revolution*, Oxford English Literary History 2 (Oxford, 2002)

Skeat, W. W., ed. and trans., *Ælfric's Lives of Saints*, EETS, os 76 (London, 1881)

Sommer, Emil Frederich, *De Theophili cum Diabolo foedere* (Berlin, 1844)

Southern, R. W., 'The English Origins of the "Miracles of the Virgin"', *Mediaeval and Renaissance Studies* 4 (1958), pp. 176–216

——, 'Foreword', *The Prayers and Meditations of Saint Anselm, with the Proslogian*, ed. and trans. Benedicta Ward (London, 1973), pp. 9–16

——, *The Making of the Middle Ages* (New Haven, CT, 1953)

Spalding, Mary Caroline, *The Middle English Charters of Christ*, rpt (Whitefish, MT, 2007)

Spector, Stephen, 'Empathy and Enmity in the Prioress's Tale', *The Olde Daunce: Love, Friendship, Sex, and Marriage in the Medieval World*, ed. Robert R. Edwards and Stephen Spector (Albany, NY, 1991), pp. 211–28

Spencer, H. Leith, *English Preaching in the Late Middle Ages* (Oxford, 1993)

Spurgeon, C. F. E., ed., *Five Hundred Years of Chaucer Criticism and Allusion, 1357–1900* (New York, 1960)

Steiner, Emily, *Documentary Culture and the Making of Medieval English Literature*, Cambridge Studies in Medieval Literature (Cambridge, 2003)

Strohm, Paul, 'Passioun, Lyf, Miracle, Legende: Some Generic Terms in Middle English Hagiographical Narrative', *Chaucer Review* 10.1–2 (1976), pp. 62–75, 154–71

Symons, Thomas, ed. and trans., *Regularis concordia*, Medieval Classics (London and New York, 1953)

Talbot, C. H., ed. and trans., *The Life of Christina of Markyate: A Twelfth Century Recluse*, Medieval Academy Reprints for Teaching 39 (Toronto and Buffalo, 1998)

Thomas, Antoine, ed., 'Les miracles de Notre-Dame de Chartres', *Bibliothèque de l'école des Chartres* 42 (1881), pp. 505–50

Thompson, Anne B., *Everyday Saints and the Art of Narrative in the South English Legendary* (Burlington, VT, and Aldershot, 2003)

Thompson, Craig R., trans., *The Colloquies of Erasmus* (Chicago and London, 1965)

Thomson, R. M., *A Descriptive Catalogue of the Medieval Manuscripts in Worcester Cathedral Library* (Cambridge, 2001)

Thorne, Samuel E., trans., *De legibus et consuetudinibus Angliae* (Cambridge, MA, 1968)

Thurston, H., 'Our Popular Devotions – The Rosary', *The Month* 96 (1900), pp. 403–18, 513–27, 620–37

Tolkien, J. R. R., '*Beowulf*: The Monsters and the Critics', Sir Israel Gollancz Memorial Lectures, *Proceedings of the British Academy* 22 (1936)

Tomasch, Sylvia, 'Post-Colonial Chaucer and the Virtual Jew', *Chaucer and the Jews: Sources, Contexts, Meanings*, ed. Sheila Delany (New York and London, 2002), pp. 69–85

Tryon, Ruth Wilson, 'Miracles of Our Lady in Middle English Verse', *PMLA* 28 (1923), pp. 308–88

Turner, Nancy L., 'Robert Holcot on the Jews', *Chaucer and the Jews: Sources, Contexts, Meanings*, ed. Sheila Delany (New York and London, 2002), pp. 133–44

Turville-Petre, Thorlac, review of O. S. Pickering's *The South English Nativity of Mary and Christ*, *Modern Language Review* 73.4 (1978), p. 870

Ulrich, Jacob, 'Miracles de Nostre Dame en provençal', *Romania* 8 (1879), pp. 12–28

van Dijk, S. J. P., 'The Origin of the Latin Feast of the Conception of the Blessed Virgin Mary', *Dublin Review* 465 (1954), pp. 251–67, 428–42

Villecourt, L., 'Les collections arabes des miracles de la Sainte Vierge', *Analecta Bollandiana* 42 (1924), pp. 21–68, 266–87

Ward, Benedicta, *Miracles and the Medieval Mind* (London, 1982)

——, ed. and trans., *The Prayers and Meditations of Saint Anselm, with the Proslogian* (London, 1973)

Ward, H. L. D., *Catalogue of Romances in the Department of Manuscripts in the British Museum*, II (London, 1883), pp. 586–740

Warner, George F., ed., *Catalogue of Additions to the Manuscripts in the British Museum in the Years 1900–1905* (London, 1907)

Warner, Marina, *Alone of All Her Sex: The Myth and the Cult of the Virgin Mary* (New York, 1976)

Waters, Claire M., *Angels and Earthly Creatures: Preaching, Performance, and Gender in the Later Middle Ages*, The Middle Ages Series (Philadelphia, PA, 2004)

Weatherly, E. H., ed., *Speculum Sacerdotale*, EETS, os 200 (London, 1936)

Weiss, Alexander, *Chaucer's Native Heritage* (New York, 1985)

Wenzel, Siegfried, *Latin Sermon Collections from Later Medieval England*, Cambridge Studies in Medieval Literature (Cambridge, 2005)

Whiteford, Peter, ed., *The Myracles of Oure Lady*, Middle English Texts 23 (Heidelberg, 1990)

Williams, C. H., ed., *English Historical Documents 1485–1558* (London, 1967)

Williams Boyarin, Adrienne, 'Anti-Jewish Parody around Miracles of the Virgin?: Thoughts on an Early Nonsense-Cento in Berkeley, Bancroft Library, BANC MS UCB 92', *N&Q* 54.4 (2007), pp. 379–85

——, 'Desire for Religion: Mary, a Murder Libel, a Jewish Friar, and Me', *'Something Fearful': Medievalist Scholars on the Religious Turn in Literary Criticism*, ed. Kathryn Kerby-Fulton, special issue of *Religion and Literature* (forthcoming 2010)

——, 'Inscribed Bodies: The Virgin Mary, Jewish Women, and Feminine Legal Authority', *Law and Sovereignty in the Middle Ages and Renaissance*, ed. Robert Sturges, Arizona Studies in the Middle Ages and Renaissance 28 (Turnhout, forthcoming 2010)

——, 'Sealed Flesh, Book-Skin: How to Read the Female Body in the Early Middle English *Seinte Margarete*', *Women and the Divine in Literature before 1700: Essays in Memory of Margot Louis*, ed. Kathryn Kerby-Fulton (Victoria, BC, 2009), pp. 69–88

Wilson, Evelyn Faye, ed., *The Stella Maris of John of Garland* (Cambridge, MA, 1946)

Wilson, R. M., *The Lost Literature of Medieval England* (London, 1952)

Winstanley, Lilian, ed., *The Prioress's Tale and The Tale of Sir Thopas* (Cambridge, 1922)

Wogan-Browne, Jocelyn et al., eds, *The Idea of the Vernacular: An Anthology of Middle English Literary Theory, 1280–1520* (University Park, PA, 1999)

Wright, C. E., 'The Dispersal of the Libraries in the Sixteenth Century', *The English Library Before 1700*, ed. Francis Wormald and C. E. Wright (London, 1958), pp. 148–75

Wright, Stephen K., 'The Durham Play of Mary and the Poor Knight: Sources and Analogues of a Lost English Miracle Play', *Comparative Drama* 17 (1983), pp. 254–65

Wrightson, Kellinde, ed., *Fourteenth-Century Icelandic Verse on the Virgin Mary*, Viking Society for Northern Research Text 14 (London, 2001)

Youings, Joyce, *The Dissolution of the Monasteries*, Historical Problems: Studies and Documents 14 (London, 1971)

Zettel, Patrick H., 'Saints' Lives in Old English: Latin Manuscripts and Vernacular Accounts: Ælfric', *Peritia* 1 (1982), pp. 17–37

Zieman, Katherine, 'Reading, Singing, and Understanding: Constructions of the Literacy of Women Religious in Late Medieval England', *Learning and Literacy in Medieval England and Abroad*, ed. Sarah Rees Jones, Utrecht Studies in Medieval Literacy 3 (Turnhout, 2003), pp. 97–120

——, *Singing the New Song: Literacy and Liturgy in Late Medieval England*, The Middle Ages Series (Philadelphia, PA, 2008)

Zitter, Emmy Stark, 'Anti-Semitism in Chaucer's *Prioress's Tale*', *The Chaucer Review* 25.4 (1991), pp. 277–84

Zumthor, Paul, *Essai de poétique médiévale*, Collection poétique (Paris, 1972)

Index

Individual Marian miracles are indexed in Appendix 4, though miracles discussed extensively, as well as important characters and recurrent themes/content, are listed here. Manuscript shelfmarks can be found under 'manuscripts', and those associated with individual miracles or groups of miracles are also included in Appendix 4. Medieval names follow common forms ('Gower, John' but 'Julian of Norwich'). Modern scholars are included only where crucial to argument.